IMAGINING GOD

IMAGINING GOD

THEOLOGY AND THE RELIGIOUS IMAGINATION

GARRETT GREEN

1817

Harper & Row, Publishers, San Francisco

New York, Cambridge, Philadelphia, St. Louis
London, Singapore, Sydney, Tokyo

The following publishers have generously given permission to use extended from copyrighted works: From Ludwig Wittgenstein's *Philosophical Investigations* the figure of the "duck-rabbit" is reproduced by permission of Basil Blackwell, Oxford. From "On Seeing the Unseen: Imagination in Science and Religion," *Zygon* 16 (1981): 15–28, by Garrett Green. Revised version reprinted by permission of the publisher. From " 'The Bible As. . .': Fictional Narrative and Scriptural Truth," in *Scriptural Authority and Narrative Interpretation*, edited by Garrett Green. Copyright ©1987 by Fortress Press, Philadelphia, PA. Reprinted by permission of the publisher.

FIRST EDITION

Library of Congress Cataloging-in-Publication Data

Green, Garrett.
   Imagining God: Theology and the Religious Imagination.

   Includes index.
   1. Imagination—Religious aspects—Christianity.   2. Revelation.
3. Religion and science—1946–   .   4. Bible—Evidences, authority, etc.
I. Title.
BR115.I6G74   1989   230   88-45691
ISBN 0-06-063465-0

89   90   91   92   93   RRD   10   9   8   7   6   5   4   3   2   1

For Joshua and Abigail

Contents

Acknowledgments

A book as long in the making as this one accumulates debts too numerous to recount, or even to recall. These pages doubtless contain ideas that came originally from others but which through long familiarity I can no longer distinguish from my own. I do want to acknowledge several people whose assistance I recall with gratitude. The book had its inception during sabbatical study in Tübingen, aided by conversations with both German hosts and other American visitors. E. Brooks Holifield probably doesn't remember the role he played in encouraging me to embark on a course that led, long afterward, to this book. Some of the earliest ideas for the book emerged out of a series of conversations with Michael Welker and Wolfgang Kasprzik. James J. Heaney urged me to expand these ideas into a book and offered continuing encouragement as the work progressed. I later benefited from suggestions made by Jack Forstman, Frederick W. Norris, and Ronald F. Thiemann, who read and commented on drafts of several chapters. To those who worked their way through the entire manuscript, I owe a special debt of gratitude. Charles M. Wood offered insightful commentary and incisive critique that led me to rethink and revise a number of points along the way. Hans W. Frei provided insights and encouragement both through his published works and in our private conversations. Eugene V. Gallagher, exceeding the obligations of departmental collegiality, helped to keep me in conversation with scholars of religion outside my own specialty. Priscilla Green, whose well-trained ear for written style and clear English prose has made the book more accessible to nonspecialists and more readable for everyone, also helped to keep alive the dream that this project would someday be completed.

I wish to thank the Alexander von Humboldt Foundation for fellowship support in Germany, and especially Professor Jürgen Moltmann, my official host and mentor during two years at the University of Tübingen. Connecticut College, through the good offices of its Dean of the Faculty, R. Francis Johnson, provided vital support in the form of sabbatical leaves and reduced teaching responsibilities during the final phase of the writing.

The book is dedicated to my children, Joshua Green and Abigail Green; more of their childhood than they know has provided a living and tangible counterpoint to the intellectual struggles recorded in these pages.

Introduction

Theologians have always employed concepts borrowed from secular culture in the task of articulating and interpreting religious truth. In Christianity this practice dates at least as far back as the Apologists of the second and third centuries, who took alien notions from an often hostile pagan world and recast them into weapons for defending Christian truth. In the crowning achievement of medieval theology, St. Thomas Aquinas appropriated resurgent Aristotelian philosophy, seen by his more timid theological contemporaries as an enemy of the faith, and forged it into a framework for the systematic construction of Christian doctrine. Among many attempts in the modern West to adapt secular ideas to Christian uses, two of the best known recent efforts are Paul Tillich's correlation of existentialist philosophy and Christian theology and the ongoing endeavors of process theologians to reconstruct doctrine on the foundation of Whitehead and Hartshorne's neoclassical philosophy.

Such projects have always invited controversy. From Tertullian in the second century to Karl Barth in the twentieth, periodic warnings wave been sounded that efforts at synthesis can become Trojan horses by which the church unwittingly invites the enemy inside the precincts of Christian truth. The wisest theologians have always trod a middle path, accepting the necessity of employing secular concepts while remaining vigilant against the dangers inherent in doing so. Mottoes for this approach are found in the ancient church in Augustine's *credo ut intelligam* ("I believe in order to understand") and in the Middle Ages in Anselm's *fides quaerens intellectum* ("faith seeking understanding").

Theological use of secular concepts and philosophies has become an especially complex and crucial issue in the modern world. One reason has been the pressing need, after the critical turn in modern thought epitomized by Immanuel Kant, for some alternative to the now discred-

ited metaphysical systems of the past. Since Kant, theologians have repeatedly encountered an impasse in which the only alternatives appear
to be either (1) critical and reductionist or (2) precritical and fundamentalist. Much of the history of religious thought since the Enlightenment
is best understood as a series of attempts to overcome this dilemma, to
achieve a workable "postcritical" theological stance.

Two other developments in modern thought since Kant further com-
plicate the theological situation. The first is the problem posed by historical criticism, symbolized by G. E. Lessing's "ugly, broad ditch"
between contingent historical propositions and theological truths based
upon them.[1] The outworkings of this problem are most apparent in the
impact of historical-critical study of the Bible and the attempts of theologians to come to terms with the issues of authority and certainty arising
from it. If this first development can be summarized as a growing awareness of the historical relativity of religious institutions and ideas, the
second is a corresponding realization that all cultural artifacts, religion
included, are social constructions. All our language—whether biblical
or secular; philosophical, poetic, or theological—is socially and culturally conditioned; and whatever we say in that language is shaped by its
social context. This new awareness of the social location of language and
thought has led some (through Feuerbach and Marx) to the radical conclusion that religion is a human projection, thereby eroding the plausibility of religious claims to transcendent truth. A less drastic reaction
acknowledges that the social location of religion at least requires a rethinking of the relation between theological and extratheological
concepts.

Two twentieth-century critiques, one theological and the other
philosophical, also bear upon the issue of the theological appropriation
of extratheological concepts. The first arose earlier this century in Protestant theology, provoked by Karl Barth's attack on the tendency of
modern theologians to employ ontological or anthropological doctrines
(borrowed from philosophy) as a foundation for theology. Barth argued
that such a method inevitably subjects theology to an alien criterion,
thus compromising its basic integrity. The other development is more
recent and motivated by very different concerns. Generally known today as antifoundationalism, this increasingly influential view among
contemporary philosophers holds that the long modern quest for an incorrigible "foundation" for knowledge has been futile and misguided.
Human knowledge neither can nor ought to be "grounded" in epistemological certainty. Taken together, both these "antifoundational" arguments suggest (1) that theology should eschew all attempts to ground

its claims in some extratheological doctrine, because such a foundation is neither possible nor desirable, and (2) that theologians can nevertheless make legitimate occasional or ad hoc use of extratheological concepts as long as they do not subvert the properly theological criteria for Christian thought.

It is possible to see in Karl Barth's mature work an example of such an antifoundational theology. During his early, "dialectical" period Barth wrote in a polemical context largely determined by his opposition to prevailing "neo-Protestant" assumptions. He struggled at every point to close off any avenue *von unten nach oben*, to oppose every viewpoint that would allow theology to begin its work with a general, nontheological ontology or anthropology. In later years he himself acknowledged the one-sidedness of the resulting emphasis on the sheer otherness of God and tried to balance it with a renewed stress on the "humanity of God." Here Barth is prepared to acknowledge that there is a human point of contact for the Word of God, and that revelation encounters us in religion. But he remained adamant to the end that the priorities must never be reversed: theologians may and indeed must employ a variety of secular concepts as long as they serve properly theological ends and do not become the explicit or implicit criteria for theological truth.

The situation today requires theologians to pay special attention to this "other side" of Barth's program, even at the risk of taking certain extratheological notions with greater seriousness than he himself might have approved. In short, we must take him at his word when he says that revelation *can* be interpreted (correctly) as one expression of human religion. As long as this thesis is not misunderstood as a foundational proposal, it allows theology to remain true to its own proper commitments without isolating it from the secular study of religion, a field whose coming of age carries important consequences for theology. Theologians today cannot ignore the field of religious studies, which increasingly shapes their social and intellectual context. I do not mean to suggest a shift in the institutional affiliation of theologians but rather in their intellectual focus—a change in the sociology of knowledge. Academic theology, whether practiced by scholars at theological seminaries or in departments of religious studies, has been undergoing a significant reorientation away from traditional theological preoccupations toward the newer agenda of religious studies. I believe that this change could be documented by empirical research: by investigating, for instance, the works cited by theologians, the topics of courses offered in seminaries, and the changing patterns of communication within professional societies. At the institutional level, the proliferation of theological consor-

tiums and other hybrid programs has blurred the very distinction between ecclesiastical seminary and secular university. The battles of a
generation ago between proponents of theology and those of religious
studies have led, not to a divorce, but to an ill-defined common living
arrangement (which, I am tempted to say, has proven exceptionally
fertile).[2]

The present work is intended to be a constructive contribution to
Christian theology that respects its contemporary context in religious
studies. My aim is to tackle a nexus of theological problems of concern to
Christians, but to do so in such a way that the issues are also rendered
intelligible in terms of the dynamics of human religion and culture
more generally. I want to address theologians in such a way that other
members of the religious studies community may profitably listen in.
The choice of imagination as a focal concept is one of those ad hoc bor-
rowings by which theologians have so often carried out their work. My
goal is a modest one: to make some progress toward clarifying theological issues that have engaged my energies for several years. The argument of the book is not "foundational" in either the theological or the
philosophical sense—neither a "theology of imagination" nor a proposal that imagination be taken as the fundamental trait of *homo religiosus* or
the essence of Christianity. Taken together, Barth's critique of theologies based on philosophical presuppositions and the arguments of
Richard Rorty and other contemporary philosophers against philosophical foundationalism suggest a way of understanding how the disciplines of theology and religious studies ought to be related: religious
studies is not the first stage of theology; rather, the two independently
interpenetrate from opposite directions. The theologian must be able to
speak the language of religious studies without allowing it to become
the criterion for theological work.

The central thesis of the book has accordingly both a theological and
a religious studies side. My contention is that conceiving the point of
contact between divine revelation and human experience in terms of
imagination allows us to acknowledge the priority of grace in the divine-human relationship while at the same time allowing its dynamics
to be described in analytical and comparative terms as a human religious
phenomenon. The argument unfolds in several stages.

The opening chapter reviews the interpretation of religion as imagination in Western thought since the Enlightenment and shows how it
led to reductionist conclusions by the end of the nineteenth century.
This discussion introduces the historical aspect of the problem of relating religion to imagination. The account is not exhaustive, treating only

selected thinkers whose views have been especially influential in creating the intellectual situation inherited by twentieth-century thinkers.

Chapter 2, which can be seen as a corresponding introduction to the problem in its theological aspect, returns to the debate in the 1930s between Karl Barth and Emil Brunner about the *Anknüpfungspunkt*, or "point of contact," between the Word of God and the human creature. Analysis of the debate shows how it led to an impasse, a dilemma in which theologians seemed to be left with a devil's choice between "natural theology" and "positivism of revelation." A closer look at Barth's position nevertheless reveals that the *Anknüpfungspunkt* might fruitfully be interpreted as the human imagination, though Barth does not develop an argument in those terms.

The next two chapters undertake the philosophical task of developing a concept of imagination adequate to the theological problem raised in the first two chapters. Chapter 3, taking recent discussions in philosophy of science as the point of departure, argues that the work of natural science necessarily involves imagination in quite specific and fundamental ways. An evaluation of Thomas Kuhn's controversial theory of paradigms leads to a reformulation of the concept in terms that avoid the confusion surrounding its use in philosophy of science. Chapter 4 extends the philosophical treatment of imagination beyond the sciences by examining its uses in literature and in ordinary language. The centerpiece of the chapter is a definition of imagination as the paradigmatic function, together with a discussion of the implications of that definition. The chapter concludes with a consideration of religious imagination.

The second part of the book takes up the specifically theological implications of paradigmatic imagination, showing how the Christian understanding of revelation, scripture, and theology can be usefully reformulated in terms of this concept. Chapter 5 reviews the doctrinal history of the *imago Dei*, examining various interpretations of the role of the divine image in the creation, fall, and redemption of humanity. The issue of idolatry, which has fascinated and bedeviled modern theologians, receives special attention. Finally, the doctrine of Christ as the image of God leads to an interpretation of faith as the "faithful imagination" of those who are transformed in Christ.

Chapter 6 develops the implications of the thesis for the doctrine of scripture. Beginning with Calvin's metaphor of the scriptures as spectacles, the chapter argues that the inspiration of scripture is its imaginative force, its power to re-form the human imagination. The unity of scripture is presented in a corresponding manner, not as agreement in doctrine or uniformity of content, but rather as the canon's ability to render a coherent gestalt, a normative pattern for the faithful imagination. The final section argues that the authority of scripture is imaginative, functioning as a normative paradigm for the Christian imagination. This view is worked out in terms of a concept of the classic, understood not as an expression of unthematized prior experience, but rather as a socially sanctioned textual norm for the shaping of imagination and hence of experience.

The concluding chapter applies this reformulation of the doctrines of revelation and scripture to the task of theology. Its central claim is that theology carries out the hermeneutical function implied by the Christian life as faithful imagination, interpreting the scriptural paradigm for the ongoing life and thought of the believing community. An examination of recent theories of metaphor introduces the broader question of theological truth claims. I argue that the common but inadequate dichotomy of "fact" and "fiction" prevents a proper understanding of how fictional narratives can function as normative scripture. Drawing on Hans Frei's clarification of the issues of historical reference and textual meaning, I show how fictional stories may allow us to see the world truly, *as* the "theater of God's glory" in Calvin's phrase. The upshot of these hermeneutical considerations is that modern "postcritical" believers can in good conscience make use of the Bible scripturally to envision themselves and the world in relation to God. Such a "second naïveté" allows one to read the Bible literally without falling into precritical assumptions. The book concludes with what I call a "hermeneutics of the cross," an argument based on the peculiar nature of the God depicted in scripture, who conquers not by force but by "capturing the imagination" of his fallen human creatures. This theological principle implies that the "fictional" status of scripture is appropriate to the nature of the God therein revealed. These conclusions require a reevaluation of typically modern assumptions about the relation between theory and practice, and suggest that interpretation—the central task of theology—is more than a merely "theoretical" undertaking.

Part I.

RELIGIOUS IMAGINATION
RECONSIDERED

CHAPTER 1

Religion as Imagination in Modern Thought

The notion of imagination has emerged recently as a prominent focus of theological attention. It appears as the key term in the titles of two books that have attracted particular attention among academic theologians in the United States, David Tracy's *Analogical Imagination* and Gordon Kaufman's *Theological Imagination,* and it pops up in scores of other contexts, often incidentally but increasingly as a focal idea. A term that once flourished in theology among only practitioners of "religion and literature," *imagination* is now attracting the attention of systematic and philosophical theologians. Yet this new interest in the notion apparently does not signal the birth of a new movement or school of thought (that is, it is not a potential rival for theologies of process or liberation); nor does it appear to constitute even a general direction or orientation for theology (as, for example, recent interest in "narrative" or the now passé fascination with "secularity"). Indeed, the recent users of the term employ it so variously that it would be misleading to say that they share a common concept. Kaufman's robust neo-Kantian idea of the constructive imagination, for example, is a far cry from Tracy's existential-mystical interest in the "disclosures" mediated by the analogical imagination.[1]

The significance of the new theological interest in imagination lies, I believe, in another direction altogether. It is not the name of a new theological program or method but rather a clue to the cultural and historical location of religion and thus to the nature of the theological enterprise itself.

The interpretation of religion as a form of imagination is in fact nothing new at all. A number of important and highly influential theories of religion over the past two centuries have in effect advanced such a thesis, although not all of them have employed the term *imagination* explic-

itly. I will review some of the more important of these theories in order
to show that they have in common an interpretation of religion as
imagination (however diverse they may be in other regards) and to il-
lustrate the problem that such interpretation poses for theology. In
short, I will argue that religion, in an age virtually defined by the paradigm of natural science, has generally been understood as the great alternative to science, as the chief example of the *other* way of thinking
and acting. This dualism characterizes the leading interpretations of religion by friends and foes alike. Both those critics who have opposed
religion as the great enemy of science and the apologists who have tried
to defend it against "scientific" critique have shared an underlying assumption that religion is a form of imagination.

Modern Ambivalence About Religion

The powerful impact of the "new science," beginning in the seventeenth century, extended far beyond the mere explanation of physical
nature almost from its very beginnings, profoundly affecting the way
Europeans thought about every aspect of nature and culture. In the case
of religion the application of new ideas from science received an added
incentive from the divided and divisive religious situation in Europe.
The fragmentation of Christianity as a result of the Protestant Reformation had brought in its wake the most devastating wars in history, and
religion, once the very glue that held European civilization together,
had become the seedbed of seemingly endless turmoil and strife. It is
hardly surprising that many intellectuals saw in the new vision of nature as a rational and law-abiding unity the promise of deliverance from
religious chaos. If the *natural* conforms to the *rational* in the physical
world, why not in the spiritual as well? And thus was born the powerful
modern notion of a "natural" religion, "as old as the Creation" and as
different from the dogmatisms of the "positive" religions as is modern
science from the dogmatic notions of the old Aristotelian natural philosophy. The heteronomous appeal to authority must yield to the autono-
mous claims of reason.

The place of religion in modern thought was thus deeply ambivalent
from the very beginning. It was viewed, on the one hand, as the source
of the fragmentation of culture, but on the other hand, it seemed to
many to hold the key to a recovery of cultural and intellectual unity.
This modern ambivalence about religion not only divides groups of people from one another but also, more significantly, runs right through
the minds of the greatest thinkers. Kant, for example, gained a reputa-

tion as the destroyer of all proofs for the existence of God, yet he insisted all the while that he was only preparing the ground "to make room for *faith*." A lifelong foe of all "statutory" religion, he labored nonetheless to show the legitimacy—even the necessity—of religious belief precisely on rational grounds. The place of religion in Hegel, to cite the other best-known example, is so deeply ambiguous that expert opinion has never decided whether he should rank as the St. Thomas of modernity who reconciled the claims of faith and reason or as the liberator of culture from religion who overcame at last the long dependence of Western thought on the Christian tradition.

For religious thinkers, those theologians and philosophers whose special concern is for the *truth* embodied in traditions inherited from premodern times, the ambiguity of religion has usually appeared in epistemological guise.[2] How is it possible to have knowledge of God once our concept of knowledge has been reformed by the empirical sciences? The main epistemological reformers, Hume and Kant, appeared to have kicked away once and for all the metaphysical ladder on which thinkers for centuries had been ascending and descending. Since the late eighteenth century, philosophers of religion and theologians have almost invariably taken this antisupernaturalist turn to be a kind of brute fact of the spirit. The way back to the old metaphysics (for most thinkers that has meant to metaphysics as such) has been guarded by an angel (or at least by a philosopher) with a flaming sword.

It is wise, of course, not to overlook the fact that there continue to be those who remain outside this modern consensus, those who are unimpressed by the problems that have typically concerned modern theologians either because they reject the turn taken by Hume and Kant or because they accept it as the last word in matters religious. On one side are the various traditionalists, literalists, and fundamentalists who simply continue to assert on authoritarian grounds the revealed truths of scripture or church doctrine. Their refusal to fade quietly into history, their surprising religious and political resiliency, ought to warn more acculturated theologians against generalizing too glibly about the "modern mind" or the "secular world" in which we all allegedly live. At the other extreme are the straightforward skeptics, those doctrinaire atheists and agnostics who believe that nothing remains to be reconstructed after the destruction of the old supernaturalism.[3] While not forgetting that the social context of theology includes both fundamentalists and skeptics in significant numbers, the theologians in the middle can probably be excused for continuing to assume both the impossibility of supernaturalist apologetics and the necessity of finding another lan-

guage for constructive theology. The positions at the two extremes rest
on paradigm commitments so radically different from those "in the middle" that attempts at reconciliation appear as hopeless as achieving
agreement between Ptolomaic and Copernican astronomers, or between
shamans and professors of medicine.

The territory in between, which has been staked out by those modern religious thinkers (who for convenience can be called "mediating
theologians") is sufficiently broad and varied that it has never been fully explored in the two centuries that have intervened. Beginning with
Kant's own constructive attempt in *Religion Within the Limits of Reason
Alone*, theologians and philosophers ranging from the near-orthodox to
the near-skeptical have sought to transfer the edifice of religious truth
—usually the Christian gospel—from the crumbling ruins of premodern orthodoxy to a surer foundation. The foundations proposed have
been as diverse as Kant's own ethical rationalism, the historical dialectic
of Hegelian philosophy, or the theories of more recent existentialists
and phenomenologists. The common thread running through these otherwise various and sometimes sharply opposed projects has been their
underlying assumption that a religious "essence" can be distilled out of
its unholy mixture with metaphysics and dogmatism and presented
pure to modern thought. This project of transposition or distillation is
the identifying mark of that broad spectrum of thinkers that I am calling
the mediating theologians.[4]

Theologians in this mediating tradition characteristically interpret
religion as imagination. The history of this interpretation is not cotermi-
nous with the use of the word *imagination* or with the development of an
explicit theory of imagination, although they have significant points of
intersection.[5] A rudimentary definition of imagination, in the sense that
it characterizes religion according to the mediating theologians, follows
from their common assumption that religious statements do not provide
information about the supernatural world. Before the late eighteenth
century—in the Deist Controversy, for example—all parties had agreed
that the argument was about the truth or falsity of certain propositions.
Toland could disagree with Locke about whether there were any truths
above reason, but they agreed implicitly that religion, whether natural
or revealed, was in the business of stating truths. This tacit assumption
did not survive the antimetaphysical turn epitomized in Kant's critical
philosophy, for (in Kant's own terminology) theological statements are
not claims to theoretical (or speculative) knowledge. They nevertheless
remain "true" in some *other* sense, called "practical" by Kant himself. It
is this move that characterizes the mediating theologies of the nine-

teenth and twentieth centuries. Initially their thesis appears quite negative: religion is *not* true in the same way that science is; theological propositions are *not* theoretical truths (neither true ones nor false ones) but
rather something else altogether. "Imagination" is what I am calling this
"something else"; it is the positive correlate of the negative thesis that
religion does not deliver theoretical truths about the supernatural
world. The subsequent development of the mediating tradition in the
nineteenth century makes clear why the term is appropriate.

From Kant to the Romantics

Kant, who borrowed the notion of *Einbildungskraft* from the psychological theory of Johann Nikolaus Tetens, helped to establish imagination as an important locus in modern philosophy. Yet Kant's theory of
the imagination is by no means clear, and some of his later statements
about it appear contradictory.[6] In the *Critique of Pure Reason* imagination
plays the important role of mediating between the sensible given and
the concepts of the understanding. Later, in the *Critique of Judgment* and
the *Opus posthumum*, he puts greater emphasis on the role of the imagination in aesthetics and the arts.[7] But the remarkable fact about Kant's
treatment of the *Einbildungskraft* is his failure to employ it in his philosophy of religion. (The term does not even appear in the index to the
critical edition of *Religion Within the Limits of Reason Alone*.) I will have
occasion later to consider how he might have done so, but it is important
first to examine what Kant did say about religion and how it relates to
the imagination.

One reason, presumably, why Kant ignored the relation of religion
to aesthetics is that he shared with earlier Enlightenment thinkers the
conviction that religion is essentially concerned with rational ideas—
specifically, with moral ones. His technical definition of religion as the
"recognition of all duties as divine commands" comes nearly verbatim
from the English Deist Matthew Tindal.[8] Kant's difference from the De-
ists lies not in the notion of religion as such but rather in his redefini-
tion of reason, to which religion must conform.

Kant's own most characteristic contributions to the interpretation of
religion come when he attempts to show the relation between "pure rational faith"—the essence of Christianity and all true religion—and the
actual historical phenomena of Christian belief and practice—what the
Enlightenment liked to call "positive" religion.[9] A clue to their relation
lies in the "as" of Kant's definition of religion. Insofar as religion is the
recognition of duties it is a matter for reason—for practical reason, to be

precise. But as soon as we think of these rational duties *as* divine commands, we enter the dubious realm of religious positivity. For Kant positivity is dubious because it threatens to replace the *pure* motive of rational faith with something *empirical* (which is by definition "impure," constituted by sense experience rather than purely by reason). For example, one who holds the "positive" belief in heaven and hell may be tempted to act out of fear of punishment or hope of reward rather than out of respect for the absolute claim of the inner moral law without regard for the consequences. Yet Kant also knows that he cannot do without positivity, since human beings are enmeshed in radical evil and can be led only gradually toward acceptance of pure morality unmixed with empirical representations.

The solution for Kant, foreshadowing similar moves by many later mediating theologians, is to distinguish between two kinds of religion, both of them true and ultimately identical in content but differing penultimately in form. He uses a number of metaphors to distinguish them: kernel and husk, inner and outer concentric circles, vehicle and essential truth.[10] All of them imply the same evaluation, which Kant can make explicit on occasion. First, the authentic form of religion is always the pure philosophical essence, and second, most of what we ordinarily call "religion" in everyday life and in religious studies belongs to the "empirical" or inauthentic form. How did that pure essence of religious truth come to be expressed in this so pervasive, yet finally unsatisfactory, form?

Kant's answer, though he never puts it quite in these terms, is to appeal to the popular religious imagination. The religion that we see around us in the world, positive religion, is religion as imagination. He characteristically uses the language of *Vorstellung*. This term is usually rendered "representation" in philosophical contexts, but it is in fact a quite ordinary German word closer to "imagination" and its English cognates when used nontechnically. Because this terminology is so common and is not employed in a technical sense by Kant, it frequently becomes virtually invisible in translation. For example, in discussing how the human inclination to evil appears in the New Testament, Kant comments that "it is not surprising that an Apostle represents [*vorstellig macht*] this *invisible* enemy . . . as being outside us and, indeed as an evil spirit."[11] His evaluation of this practice becomes explicit in a comment on the Christian tendency to represent (*vorzustellen*) the difference between moral good and evil in terms of heaven and hell. "Though this representation [*Vorstellung*] is figurative [*bildlich*]," he writes, "and, as such, disturbing, it is none the less philosophically correct in meaning."[12]

Kant prefers the nonimaginative use of pure practical reason but acknowledges the need (for the time being, at least) for the imaginative expression of religious truth.

Kant's interpretation of religion as imagination becomes especially clear when he discusses the danger of religious illusion.[13] In an oft-cited passage he says that "we create a God for ourselves" when we imagine him anthropomorphically, something that is "scarcely to be avoided" and "harmless enough" for theoretical purposes. The same use of imagination becomes "highly dangerous," however, "in connection with our practical relation to his will." The danger, which Kant equates with the biblical error of idolatry, arises from the possibility of honoring the *Vorstellung* in place of the *Ideal*, the subjective image of God in place of the ideal concept of pure reason. In the same context he describes this error as the elevation of *das sinnliche Vorstellungsvermögen*, the faculty of sensuous imagination, to the dignity of intellectual ideas. Any lingering doubts that what Kant is describing here should be called "imagination" are removed by an explicit statement (albeit expressed parenthetically in a footnote) that the *Einbildungskraft* is the source of the images.[14] Even without this explicit reminder, it should be apparent that for Kant any *Vorstellung* must be produced by the imagination; if the *Vorstellung* does not involve outer sense, its origin can only be the productive (as distinguished from the reproductive) imagination.[15]

Two conclusions are important for understanding Kant's place in the modern tradition of interpreting religion as imagination. First, without developing an explicit theory, Kant interprets empirical religion—that is, the actual, "positive" religious beliefs and practices of people—as constituted by images (*Vorstellungen*) flowing from the imagination (*sinnliches Vorstellungsvermögen* or *produktive Einbildungskraft*). His primary concerns as a philosopher of religion follow from this view. His critical intent is to demonstrate the inauthenticity and warn against the moral danger of false religion, which he shows to be the product of what might be called bad imagination. His corresponding constructive concern is to demonstrate that true religion, though it, too, is the product of imagination, can be justified as a legitimate expression of pure moral religion, its only adequate foundation.

The second point follows from Kant's concern to ground religious positivity in pure rational faith: religion as imagination is religion inadequately expressed. *As imagination* it is indistinguishable from illusion and therefore in need of apologetic support, some defense against the charge that it is *mere* imagination. Here, too, Kant anticipates a familiar feature of mediating theology—its basically apologetic motive. The same motive may help to explain why many of the thinkers in this tradition hesitate to use the *term* imagination to describe religion, even though it would seem to be appropriate. To modern ears it simply sounds too much like admitting that religious belief is imaginary.

One way to characterize the development of Kant's thought into a full-blown idealism by his immediate successors in Germany is to say that the productive imagination commandeers the whole operation. For Fichte imagination becomes the motive force of the entire philosophical system, so that "all reality . . . is produced simply by the imagination."[16] He identifies the human spirit itself with *Einbildungskraft* and makes it the source of all our images and ideas that go beyond sense experience. Fichte's claim that "the whole operation of the human spirit proceeds from the imagination" attracted the attention of Schelling and Coleridge and became one of the sources of the Romantic emphasis on the imagination.

More influential for the development of religious thought was Hegel's brand of idealism, and for him, as for Kant, the significant term is not *Einbildungskraft* but *Vorstellung*. Hegel makes *Vorstellung* into the distinguishing feature of religion, the key to its nature and its place within the System. To offer a translation of this controversial term is already to commit oneself to some interpretation of its meaning in Hegel's thought; and once again there is a formidable tradition among translators in favor of "representation." Despite the risk of confusing some other aspects of Hegel's thought, I believe that his interpretation of religion can best be clarified by rendering *Vorstellung* as "imagination" where it refers to a form of consciousness or general procedure and as "image" where it denotes the specific components of that consciousness.[17]

The sense in which Hegel interprets religion as imagination is clearest when seen in the context of Absolute Spirit, that highest realm in the odyssey of *Geist*, where subjective and objective Spirit unite as self-thinking Thought.[18] The three forms in which Absolute Spirit manifests itself—art, religion, and philosophy (in ascending order)—are identical in content, differing only in their form. Religion is thus a particular form of consciousness, distinguished on the one hand from art and on the other from philosophy. What differentiates them is the medium through which they express the truth: art employs "the most sensuous medium, philosophy the most conceptual."[19] In art the Absolute is apprehended as beauty, a sensuous *Scheinen* in which the infinite truth appears "occluded" by the finite medium.[20] Religious consciousness represents an advance over the aesthetic because it involves thought as well as sense. It represents "an intermediate way of apprehending the

Absolute" that could be described as "the product of a marriage between imagination and thought."[21] *Vorstellung* can be translated as "imagination," in other words, only if it is understood as a form of thought: imaginative or figurative thinking. *"Vorstellungen* in general," Hegel states, "can be viewed as *metaphors* of thoughts and concepts."[22] Religion, in other words, is the metaphorical expression of the truth.

In Hegel's final step the purification of form is completed, and Absolute Spirit becomes the pure thought, the *Begriff*, which has been the goal of the dialectic from the beginning. This move has given rise to a long-standing debate about whether Hegel in the end vindicates religion (and thus Christianity, which he interprets as the "Absolute Religion") or leaves it behind as unneeded once the truth has achieved its pure philosophical expression.[23] This controversy, which I will not attempt to resolve here, has an important bearing on the present topic because it arises out of the built-in ambiguity of imagination. Hegel himself believed that his System was the vindication of Christianity because he thought that metaphorical truth could be expressed, and expressed more adequately, in nonmetaphorical terms—what he calls *Begriff* or pure philosophical thought. "Hegel's Science," in Michael Rosen's trenchant words, ". . . is the *radically non-metaphorical discourse*. Its deep truth is imageless."[24] To dispute Hegel's claim to have preserved the full truth of Christianity in philosophical form is to disagree that metaphoric discourse is translatable into nonmetaphoric terms. If religion is imagination and the "deep truth" is imageless, it is clear why Hegel must insist on the final *Aufhebung* of Christianity into philosophy, the translation of Absolute Spirit out of the occluded medium of religion into the sheer transparency of the *Begriff*. The change is finally not a change of medium at all, but rather a leaving behind of every medium. After the Spirit's long odyssey, the very essence of which is mediation, it arrives at last at the point where it needs no medium because it has become fully explicit (*an und für sich*), the utter identity of subject and object.

For all their vast differences about the nature of religion and the nature of science, there are some striking parallels between Kant and Hegel. They agree that religion is imagination, and they both mean by this term that religious truth is inextricably linked with images dependent on sense experience. Furthermore, they agree that religion nevertheless really does express truth, that the highest expression of this religious truth is found in historical Christianity, and that philosophical reason is capable of freeing the pure religious essence from its entrapment in imaginative forms. Both concede to positive (imaginative) religion a penultimate legitimacy while nevertheless insisting that it can and must ultimately leave positivity behind. And finally, for both Kant and Hegel this state of affairs requires a religious apologetic in the form of an argument to show how religion can be both imagination and truth. Kant performs this task by distilling out the religion within the bounds of reason and showing its identity to essential Christianity. Hegel does it through the dialectical *Aufhebung* of religion, which he understands to be not the triumph of philosophy over religion but the attestation (*Beglaubigung*) of Christian truth by philosophy.[25]

Not everyone, of course, agreed with Kant and Hegel that imagination is an inferior form of the truth in need of attestation by philosophy. The exalted position of the *Einbildungskraft* in Fichte and Schelling is an early indication of the tendency, reaching its culmination in Romanticism, to make of imagination the supreme human faculty. Indeed, it is characteristic of the Romantics to treat imagination as more than merely human, as the point of contact between divine and human creativity. Coleridge's famous definition of the "primary imagination" makes of it not only "the living Power and prime Agent of all human Perception" but also "a repetition in the finite mind of the eternal act of creation in the infinite I AM."[26] If thinkers in this tradition interpret religion as imagination, it is because they understand the imagination as virtually religious.

Coleridge is undoubtedly a figure of great importance for theology, but it is easier to chart his influence than to describe his theory of the imagination and its implications for religion. He is the despair of more philosophically minded commentators, who tend to find his ideas "cloudy and imprecise"[27] and would be happy to leave him to the literary critics. Still, his influence is undeniable in two particular areas. First, he became the chief spokesman for the importance of the imagination in literature and did much to establish the Romantic concept of imagination in critical tradition. Coleridge is also generally credited with reviving Anglo-Saxon theology by freeing it from a devil's choice between Palean rationalism and the utilitarianism of Bentham.[28] The connection between these two accomplishments is indirect and can be seen only by delving into the content of his often murky ideas.

The most famous of Coleridge's theoretical contributions is the dichotomy of imagination and fancy, which depends in turn on his distinction between primary and secondary imagination. His "desynonymizing of Fancy and Imagination" goes against a long tradition that had treated the two terms as either equivalent or differing only in degree.[29] Basil Willey has shown that the key to the distinction lies in the contrast between primary and secondary imagination, for it is the latter that Coleridge contrasts with fancy. Briefly, the "Fancy must receive all its materials ready made from the law of association,"[30] whereas the (secondary) imagination fuses its images into a genuine new unity. A good analogy is the difference between a chemical mixture (fancy) and a compound (imagination), for in the latter case the individual components (images) lose their individual properties when they are fused into unity.[31]

Despite the ringing biblical tones of Coleridge's definition of the primary imagination (quoted above), he attributes to the secondary imagination the higher and more important power. It is the poetic, or creative, faculty. The primary imagination is "necessary," shared by everyone; the secondary is under the free control of the will—the mark of genius, the quality that Coleridge discovered in Wordsworth and that, he said, gave him his original insight into its difference from mere fancy. Together the two levels of imagination constitute the "esemplastic power," Coleridge's coinage from the Greek meaning "to shape into one."[32] Their combined effect can be observed in metaphor, where the primary imagination supplies the component images that are then forged into a creative unity by the secondary imagination.[33] Willey traces the distinction between fancy and imagination ultimately to Coleridge's overriding concern to distinguish "a living whole or organism" from "a mechanical juxtaposition of parts."[34]

The same central concern to defend the organic against the merely mechanical appears in Coleridge's religious ideas, in his efforts to free religion from the stultifying atmosphere of rationalist orthodoxy that characterized English theology at the beginning of the nineteenth century. It is surprising that Coleridge, having articulated so powerfully "religious" a conception of the imagination, did not employ it in the religious writings that occupied so much of his energies in the final two decades of his life. Indeed, the very word all but dropped out of his vocabulary. His reasons may, in fact, have been theological, for according to Engell, Coleridge reached a point where he "felt that the imagination had betrayed him into a mistaken pantheistic attitude."[35] Whatever the personal motivation may have been, reason eventually usurped the dominant role of imagination in Coleridge's thought, combining within itself the sense, the understanding, and the imagination.[36]

But the eclipse of the term has less to do with the substance of Coleridge's thought than may appear at first to be the case. Like other modern thinkers, particularly those with strong apologetic interests,

Coleridge became uncomfortable with the concept of imagination while continuing to make anonymous use of it in the interpretation of religion. In place of the distinction between imagination and fancy that he had developed in his aesthetic theory, he introduces a contrast between reason and understanding when he turns to ethical and religious matters. Willey calls it the "same distinction transposed into another key."[37] In other words, Coleridge posits,

> Understanding is to Reason as Fancy is to Imagination.

Just as Wordsworth had opened his eyes to imagination, so Kant taught him to value reason as a higher power than mere understanding. The understanding, like fancy, is necessary but passive and wedded to the senses; reason, like imagination, is free and creative, the "organ of the supersensuous."[38] Like the imagination in poetry, reason unifies the faculties and opens them to the higher truth that lies beyond sense experience. Though Coleridge credits Kant with showing him that reason leads us beyond the sensuous, he attributes to it a potency that Kant did not allow: the power to *know* the truth directly.[39] Lacking the powerful systematic articulation of Kant's concepts, Coleridge's exalted view of reason remains a suggestive but undeveloped possibility without significant influence on later epistemology. Understood as imagination "in another key," however, it contributes to the growing tendency to see religion as an imaginative expression of the human spirit.

Whether he calls it reason or imagination, in the end Coleridge holds a quite un-Kantian notion of the relation between images and truth. "An IDEA, in the *highest* sense of that word," he writes, "cannot be conveyed but by a *symbol*."[40] Unlike Kant and Hegel, who want to leave the sensuous behind in the final ascent to truth, Coleridge holds symbols to be indispensable,

> the living *educts* of the Imagination; of that reconciling and mediatory power, which incorporating the Reason in Images of the Sense, and organizing (as it were) the flux of the Senses by the permanence and self-circling energies of the Reason, gives birth to a system of symbols, harmonious in themselves, and consubstantial with the truths, of which they are the *conductors*.[41]

The imagination appears here, in Coleridge's metaphor, as a kind of fusion of incarnation and electricity, and the mention of a "system of symbols" could have come from an anthropologist writing about religion a century later. The context makes clear that for Coleridge imagination is no mere second-best form of truth but its highest expression. Had he possessed the system-building genius of a Hegel, one can imagine him reversing the priorities of the highest forms of spirit, placing the religious imagination above philosophy in the ascent of the spirit to truth.

Even such basic differences of priority should not blind us to the widespread agreement among modern thinkers that religion is a kind of imagination and, as such, basically distinct from science. Since imagination is characteristically the *other* way of apprehending, its evaluation depends heavily on how the particular thinker understands the non-imaginative alternative, whether it be called science, or *Wissenschaft*, or philosophy. Kant, for example, was deeply committed to the modern spirit of Enlightenment and felt the need to bring religion into harmony with it. For Coleridge, by contrast, the modern spirit appeared in the form of a shallow and mechanical rationalism to which religion, precisely because it did *not* share in that spirit, offered an attractive alternative. But in both cases the essential dichotomy between two ways of thinking remained unquestioned.

The Critics of the Hegelian Left

In Coleridge and the English Romantic poets, imagination achieved its most exalted status, and it has continued to function as an important concept in literary criticism. English-speaking theologians, on the other hand, have generally employed the term, if at all, only when dealing explicitly with the arts (for example, in the field that has become known as "religion and literature"). The identification of religion with imagination produced its most notable fruits in nineteenth-century Germany among theologians and philosophers of the Hegelian Left. The consequences for theology were traumatic and controversial but far more important for religion in the long run than the influences of Romanticism. The ideas of three of these thinkers continue to influence both religious studies and Christian theology today in powerful explicit and implicit ways. The starting point for each of them was Hegel's distinction between religious imagination and scientific conceptuality.

Of all the ways this dichotomy has been articulated, perhaps the most fateful (certainly the most notorious) for the interpretation of religion has been the one stemming from David Friedrich Strauss.[42] For him the great challenge of the modern spirit was posed by *historical* science, which he applied to the New Testament in *The Life of Jesus Critically Examined* (1835) with a thoroughness that shocked his contemporaries. Beginning as "the most gifted of all Hegel's followers,"[43] Strauss recognized a basic ambiguity in the distinction between *Vorstellung* and *Begriff*: how are they related to the history narrated in the New Testament Gospels? "Does the historical character adhere to the content [of the Christian faith]," he asked, "thus demanding recognition from the concept [*Begriff*] as well as the imagination [*Vorstellung*], since the content is the same for both, or is it reduced to the mere form [of imagination], to which conceptual thinking is not bound?"[44] Strauss, at least at the time of the 1835 edition of the *Leben Jesu*, unhesitatingly opted for the latter alternative. He was still an ardent enough Hegelian to believe that the truth of the gospel lies wholly in its ideal content, which can be sharply distinguished from its imaginative form. The important point for the history of interpreting religion as imagination, however, is Strauss's historical-critical investigation of the Bible itself rather than his own dogmatic and philosophical attempts to cope with its conclusions.[45]

The effect of applying the historical question to the Gospels was to transform the distinction between *Vorstellung* and *Begriff* into a contrast between myth and history. Strauss discovered that the religious imagination is the historical imagination of religious people, and the result is what he called *myth*, a term that has fascinated and frustrated theologians ever since. "For Strauss," in Hodgson's words, "the terms *Religion, Vorstellung,* and *Mythos* become largely synonymous."[46] Strauss brings out the particular force of mythological interpretation by comparing it with ancient allegorical and modern rationalist interpretations. He points out that the orthodox and the rationalists, despite their opposing views on the divine origin of the biblical text, agree in treating it as a historical record. The mythological and the allegorical interpretations, on the other hand, both maintain that "the historian apparently relates that which is historical, but they suppose him . . . to have made use of this historical semblance merely as the shell of an *idea [eines Ideellen]*—of a religious conception [*Vorstellung*]." They differ, of course, about the source of this process, the allegorical view attributing it directly to divine agency while the mythological view ascribes it to the "spirit of a people or a community."[47]

With Strauss it becomes obvious that *Vorstellung* means imagination, and that mythology is imagination in the religiohistorical mode. His famous English translator, George Eliot (Mary Ann Evans), generally renders *Vorstellung* as "image" or "imagery," though she is not always consistent; one can speculate whether her own more literary than philosophical orientation may have influenced her choice of English equivalents. At any rate, Strauss's *Life of Jesus* in Eliot's English became as widely known, and as notorious, in England and America as the original had been in Germany.[48] The suggestive and explosive idea that religion is imagination could no longer be confined to the academy.

Strauss was not the only figure of the Hegelian Left to develop the radical consequences of Hegel's identification of religion with imagination. The other notorious book of the age, also made popular in the English-speaking world through the mediation of George Eliot, was Ludwig Feuerbach's *Essence of Christianity*, which offers a kind of psychological complement to Strauss's historical reduction of religious imagination. Feuerbach does not even attempt to mollify the sensibilities of the pious, and his book bristles with the vocabulary of the fictive imagination, especially *Illusion*. "Religion," he announces, "is the dream of the human mind." Especially telling is the sharply dualistic character of Feuerbach's terminology: no longer is *Vorstellung* opposed to the *Begriff* of pure Spirit but to "reality," "the world," "the facts." In the dream world of religion we see things "not in the light of reality and necessity but in the entrancing splendor of imagination and caprice"—and here Feuerbach uses the German word *Imagination*.[49] He defines religion in good Hegelian terms as the consciousness of God but then—in a move that Hirsch calls the "precise reversal of the Hegelian philosophy of religion"[50]—identifies this God-consciousness simply as indirect human self-consciousness. Most radical from the standpoint of religious believers is Feuerbach's insistence that the religious person is unaware of the identity of divine and human consciousness—indeed, that "ignorance of it is fundamental to the peculiar nature of religion." The very "antithesis of divine and human," he argues, "is altogether illusory [*ein illusorischer*]."[51] The heart of his argument is an exposé of the "mystery of religion": *homo religiosus* "objectifies his nature" and then takes himself to be the object of his own creation. Eliot, in words that foreshadow Freud, translates *vergegenständlichen* as "project": "Man . . . projects his being into objectivity and then again makes himself an object to this projected image of himself thus converted into a subject."[52] Like other radical revisers of Hegel, Feuerbach retains the scheme of historical dialectic. He sees mankind progressively awakening from the religious dream or—in another of his metaphors anticipating twentieth-century writers—coming of age, outgrowing the need for the illusion of religion, the "childlike condition of humanity."[53]

Though Feuerbach's reduction of religion to imagination ranks as a potent theological critique in its own right, it remained to that other inverter of Hegel, Karl Marx, to forge Feuerbach's insight into the most powerful antireligious weapon of the modern age. Marx, acknowledging that after Feuerbach the "criticism of religion is in the main complete," goes on to explain *why* human beings should be so intent on imagining other worlds; he exposes the *point* of religious imagination.

The dirty little secret of religion, he says in effect, is that some people profit from the illusions of others. He believes that the "criticism of religion is the premise of all criticism"[54] because no social progress can be made until the oppressed are freed from the religious illusions that blind them to the real identity of their oppressors. Marx outdoes even Feuerbach in the richness of his imagination-vocabulary. Like Feuerbach, he favors those terms like *Illusion* and *Phantasie* that underscore the fictive (for Marx, one must say the deceitful) character of religious imagination. Religion is the *"fantastic realization* of the human essence," the *"illusory* happiness of the people," the "imaginary flowers on the chain" of the oppressed that antireligious criticism must "pluck away" (literally, "pick to pieces").[55] In this context the real force of the most famous of all Marx's metaphors of religion—the *"opium* of the people"— becomes evident. Opium (as Coleridge also knew) induces dreams, fantasies; but the dreams, which dull the critical faculties and disguise reality, are *deliberately* induced. Marx believes that the capitalist class has drugged the proletariat with religious fantasies in order to exploit their labor. For this reason he wants "to turn the *criticism of theology* into the *criticism of politics,"*[56] by snatching the opium pipe away from the working class so that in the pains of withdrawal they will recognize the true source of their misery and their own power to overcome it. Feuerbach was right in the content of his criticism but failed to understand its political implications; he thus epitomizes the philosophers, who "have only *interpreted* the world in various ways" without understanding that "the point is to *change* it."[57]

Religious Imagination and Modern Atheism

The reluctance of modern theologians to identify religion explicitly with imagination is understandable in view of what happened to the thesis at the hands of the antitheologians of the Hegelian Left. After Strauss, Feuerbach, and Marx, most theologians were more frightened by the reductionist dangers inherent in the idea than attracted by its potential usefulness for systematic theology. But why did the interpretation of religion as imagination take such a negative turn? The imagination itself had frequently been viewed as an important and constructive faculty, becoming virtually a divine sense for the high Romantics. A constructive theological development of imagination was suggested by the work of Coleridge and others. Why did it remain largely without issue in nineteenth-century theology? Before turning to the contemporary possibilities for accomplishing what the nineteenth century could not, I will examine these historical questions.

The modern critique of religion is complicated by the fact, mentioned earlier, that there are really two distinguishable traditions of atheism in post-Enlightenment thought, even though they may be combined in a particular thinker.[58] The atheism of the imagination, rooted in Hegel and developed into a formidable critique of religion by Feuerbach and Marx, has influenced various subsequent theories of religion. Especially influential in the twentieth century have been the sociological theory of religion proposed by Durkheim and the psychoanalytic interpretation advanced by Freud. But the tradition represented by these thinkers should be distinguished from the skeptical atheism stemming from Hume, which flourished in the positivist environment of French and English Victorian thought and is typically represented in the twentieth century by a figure like Bertrand Russell. The skeptical atheist opposes theology polemically from without, challenging the truthfulness or meaningfulness of its assertions. The imaginative atheist, on the other hand, undermines theology from within by interpreting its own categories to reach negative conclusions. One kind of atheist says that theological assertions are simply wrong; the other claims to understand them better than the theologians do.[59] Thus the skeptical atheist characteristically *refutes* religion, while the imaginative atheist is more likely to *reinterpret* it.

What happened in the nineteenth century is that these two atheistic traditions converged to produce a result more persuasive than either taken alone. The convergence is especially evident in the role played by imagination. In the Hegelian context, as we have seen, the imagination is deeply ambiguous, connected to the sources of knowledge as well as illusion. For a Victorian positivist, on the other hand, imagination is simply the subjective opposite of "objective reality" or "the facts." Imagination from this perspective is the realm of the merely imaginary, and the job of the critic is to replace the imaginations of earlier and more ignorant ages with the truths uncovered by modern science. The more positivistic the cultural atmosphere of Europe became, the more inevitably the identification of religion with imagination—regardless of the original intent of the proposer—came to be heard as the claim that religion is simply illusory and false.

Since that time one of the two pillars supporting this hybrid atheism has collapsed. The demise of positivism and the view of science that it fostered has undermined the consensus of the late nineteenth and early twentieth centuries and gives us cause to reexamine the implications of identifying religion with imagination. I will argue that recent developments in the philosophy of science have shown the simplistic equation of imagination with the imaginary to be untenable, and that the interpretation of religion as imagination thus no longer implies necessarily its reduction to mere subjectivity.

Without the admixture of skeptical atheism, however, the atheism of imagination also appears in a different light. The virulent antireligious polemics of Marx, for example, attribute a power to religion that would be quite unthinkable for a positivist. If we can bracket the negativity of the Marxist evaluation of religion long enough to examine the view of imagination that it implies, it becomes evident that the prophets of dialectical materialism attribute a formidable cultural and psychological potency to the "spiritual" faculty of imagination. They would have us believe that religion, in the words of Friedrich Engels, "is nothing but the fantastic reflection in men's minds of those external forces which control their daily life, a reflection in which the terrestrial forces assume the form of supernatural forces."[60] Marx and Engels are convinced that this "religious reflex" will vanish when the social conditions that it reflects have been abolished.[61] Yet in the meantime this illusory imagination retains a powerful hold on people, powerful enough to cause them to betray their own self-interest. Such a view of religion takes it very seriously indeed as a force in human individuals and societies. The argument between Marxists and religious believers—and it remains a real one—is not over the cognitive status of theistic beliefs but about the social uses of imagination. The atheism of imagination is a more formidable opponent of theology than positivist skepticism because it takes religion seriously.

Feuerbach believed that what he had done was to reduce theology to anthropology by uncovering the psychological motives of religious imagination. It would be hard to deny that the modern interpretation of religion as imagination has tended in the direction he anticipated in 1841. Especially sobering is the evidence for this tendency among the friends of religion as well as its foes. The description of religion as a kind of imagination (whether this term is used or one of its surrogates) seems inevitably to have led in a reductionist direction, implying that religion is the product of human needs, the projection of this-worldly subjectivity onto an illusory screen of other-worldly objectivity.

Throughout this book I will argue that imagination, adequately conceived as a human activity and rightly employed as a theological concept, need not lead to reductionist conclusions. Those conclusions appeared inevitable to earlier generations for contingent historical reasons that I have tried to clarify—reasons that are no longer binding on us. In order to overcome them we will need to break the well-entrenched modern habit of thinking of religion as the opposite of science.

The case will be made largely in terms of Christian theological categories and concerns. This is the tradition I know best, about which I care most deeply, and in which I have the training to undertake such an endeavor. I am nevertheless convinced that the argument has important implications for other religions as well, and I hope that scholars who are competent in those traditions will be challenged to extend my ideas in directions that I have not pursued. Christian theology today, whether undertaken in the setting of the seminary or the university, finds itself increasingly in the context of religious studies and simply cannot proceed as though the broader world of religion did not exist or were unimportant. I have therefore proceeded from the thesis that *religion* is an activity of the human imagination, even though I am offering arguments only for the Christian case. I also believe that the case must be made for each tradition on its own terms, for reasons that are endemic to religion and will become apparent as the argument unfolds. To use imagination as the cornerstone for a theory of religion-in-general, from which the various religions could be derived, would be to misunderstand profoundly the nature of both religion and imagination.

CHAPTER 2

A Theological Dilemma: "Natural Theology" or "Positivism of Revelation"

Some of the most influential twentieth-century thinkers have continued and extended the anthropological reduction of religious imagination that emerged so powerfully in the nineteenth century. The examples of Durkheim and Freud, both outspoken proponents of "science" as the alternative to an outmoded "religion," have already been mentioned.[1] But the twentieth century has also witnessed a great theological revolt against the "anthropologizing" of religion and the kind of theology that invites it. This chapter examines that revolt with particular attention to its consequences for the role of imagination in religion. The resulting situation, best characterized as a dilemma for theological method, sets the stage for a fresh look at the imagination as a key to resolving that dilemma.

The tradition of mediating theology—those thinkers who have sought to reconcile the assumptions of post-Enlightenment intellectuals with the historic truth claims of Christian doctrine—has generally remained impotent in the face of the "atheism of imagination." Mediating theologians typically have either ignored its challenge or they have simply asserted that its conclusions are unjustified while continuing to practice theology in ways that remain vulnerable to its criticism. At its worst, this kind of theology has acquiesced in the reduction of religious truth to subjective imagination while continuing to insist that such interpretations are compatible with the truth claims of historic Christian theology.

The most important challenge to the mediating tradition in modern theology originated in German Protestant circles in the years following the First World War. The movement that formed around Karl Barth, whose *Epistle to the Romans* is generally regarded as its manifesto, came to be known as dialectical theology and flourished during the 1920s. The public exchange that took place in 1923 between Barth and Adolf von Harnack, the elder statesman of Protestant liberalism, epitomizes the gulf in religious sensibility and theological assumptions that had opened up between the reigning academic theology and the young Turks.[2] Even more significant for the issues relevant to religious imagination are the controversies a decade later between Barth and his erstwhile "dialectical" allies, culminating in the 1934 debate about nature and grace between Barth and Emil Brunner. At the center of their disagreement was the issue of the so-called *Anknüpfungspunkt*, the anthropological point of contact for revelation. I want first to recall the salient features of that debate and describe the theological impasse to which it led. I will then show how the issues can be sharpened and clarified by reformulating them as an argument about theology and the religious imagination. Subsequent chapters will demonstrate how the concept of imagination can be developed and employed to clear away the conceptual confusion that led to the dilemma about revelation and theological method.

The Debate About Nature and Grace

The intensity of the polemics that exploded into public controversy between Barth and Emil Brunner in 1934 is understandable in retrospect in the light of two factors. First, the debate occurred against the background of a decade of partisan unity among the advocates of dialectical theology, expressed concretely in the publication of the journal *Zwischen den Zeiten* from 1923 to 1933. Originally inspired by Barth's *Romans* commentary, these young theologians had made a decisive break with the dominant tradition of Protestant theology since the Enlightenment. This tradition, which counted Schleiermacher as its greatest thinker, had achieved virtual dominance of academic theology in the liberalism that held sway in the German theological faculties in the decades preceding the First World War. The young theologians believed that dialectical theology had at long last recovered the genuine spirit of the Protestant Reformers and was able to proclaim it in words that spoke to the situation of the church in the twentieth century. In *Nature and Grace* Brunner blamed Barth for shattering this unity by his intransigent stance and his anathematizing of former compatriots. Barth's *No!* in turn charged Brunner with betraying the common cause by embarking on a theological program that professed loyalty to the newly recovered principles of the Reformation while in substance succumbing to the old assumptions of the modernist tradition from which they had so recently declared their independence.

The other factor that intensified the emotional tone of the theological debate was Hitler's rise to power in 1933, especially the emergence of the "German Christians" and the increasing political pressures on church and university affairs that were shortly to force Karl Barth to leave his academic post and return to Switzerland. It is no mere coincidence that the exchange about nature and grace took place in the same year as the *Theological Declaration of Barmen*. The seemingly "academic" issues of nature and grace, of natural theology and revelation, were fraught with immediate political implications to an extent unparalleled in modern church history. Barth was convinced that the "German Christians" were the final poisonous fruit of two centuries of corrupt theological tradition. It was no time to mince words when the church was in mortal danger.

But the substantive issues of the controversy have an importance that extends far beyond the European crisis of the 1930s. The urgency of that situation simply served to force out in particularly dramatic fashion problems that had long troubled theology. The central issue that emerged in the debate under the classical rubric "nature and grace" was the knowledge of God—and therefore the possibility of theology—in an age when theologians had long since abandoned the metaphysics undergirding the old orthodoxy but had not yet succeeded in finding a workable alternative. This much, at least, was taken for granted by the dialectical theologians, who had no interest whatever in resuscitating supranaturalist philosophy but were equally agreed that Protestant liberalism had betrayed the essential content of Christian belief by identifying it too closely with merely human possibilities and institutions, whether individual or cultural. But the further they proceeded in articulating positive alternatives to that tradition, the more apparent it became that they did not share a common vision of the future of theology.

The keynote had been sounded in Barth's *Romans* commentary, which is filled with negative and paradoxical images of the divine-human relationship, the feature that earned the label "dialectical" for the enterprise that its proponents preferred to call "theology of the Word of God." Not continuity but discontinuity was the hallmark of this relationship: grace is related to nature as a tangent to a circle; revelation is not a "content" but rather a "vacuum"; salvation comes in the form of judgment, *krisis*. As a battering ram against *Kulturprotestantismus* this was effective polemics. But it was another matter to construct an adequate positive account of revelation, of the relation of the Word of God to the word of man.

Brunner's concern to articulate this relationship led him to make a series of attempts in the late 1920s and early 1930s to describe the *Anknüpfungspunkt*, the point at which the divine Word makes effective contact with human nature. At the same time, he became increasingly critical of Barth's wholesale rejection of natural theology and tried to argue for a new *theologia naturalis* in keeping with the teachings of the Reformation. Brunner was convinced that theology must address directly the homiletic question, "What does is mean to *say* the Word of God to a human being?"[3] It is essential to understand *how* revelation becomes effective in proclamation, and this means that the question of the *Anknüpfungspunkt* cannot be evaded. Seeking to follow the examples of Pascal, Hamann, and Kierkegaard, Brunner begins with the assumption that the question of God is fundamental to human existence; it is, in fact, "identical with humanity" itself and therefore constitutes the point of contact for revelation. The error of "every Pelagian or Pelagianizing theology,"[4] Brunner insists, is not in seeking an *Anknüpfungspunkt* but rather in trying to identify it positively instead of negatively. "Life in all its manifestations," according to Brunner, "is essentially asking the question of God and is therefore ambiguous, *grandeur et misère de l'homme*," in his favorite phrase from Pascal.[5] Brunner wants to say that the human quest for God is futile, that it cannot achieve genuine knowledge of God apart from revelation, and yet that the quest itself provides the point of contact for God's Word. The view is not "synergistic," he argues, because God—as creator rather than redeemer—is the author of this *Anknüpfungspunkt*, which lies at the heart of human nature and cannot be effaced by sin.

When Barth published the first half-volume of his *Church Dogmatics* in 1932, he drew heavily from Brunner in characterizing the wrong reasons for pursuing dogmatic prolegomena. According to the prevailing but mistaken view, Barth argues, modern paganism has created the need for a second, apologetic task that theology must discharge before it can proceed to its primary task of dogmatics. Theology carries out the preliminary task by rejecting modern rationalistic self-sufficiency and relating theological propositions to the true *Anknüpfungspunkt*, the natural human search for God that has not been disrupted by sin. Barth rejects this program on the grounds that it raises the false question of the possibility of revelation instead of presupposing that revelation itself creates the necessary human "point of contact."[6] We cannot establish the knowability of the Word of God, he argues, "by turning our backs on [it], as it were, in order to contemplate ourselves and to discover in ourselves an openness, a positive or at least a negative point of contact [*Anknüpf-ungspunkt*] for the Word of God."[7] Barth does not base his objections on the weakness of any specifically proposed points of contact. His critique is more radical: any account whatever of the anthropological point of contact with the divine Word is illegitimate, since to know about the *Anknüpfungspunkt* in abstraction from revelation contradicts the character of revelation as grace. We do not understand revelation by learning how people are able to receive it but rather by learning that it comes precisely to those who are *un*able to receive it. It is important to note that Barth never denies that there *is* a point of contact for revelation. His concern is epistemological and methodological: the issue is whether we can *first* establish the existence of an *Anknüpfungspunkt* and *then* understand revelation or whether the point of contact is itself real and knowable only on the basis of revelation. The reversal of the usual order of possibility and actuality—a feature fundamental to Barth's theology—plays a key role here. "By hearing it [the Word of God]," he writes, "we have the possibility of hearing it."[8]

This stance appeared to Brunner, as it has to so many of Barth's critics, simply to isolate theology in a realm of its own and to abandon any hope of seriously addressing the modern secular world. Brunner presented his alternative proposal for a new natural theology in its most developed form, together with his most explicit challenge to Barth, in his 1934 essay *Natur und Gnade*, which provoked Barth's notorious reply entitled *Nein!*[9] Although the polemical intensity did not contribute to the balance or precision of the theological arguments, it did serve to focus the critical issues sharply.

The main part of the debate is structured around six theses, in which Brunner first summarizes his understanding of Barth's position before elaborating a list of countertheses containing his own views. Barth rejects the theses attributed to himself and speaks instead to each of Brunner's countertheses in turn. Four of the points (the second, third, fourth, and sixth theses) have to do with distinguishing aspects of nature and grace: general and special revelation; the grace of creation and the grace of preservation; the "ordinances" of creation; and the relation of old and new creation. In each case Brunner endeavors to treat the two aspects separately, arguing for a distinct, though ultimately subordinate, "natural" theology; and Barth, applying what he later calls his christological concentration, refuses to allow an independent thematic treatment of nature apart from the revelation in Jesus Christ.

The central issues emerge most clearly in the two theses that speak directly to the connection between nature and grace. In the first thesis, Brunner attributes to Barth the proposition that the image of God in creation is utterly destroyed by sin, leaving no remainder. In his counter-thesis Brunner introduces a distinction between the formal *imago Dei*, essential humanity, consisting of human personhood and responsibility that is not impaired by sin, and the material *imago* that is lost in the fall. Barth, in his rejoinder, does not deny that the sinner remains a responsi-ble subject but finds in this truism no grounds for an independent natu-ral theology apart from grace.

The fifth thesis takes up the theme of the *Anknüpfungspunkt* directly. According to Brunner's summary, Barth rejects all discussion of a "point of contact" because it would contradict the sole efficacy of Christ's grace. Brunner himself, on the other hand, maintains that the unimpaired for-mal *imago Dei* is the (natural) point of contact for God's grace, though he admits there is no material point of contact, since the Word of God must create its own ability to be heard. His most important contention is that this natural *Anknüpfungspunkt* consists in man's ability to be addressed (his *Ansprechbarkeit*) and includes all that the natural man knows, how-ever confusedly, about God. At this point Barth accuses Brunner of a fundamental contradiction that serves to mask his covert agreement with Thomistic and Protestant modernist doctrines of continuity be-tween nature and grace. If Brunner had really meant to restrict the *An-knüpfungspunkt* to a purely *formal* divine image, consisting merely in the fact that man remains man and therefore capable of responsibility and decision even as sinner, his point would have been true but trivial, of-fering no basis for a natural theology. But Barth accuses him of smug-gling a substantial amount of "matter" into this human "form." "The realm over which this 'addressibility' extends," Brunner had written, "encompasses not only the *humanum* in the narrower sense but every-thing connected with the 'natural' knowledge of God," including "that which natural man knows of God, the law, and his own belonging to God," however confused it may be.[10] Such statements, Barth argues, make a mockery of Brunner's claim that the anthropological point of contact is purely "formal." Despite his announced intention of remain-ing true to the Reformation *sola gratia* and *sola scriptura*, Brunner has laid the foundations for a natural theology in which the possibility of revela-tion depends on a prior human potentiality unimpaired by sin and therefore not in need of divine grace.

Resolving the Theological Dilemma

The Barth-Brunner controversy of 1934 exposed a raw nerve of mod-ern theology. Far from resolving the issues it raised, it ended in a stand-off that bequeathed to later theology a dilemma that it has not been able to overcome. In order to explain what it means to say that human beings receive divine revelation, the theologian must be able to describe—to theological outsiders as well as insiders—what happens to human nature in the encounter and cannot thereby avoid saying how or where the divine Word becomes humanly effective. Here is the undeniable force of Brunner's insistence on the *Anknüpfungspunkt*. Yet if the theologian offers an anthropological account of the point of contact, one that does not presuppose revelation—and here is the undeniable force of Barth's objection—the event apparently has its ground in a human possibility rather than in the free grace of God. To say that revelation is *grace* is surely to say at the very least that it is not the actualization of some existing human potentiality but rather the reception of something novel, something alien, something incapable of anticipation and not at the disposal of the human recipient. In short, the event of grace appears to require a theological explanation that cannot be given without denying the grace of the event.

As long as this dilemma remains unresolved, theology is faced with a devil's choice. Seizing the first horn of the dilemma leads to an accommodating modernism, the "neo-Protestant" heresy attacked by Barth, whose chief identifying mark is "natural theology" by whatever name it may be called. Choosing the other alternative, however, threatens to land theology in an isolated dogmatic purism in which revelation is protected from anthropological reduction at the price of refusing to speak of it in any but self-referential terms. The theologian is left speaking a language whose conceptuality is internally coherent but powerless to communicate its content because it is unrelated to all nontheological discourse. This alternative can be described as a "positivism of revelation," borrowing the phrase sometimes used by critics of Barth.[11]

One way to state the thesis of this book is to say that the dilemma can be resolved by identifying the point of divine-human contact as imagination. Before that thesis can be adequately developed theologically, the concept of imagination on which it depends will need to be examined in detail, which is the task of the next two chapters. In the meantime it will be informative to look again at the issues raised by the Barth-Brunner controversy, with the advantage of both historical hindsight and philosophical distance from the prevailing assumptions of German theology in the 1930s.

An advantage of reexamining the debate about the *Anknüpfungspunkt* from this perspective is that the intellectual context no longer appears so self-evident or inevitable as it did at the time. It may therefore be possible to recognize assumptions or presuppositions of the participants that clouded the central issue and blinded them to possible solutions. In the clearer (if drier) atmosphere of more recent Anglo-American philosophy, we may be able to view theology in a broader context without compromising its integrity by trying either to deduce it from an ontological theory or to ground it on an anthropological presupposition. The goal will be to do justice to Brunner's legitimate search for an answer to the question, "What does it mean to *say* the Word of God to a human being?" without falling into the "neo-Protestant" assumptions that Barth exposed. The argument assumes (1) that in substance Barth was right to reject natural theology as proposed by Brunner and others in the 1930s, but (2) that this does not mean that Brunner's question was wrong and does not preclude an independent account of the human point of contact for divine revelation. The challenge is rather to find a way of describing the *Anknüpfungspunkt* that not only does justice to the character of revelation as grace but also makes clear in purely "formal" or theologically neutral terms what it means to say that human beings receive that revelation.

Behind Barth's vehement polemic against natural theology is a historical thesis, a critical reading of modern philosophical and theological thought. According to this historical critique, modern thinkers have come to view church and faith as parts of a larger "context of being" and dogmatics as a special case of a general scientific problem-complex. In post-Cartesian thought, Barth argues, this general context can mean only one thing: "a comprehensively articulated self-understanding of human existence, which . . . can also become the preunderstanding of an existence in the church or in faith and hence the preunderstanding and criterion of theological knowledge."[12] Barth assumes, in other words, that any attempt to place faith in a broader context will inevitably mean subjecting theology to the criteria of a philosophical ontology as its presupposition and ground. Whether or not modern theologians *had* to ground dogmatics ontologically (this point may be left open for the time being) Barth is surely right that nearly all have in fact tried to do so. His own unwillingness to follow such a program led him to reject not only Brunner's natural theology but also the existentialist "preunderstanding" proposed by Gogarten and Bultmann.[13] All such attempts to ground dogmatics have in common the acceptance of an anthropological presupposition as the condition for theology. But this means that the theologian already knows something important—indeed, the essential fact—about human nature and the human condition prior to, and therefore apart from, divine revelation. From the standpoint of a theology of grace based on the principles of the Reformation, Barth concludes that this program is impossible, since it implies that knowledge of God can be obtained directly from creation by fallen human beings.

In the context of his attack on Brunner's proposal for a natural theology, Barth's comments about the *Anknüpfungspunkt* of revelation are therefore almost entirely negative. He wants to preclude every attempt to "ground" theology philosophically or in any other nontheological way, which means on any foundation other than revelation itself. To his critics that refusal has seemed effectively to isolate theology from other human intellectual endeavors in a self-enclosed fideism—the quality of Barth's thought that has invited the label "positivism of revelation."

Recent developments in Anglo-American philosophy, however, suggest another way of understanding Barth's consistent refusal to undergird theology with a philosophical foundation. Some philosophers have been arguing (and certainly not out of theological motives!) that all proposals to "ground" knowledge epistemologically are based on untenable assumptions about the nature of knowledge and should therefore be rejected.[14] This antifoundationalist critique—whether or not one is prepared to accept all of its claims—has surely demonstrated that to refuse, as Barth does, to ground one's arguments philosophically does not automatically constitute an irrational or fideist position. Before passing judgment, one must examine more closely the specific reasons for that refusal.

If we first look carefully at what theologians were saying in the 1930s under rubrics like "philosophy" and "anthropological point of contact," it becomes apparent that real and important *theological* disagreements were never clearly distinguished from certain shared assumptions about the nature of *philosophical* doctrines. Both Brunner and Barth took for granted in 1934 what today would be called a foundationalist view of philosophy, according to which the principal task of philosophical inquiry is to "ground" the concepts we use, to provide our discourse with an epistemological starting point in incorrigible or self-evident assumptions. Barth rightly saw that proposals to base theology on a philosophical anthropology or ontology were attempting to borrow "scientific" credibility from philosophy, understood as what today would be called the "foundational" discipline.[15] He recognized (borrowing the recent formulation of Ronald F. Thiemann) that "modern doctrines of revelation inevitably become epistemological doctrines," in which the "key theological task becomes the devising of a category which will be congenial to a general epistemology and yet establish the uniqueness of the process of religious knowing."[16] Barth correctly understood that theology must eschew foundationalism, since its only proper "foundation" is the Word of God, revealed in scripture and guaranteed by the Holy Spirit. Any other, nontheological ground would constitute a prima facie rejection of that axiom. Since Barth, like others of his generation, assumed that the business of philosophy is to provide such grounding, he naturally opposed every "philosophical" treatment of theological subject matter as an unwarranted distortion of theological method. Brunner, dissatisfied with the consequent isolation of theology from general human discourse, sought to find a philosophical starting point (a "natural theology") consistent with the theological principles that both he and Barth had been defending against Protestant liberalism on the one hand and Roman Catholic doctrine on the other. But since he, too, had a foundationalist understanding of philosophy, he proposed an anthropological "point of contact" grounded in the "human quest for God"[17]—in other words, precisely the sort of extratheological foundation that Barth showed to be inconsistent with proper theological method.

The polemical side of Barth's case against Brunner can thus be explained as a legitimate rejection of theological and philosophical foundationalism. But the key to the theological issue at stake has more to do with the positive aspect of the issue: how to describe the human point of contact for divine revelation. It is possible to characterize Barth's rather elusive position if we bracket the negative polemics, attending especially to the metaphors that he employs in describing the human reception of revelation. One of the passages that provoked Brunner's ire in *Nature and Grace* is Barth's excursus on the notion of an *Anknüpfungspunkt* in the first volume of the *Church Dogmatics*.[18] It occurs in the context of section 6, "The Knowability of the Word of God," where Barth singles out Brunner as the example of how not to employ the term theologically. Barth speaks of the *Anknüpfungspunkt* as a *Gottförmigkeit*, a "God-shaped" aspect of the fallen creature, denying Brunner's contention that such a feature remains in human nature from creation after the fall. "The image of God in man . . . that forms the actual point of contact of the Word of God," Barth writes against Brunner's view of the *imago*, "is the *newly* created *rectitudo*, awakened by Christ from actual death to life and thus 'restored,' now actually as the possibility of man for the Word of God."[19] In faith—that is, by grace and not by nature—the human being does indeed become *gottförmig*, "theomorphic," capable of truly hearing and responding to God's Word.[20] When Barth comes to the corresponding point in his doctrine of God (section 26 on "The Knowability of God"), he again speaks directly to the issue of the *Anknüpfungspunkt*. His point is to show that the alleged biblical *loci classici* for natural theology do not in fact support the claim that there is a separate human basis for knowing God independently of God's self-revelation. He acknowledges that what Paul (author of the main New Testament texts in question) describes can be called an *Anknüpfungspunkt*. What is important is to understand that "this 'point of contact,' precisely from the human side, is not treated as already posited, but rather is *posited anew* in and with the proclamation of the gospel."[21]

With only a slight shift of emphasis, Barth's account of how revelation is received can be redescribed as a conversion of the imagination. His metaphoric language provides a clue. In describing the *Anknüpfungspunkt*, his language shifts from static and local metaphors to dynamic images of shaping or forming. Instead of talking in terms of a *point* of contact, in which it would be important to know what *parts* of human nature remain upright, he prefers to depict a drama of transformation, a story in which the human creature is originally formed by God, becomes de-formed or misshapen by sin, and is finally re-formed by grace through being con-formed to the image of God in Christ. The kind of transformation that Barth describes as the effect of divine revelation involves the human being at that point most precisely designated as imagination. At the very least his metaphors coincide with dominant metaphors implicit in the language of imagination itself: shaping or formation according to an image. The more difficult task will be to demonstrate that this coincidence of imagery is not merely coincidental but reflects a genuine "fit" between the substance of the Christian doctrine of revelation and the human act of imagining.

Once the issue of philosophical foundations is disentangled from the theological question of the *Anknüpfungspunkt*, a space begins to open up between the false alternatives of "natural theology" and "positivism of revelation," a space that becomes visible in Barth's suggestively metaphorical terminology. As long as theologians persist in describing the reception of revelation solely in biblical and dogmatic terms, the problem of "revelation-positivism" remains. Outsiders—even if we grant them an earnest and sympathetic willingness to understand believers—will remain unable to conceive what sort of thing this "revelation" is, since its theological description contains nothing to enable outsiders to compare it to other events or experiences with which they are familiar. The revelation-positivist may at this point counter that divine revelation is in fact incomparable and unlike any previous experience that the outsider has had: the only way to understand revelation is to experience it. But the pious plausibility of this rejoinder masks a conceptual confusion, a refusal to distinguish two levels of comparability. A full defense of this claim requires the lengthier argument of the following chapters. For now, it can be briefly explained by saying that the revelation-positivist fails to distinguish material from formal comparability. The *content*—better: the shape, substance, or "meaning"—of revelation is indeed unique and discontinuous with other "contents." But if revelation is a real event in the human world—a point on which Christians have always insisted—it has *formal* similarities with other events in that world (what else could we mean by calling it an "event"?). For theology to deny *that* kind of comparability, I believe, would be truly to succumb to the "death by a thousand qualifications,"[22] emptying the language of Christian faith of its substance and persuasive power.

The formal comparability of revelation to other human events and experiences implies and authorizes a philosophical task for theology. The legitimacy of this enterprise, not evident in the 1930s, depends upon our replacing the notion of philosophy as the foundational discipline for theology and other enterprises of the mind with a more modest view of philosophy as "descriptive grammar," an analytical tool for investigating the logic of various human endeavors and a therapy for conceptual conundrums resulting from "grammatical" confusions. Such a philosophy could scarcely lead to a project like "natural theology," and theologians can employ it without any greater risk to the integrity of their discipline than that entailed by the use (for example) of English or of mathematics.[23] The criteria for an acceptable philosophical theology would be drawn, not from a prior "ontology" or "context of being," but from the grammar of theology itself.

Viewed in this way, the issue of the *Anknüpfungspunkt* appears to be not a methodological debate about the proper relation of philosophy to theology in general but rather a substantive theological dispute— having important methodological consequences—about the relation of human experience and thought to divine grace. Barth's critique of Brunner's proposal for a natural theology appears to be justified, but not to entail the sweeping consequences that have sometimes been attributed to it. In particular, it does not entail the conceptual isolation of theology from other disciplines engaged in the interpretation of human experience. Barth shows convincingly that Brunner's specific proposal to correlate biblical revelation with a universal human "quest for God," or with essential human "addressability," is not theologically neutral or purely "formal," as Brunner had insisted, but compromises the gratuitous character of God's revelation while underestimating the negative potential of human religion. Nothing in that critique, however, rules out the possibility of a *truly* "formal" description of the human point of contact for revelation, one that does not compromise the prevenient nature of revelation by making prejudicial anthropological assumptions.

Imagination, properly understood as the name of a basic human ability—one of the things that people *do* in the course of living in, acting on, and thinking about the world—identifies that specific point where, according to Christian belief and experience, the Word of God becomes effective in human lives. More formally: imagination is the anthropological point of contact for divine revelation. It is not the "foundation," the "ground," the "preunderstanding," or the "ontological basis" for revelation; it is simply the place where it happens—better, the way in which it happens. If the term were not so freighted with historical baggage, one could speak quite properly of the *faculty* of imagination, not in the substantival sense of the old faculty psychology but in the original verbal meaning of the word: a faculty is an ability, a skill, a way of behaving that allows one to do something. What it is that one does with imagination— more simply, what it means to imagine—is the crucial issue. In the following chapters I will examine that issue, arguing that the concept of imagination offers theology a means for resolving the dilemma of "natural theology" or "positivism of revelation." Describing the point of divine-human contact in terms of imagination allows theology to do justice to both aspects of revelation: (1) as a divine act of grace, reducible to no human ability, attribute, or need and (2) as a human act of faith, comparable in significant respects to other forms of human experience. The first aspect is the one for which Karl Barth fought so doggedly against every form of "natural theology"; the second recognizes the legitimacy of Brunner's question (and Bonhoeffer's misgivings) and reminds theologians that the Word, having become flesh, remains a part of the human world with real and intelligible relations to the other parts. The uniqueness of the revelation to which Christians bear witness is best served, not by trying to immunize it against criticism by isolating it conceptually, but rather by freely exploring its manifold relations with other human phenomena. One of the things that people do is to imagine, and one of the things they imagine is what theologians have called revelation. The task at hand is to show why this thesis need not expose theology to the anthropological reductionism of the nineteenth century.

CHAPTER 3

The Priority of Paradigms: Clues from the Natural Sciences

The dilemma epitomized by the debate between Barth and Brunner has outlived the immediate issues so vehemently argued in the 1930s. In some respects the problem has intensified, due in part to the shift in the social location of Christian theology from the traditional seminary to the emerging discipline of religious studies.[1] Most attempts in the past half-century to relate theology to other human phenomena—whether popular proposals for theological "relevance" or systematic programs for the "correlation" or "foundation" of Christian truth claims—have avoided the problem of "natural theology" only by ignoring it. Yet the alternative seems always to entail an unacceptable isolation of theology from common norms of public discourse, the recurrent suspicion of "revelation-positivism." Though it would be difficult to prove, I suspect that, precisely because this dilemma has been so deeply felt, theology in the intervening years has struggled hard to repress it. As with other problems felt to be fundamentally insoluble—from the private inadequacies of individuals to the public threat of nuclear annihilation—the more powerfully the dilemma is experienced, the greater the stake in not facing up to it. It remains the bad conscience of liberal theology (many theologians suspect that Barth was right about natural theology but, seeing no acceptable alternative, direct their attention elsewhere). Those who seize the other horn of the dilemma have often been called "Barthians," theologians whose allegiance to biblical revelation is purchased at the price of defining theology into an intellectual ghetto.

Imagination as *Anknüpfungspunkt*

The task at hand is to show how attention to imagination can offer a way out of this impasse. I will argue that the devil's choice between a modernism that excludes grace a priori and a theological positivism that leaves revelation isolated from common human experience is the result of conceptual confusion rather than substantive contradiction. The situation can be clarified and the underlying issues of theological method and anthropology brought to light by developing the thesis that the *Anknüpfungspunkt*, the link between divine revelation and human experience, is the imagination.

The way is fraught with danger. Appeals have frequently been made to the religious import of the imagination. Sometimes, as in high Romanticism, those appeals have been extreme and even preposterous; more often they have simply been loose, too vague to be of much use in the work of serious theology. And lurking behind every such proposal is the threat of anthropological reductionism, the atheism of imagination inherited from the nineteenth century, ready to dissolve every religious truth claim into an airy cloud of illusion. But the most ominous threat of all is a specifically theological one: is not the imagination precisely the kind of tendentious anthropological presupposition that provoked Barth's "Nein!" to the whole tradition of modern Protestant theology as well as traditional Roman Catholic natural theology? A "natural theology of the imagination" would, after all, be a quite conceivable program. First of all, the imagination would need to be grounded philosophically as the definitive human faculty and the source of human piety—in short, as the religious a priori and therefore the foundation for theology. An analysis of the structure of *homo imaginans* would then provide the anthropological base with which the truths of revelation could be correlated. Human imagination could then be interpreted as an implicit relation to the divine—no doubt inadequate from a Christian perspective but nevertheless the precondition for faith, the outstretched hand waiting to be filled by the revelation of God, the anthropological question awaiting a theological answer. Such a program is surely conceivable, and it might even have advantages over other proposed anthropological starting points: the human quest for God, the feeling of absolute dependence, the moral conscience, ultimate concern. But it would just as surely remain vulnerable to the very arguments brought by Barth against the methods of such theologians as Brunner, Gogarten, Bultmann, and Tillich.

If the proposal to interpret imagination as the human point of contact for revelation is to offer a solution and not just another variation on earlier mistakes, therefore, the concept of imagination will have to be employed in such a way that it does not constitute an ontological or anthropological presupposition or preunderstanding of revelation. To this end, it will be helpful from the outset to think of the imagination not as the "faculty" or the "ground" of revelation but simply as its *locus*. The implications of this distinction may become clearer by looking at a parallel case: Barth's treatment of *religion* in section 17 of the *Church Dogmatics*.[2] Far from denying that Christianity is a religion (as a consistent "positivism of revelation" would have to do), Barth emphasizes that revelation encounters us precisely in the form of human religion, though "hidden" within it. The crucial point for theology is whether religion becomes the criterion for revelation—Barth's charge against the dominant trend in modern Protestant theology—or vice versa. In keeping with the christological doctrine of *assumptio carnis*, revelation appears in the form of human religion, which in itself is "unbelief." By the grace of God this all-too-human religion is nevertheless transformed (*aufgehoben*)[3] into the "true religion" of revelation. Religion is thus the locus, the stage, the garment of revelation. It occupies this position without constituting any anticipation, preunderstanding, or capacity for revelation; on the contrary, it is not even neutral, for religion by itself remains a *mis*understanding, the embodiment of human resistance to revelation.

In a similar way, and for similar reasons, I will argue that imagination can be acknowledged as the point in human experience where revelation is encountered without thereby implying any inherent "natural" connection with God. Nothing about the imagination per se, properly conceived, implies the possibility of revelation; nor does anything in the *concept* of imagination prohibit someone from interpreting all religious imagination as imagin*ary*, rooted in the illusory projection of human experience. For this reason neither transcendental analysis nor psychological investigation of imagination is likely to be very fruitful theologically: no clues to transcendence, no traces of God can be expected from an inquiry into the imagination as a human faculty, for the religious imagination has the same anthropological structure as all imagination. That structure is nevertheless important to theology, since it is the matrix in which revelation occurs and the basis for viewing revelation, as a human event, in significant relation to other human phenomena.

Imagination in Science and Religion

Since the rise of the "new science" in the seventeenth and eighteenth centuries, every aspect of Western culture has been profoundly affected by its influence. Historical and philosophical investigations of modern science therefore have implications not only for the natural sciences but also for other areas of culture that take their cues, directly or indirectly, from science. Religion is a prime example of this cultural tendency, for it has typically been defined by modern thinkers in explicit or implicit contrast to science.[4] Any attempt, therefore, to change the way we think about religion requires a change in our thinking about science as well.

Some recent developments in philosophy of science suggest just such a change in the picture of science—a change laden with unexplored implications for religion. To orthodox ears, talk about the "religious imagination" arouses suspicion because it seems to imply that the objects of religious belief are imaginary, mere figments of the subjective imagination. We have seen that there are good grounds for this suspicion in view of the history of modern religious thought.[5] Some of the most powerful antitheologies of the modern world, the critiques of religion by Feuerbach, Marx, and Freud, have been based on the conviction that religion is "really" about unconscious aspects of human finitude, a projection of subjective wishes or fears onto the heavenly screen of the imagination. The close association of religion, imagination, and illusion reflects the common modern dichotomy between a "science" that deals only in empirical facts and a "religion" confined to an inner world of faith, fantasy, and feeling. Despite repeated assaults by philosophers and theologians, the dichotomy persists (sometimes in attractively subtle forms) in the thinking of many, including both religious skeptics and apologists, and its persistence prevents an adequate understanding of either science or religion. The recent philosophical rethinking of science holds the promise of finally dissolving such misinterpretations by radically revising our picture of how scientists think and act when they are doing science.

The central insight of these philosophers of science may be summarized in the thesis that imagination plays a fundamental role in the origin, development, and ongoing work of the natural sciences.[6] If this account of science is correct, imagination is not a peripheral or incidental factor but the key to the scientific knowledge of nature and therefore of profoundly philosophical significance. It does not have to do just with the subjective side of human experience but is essential to the objective and factual investigation of natural phenomena as well.

A number of thinkers have contributed to this reconception of science, including philosophers like Stephen Toulmin, Paul Feyerabend, and Norwood Russell Hanson, but its focus has been the work of Thomas S. Kuhn, whose book *The Structure of Scientific Revolutions* has been at the center of an ongoing discussion ever since its original publication in

1962.[7] Kuhn's historical and philosophical arguments, despite continuing controversy, show a number of traditional assumptions about the nature of science and scientific method to be untenable. At the same time he brings to light some important features of scientific thinking and research that have long been overlooked or misunderstood.

This new view of science requires a rethinking of the relationship of science and religion and therefore—in view of the special place of science in modern thought—a rethinking of religion itself. Throughout the debates about "science and religion" since the nineteenth century, critics and apologists of religion alike have usually shared a common assumption: that religion is to be distinguished from science by some fundamentally different way in which it thinks or knows. The key to religious knowledge, according to both sides, lies in its *difference* from scientific knowledge. Imagination has usually been assigned to the "religious" side of these dichotomies. The importance of the new philosophy of science for theology is to show that imagination cannot be the basis for contrasting religion and science: instead, it names a feature that they have in common. The discovery that imagination plays a crucial role in scientific theory and practice calls into question familiar dichotomies between what counts as subjective and objective, theory and fact, interpretation and observation, forcing a fundamental rethinking of the relationship between science and religion. No longer can theology view science as typifying the "other" way of thinking; on the contrary, attention to imagination can clarify the nature of theology by showing significant parallels to the natural sciences. The point of this comparison is neither to cast doubt on the credibility of the sciences (because scientists, too, are forced to use their imaginations) nor to wrap theology in a white coat of "scientific" respectability. Rather, by concentrating first on the role of imagination in the sciences, we can discover important aspects of its structure that will illuminate its role in religion as well. Also, by examining the imagination first in the natural sciences, those most "objective" of modern disciplines, we have a better chance of avoiding certain prevalent assumptions about the merely "subjective" or illusory nature of imagination.

The Discovery of Paradigms in Science

Philosophically the most important term in Kuhn's theory is the concept of "paradigm," which has been the point of greatest controversy in subsequent debate. I want to examine it in some detail, not only because it is central to the discussion but also because I believe that it is the key to understanding the role of imagination in science, which in turn sheds new light on religious imagination. I want first to outline the role of paradigms in Kuhn's original account of science and then to examine his response to criticism of the concept. I then will argue that, despite criticisms brought against Kuhn's use of the term, the concept of paradigm can be clearly defined as an essential feature of natural science and used to specify the way in which imagination functions in science. This clarification of scientific imagination will prepare the way for consideration of the religious use of imagination in the following chapter.

Kuhn's point of departure for his philosophy of science is the history of science, and the clearest way to gain an overview of his theory is by looking at the way it changes our picture of scientific history. He begins by characterizing what we may call for convenience the traditional view, according to which science develops piecemeal by a continuous and cumulative process, gathering facts by empirical observation, then formulating, testing, and revising theories against established facts and new observation. In contrast to this view Kuhn presents a dialectical account of scientific development, in which periods of "normal science" are interrupted and transformed by "scientific revolutions" that change the rules, the methods and instrumentation, and even the meaning of the basic concepts used in scientific thinking. The philosophic key to this historical process is the role of paradigms, which account for both the unity of normal science and the discontinuities of scientific revolutions.

Paradigms, Kuhn writes, are "accepted examples of actual scientific practice . . . which . . . provide models from which spring particular coherent traditions of scientific research" (10). On the basis of such accepted paradigms, normal science is largely a matter of what Kuhn calls puzzle solving, "achieving the anticipated in a new way" by working out the implications of the paradigm in concrete research programs (36). The paradigm limits scientific attention to a particular narrow range of phenomena and implies the rules under which research is to proceed. This limitation is not a disadvantage but is in fact the main advantage of the paradigm, since science otherwise would have no basis for attaching more significance to some facts than others and no criteria for choosing among possible research projects. Radical novelty is thereby excluded from the normal work of science, allowing it to get on with its business. "Normal science," says Kuhn, "does not aim at novelties of fact or theory and, when successful, finds none" (52).

The significant characteristics of paradigms, which remain largely invisible in normal science, come to light most clearly in scientific revolutions; that is, at those points in the history of science where accepted paradigms break down, novelty does occur, and new paradigms become the basis for a new kind of normal science. The midwife of change is a growing awareness of anomaly, brought on by an increasing number of problems that cannot be solved by normal scientific means and therefore place the scientific community and its paradigms under mounting pressure. Without such a crisis discoveries will often go unnoticed even if they are made by individual scientists, as Kuhn demonstrates from the histories of several sciences. Particularly significant is Kuhn's contention that scientists do not simply reject the old paradigm that led to the crisis; rather the "decision to reject one paradigm is always simultaneously the decision to accept another" (77). Ptolemaic astronomers, for example, were able to cope with observed anomalies for centuries by ad hoc amendments to their theory; only after Copernicus offered a new paradigm were scientists able and willing to see the anomalies as counterinstances, grounds for falsification of the old paradigm. In a similar way physicists continued to see anomalies as puzzles to be solved on the basis of Newtonian physics until Einstein's new paradigm enabled them to see the anomalies as evidence of the inadequacy of the Newtonian paradigm itself.

The period of revolutionary science ends only when the scientific community has accepted a new paradigm, which then forms the basis for a new tradition of normal science. But the nature of the change is perhaps the most noteworthy aspect of Kuhn's theory and highlights the logical peculiarity of paradigms. The transformation is not gradual and cumulative but logically (and psychologically) discontinuous, like a visual gestalt shift in which the elements of perception suddenly come together in a new and unanticipated configuration. Kuhn's very language at this point should arouse the attention of philosophers of religion, for he speaks of "conversion to the new paradigm" (19). His appeal to religious metaphor is occasionally quite undisguised. He writes for example: "The man who embraces a new paradigm at an early stage must often do so in defiance of the evidence provided by problem-solving. He must, that is, have faith that the new paradigm will succeed with the many large problems that confront it, knowing only that the older paradigm has failed with a few. A decision of that kind can only be made on faith"(158). Although scientists committed to a new paradigm may present arguments in an effort to persuade their skeptical colleagues, they cannot have recourse to step-by-step proofs to compel assent, since the very rules and concepts previously employed are called radically into question by the new paradigm. For this reason Kuhn speaks of competing paradigms as "incommensurable" (112). Once a new paradigm is established it can be applied and further articulated but not proven or corrected, for "paradigms are not corrigible by normal science at all" (122). Only a new crisis followed by a new revolution occasioned by another paradigm can bring about such a change—which again will involve a discontinuous shift of vision.

The first edition of Kuhn's book provoked a wide range of responses, including criticism of various kinds and degrees, some of which would take us beyond the issues of consequence for theology.[8] But one area of criticism does require attention here because it is directly pertinent to the nature of imagination in science and religion, and because it has provoked Kuhn to qualify his original theory. The notion of paradigm in Kuhn's book, according to this critique, is vague, confused, contradictory—or all three at once. One critic listed twenty-one different ways in which Kuhn used the term *paradigm*.[9] Kuhn responds to this criticism in the second edition of the book by appending a "Postscript" dealing with the concept of paradigm (174–210). Acknowledging considerable ambiguity in his use of the term, he tries to clarify by distinguishing the principal uses of the word and assigning them new designations. The more general, sociological meaning of paradigm, referring to what is shared by a community of scientists, he proposes to call a "disciplinary matrix," which includes such components as "symbolic generalizations," models, and values. The more specific use of "paradigm" to refer to concrete examples of scientific research—also a component of the disciplinary matrix—he now wants to call "exemplars." He recognizes exemplars to be the most philosophically important component and the most controversial aspect of his theory. They are shared examples through which scientists learn to see certain problems as like one another. They signal the "gestalt in which the situation is to be seen" and are therefore the means of bringing about "a time-tested and group-licensed way of seeing" (189).

I believe that Kuhn, under the pressure of his critics, prematurely abandoned his most promising concept.[10] In view of the criticisms that have been made of his use of the term, however, and the confusion about precisely what it designates in his theory, I want to examine it more closely and specify what I take to be its distinctive features. In general, I will assume that "paradigm" properly denotes what Kuhn now calls "exemplars," but there are compelling reasons for retaining the original term. Taking a cue from Stephen Toulmin's critique of Kuhn, I will be concerned not primarily with Kuhn's original *historical* thesis of alternating phases in scientific development, but rather with the *logical* distinction that gave rise to it.[11] Properly delimited, the concept of paradigm identifies an important aspect of imagination, one that is central to both science and religion. It therefore supplies the key to the distinctive nature of religious imagination and an important clue to the task of theology.

The Priority of the Paradigm

If the new philosophy of science contributes negatively to theology by undermining some cherished but misleading dichotomies, it also has a positive contribution to make by allowing theologians to learn something indirectly about the role of imagination in their own field. That role can be described by adapting Kuhn's key concept: like the natural sciences, theology employs paradigms in thinking about its object. In order to conceive of God—to take the primary theological object—we necessarily make use of analogies drawn from our common experience, from the world of the familiar. Analogy, of course, has been a mainstay of theology since ancient times, and virtually every theologian has been willing to acknowledge its necessity. But disagreements arise whenever someone proposes a specific analogy for imagining God. The "nature and grace" debate between Brunner and Barth was one battle in this intermittent war. For them the sticking point was not whether an analogy was needed, but whether it can be taken from the natural world or must be given by the grace of God. The recent discussion in philosophy of science suggests an approach to these issues that can break the deadlock. In the sense to be developed here, a *paradigm* is not a simple synonym for *analogy* in the traditional theological sense. In order to bring out the peculiar function of paradigms in the religious imagination, it will be useful to examine the concept closely, paying special attention to those features of paradigms brought to light by recent philosophy of science. At the same time it will be necessary to define the term more precisely so as to avoid the confusion that led even Kuhn to retreat from its use.

The term *paradigm* itself, though only recently in vogue among philosophers, has been around for a long time. The Greek word *paradeigma*, meaning a pattern or model, was used in several ways by ancient writers.[12] Concretely, it referred to an architect's model or plan for a building, or the model used by a painter or sculptor. It could also mean a precedent or example—or by extension a lesson, a warning, or an argument or proof by example. In law, it referred to a leading case or precedent. It also had a philosophical, even theological, use in Plato: *paradeigmata* were the divine exemplars after which earthly things are modeled. The verbal form *paradeigmatizo* meant "to make an example of" or "to show by example."[13] The common denominator in all these uses is a pattern after which something can be modeled or by which something can be recognized. Kuhn's use of the term *paradigm* to interpret the history of science is consistent with the ancient meanings: it represents the essential pattern by which scientists learn to see an aspect of nature and is therefore the key to the terminology, instrumentation, methods, and data for a science or part of science under its sway.

To understand properly the recent attention given to paradigms by philosophers, it will be helpful to recall a chapter from the history of modern psychology. The early gestalt psychologists challenged the assumptions of the prevailing associationist theory, which explained perception by the cumulative adding together of atomistic sense data to form larger wholes. Gestalt theorists such as Max Wertheimer, Wolfgang Köhler, and Kurt Kaffka pointed to experiments suggesting the reverse: that our perception of "parts" depends on our prior grasp of a "whole." Especially suggestive were certain "optical illusions" or shifting-perspective figures in which the entire figure is perceived differently by different observers, or by the same observer at different times. The most famous example (among philosophers, at least) is the so-called duck-rabbit, used by Wittgenstein in his *Philosophical Investigations*.[14] The same arrangement of lines on paper can be seen alternately as a duck or a rabbit. The "parts" reported by the observer (e.g., bill, ears, eye) are relative to the *aspect* (as Wittgenstein called it), the gestalt according to which the observer is seeing the figure.

The discoveries of gestalt psychology raise both psychological and philosophical issues that need to be carefully distinguished. Hanson calls attention to situations in which one person perceives something differently from another—for example, when a physicist sees a pattern in an X-ray tube that the lay observer does not; or when a musician hears the oboe out of tune while the untrained ear does not. In each case both parties receive identical sense data and yet see or hear differently; in Wittgenstein's terminology, one perceives an aspect that the other does not. Hanson distinguishes the psychological from the logical (or philosophical) issues as follows:

> *Why* a visual pattern is seen differently is a question for psychology, but *that* it may be seen differently is important in any examination of the concepts of seeing and observation. Here, as Wittgenstein might have said, the psychological is a symbol of the logical.[15]

Whatever the psychological roots of gestalt phenomena may be (an interesting and important issue, but a different one), their philosophical importance has to do with their logic, not their origins. The point is that our perception and understanding do behave in such a manner, and the philosopher's task, as Wittgenstein might have said, is to explore their grammar. As Wittgenstein did say about the experience of shifting aspects, "Its *causes* are of interest to psychologists" but philosophers "are interested in the concept and its place among the concepts of experience."[16]

The main *philosophical* issue raised by experiments in gestalt psychology concerns the grammar of wholes and parts. According to conventional wisdom as well as associationist psychology, a whole is the sum of its parts. The gestalt position has often been summarized in the misleading thesis that the "whole is more than the sum of its parts." The weakness of this formulation is that it fails to grasp the most important insight of gestalt theory: that the whole can be neither more nor less than the sum of its parts since it is not a *sum* at all. (If one is partial to mathematical analogies, it would be better to call the whole the *product* of its parts.) Köhler, describing what he calls "insight," contends that "organization in perception . . . as an action does not occur within the mental world. Only the *result* of the organizing process," he says, "is usually experienced." Important intellectual achievements appear to result from "an abrupt reorganization of given materials, a revolution, the result of which suddenly appears ready-made on the mental scene." Such insights, he notes, characteristically occur at times of great passivity—what Köhler calls the "three B's . . . the Bus, the Bath, and the Bed"—though he is careful to add that they are always preceded by a period of "active mental work."[17] Insight, like other gestalt phenomena, is not the result of some additional factor; if it were, something would have to be added to the duck-rabbit-as-duck before it could be perceived as rabbit. The logical, philosophical, or grammatical point (its negative side, at least) has been put this way by one philosopher: "Wholes are . . . quite incomparable with additive aggregations."[18]

Ignoring the logic of wholes and parts leads to a common "grammatical" error that can be called the *atomistic fallacy*. Kuhn describes the "shared paradigm" common to a community of scientists as "a unit that cannot be fully reduced to logically atomic components which might function in its stead."[19] He is recognizing a feature of science that closely parallels what the gestalt psychologists learned about perception. The pattern, the peculiar way in which the components are organized into a coherent whole, is the essential point, the *sine qua non* for the consensus on which scientific research depends. The error of associationist psychology in explaining perception has its parallel in scientific theory. "There is no inductive method which could lead to the fundamental concepts of physics," according to Einstein; "in error are those theorists who believe that theory comes inductively from experience."[20] Hanson accounts for the atomistic fallacy in this way: "In general, though each member of a class of events may be explained by other members, the *totality* of the class cannot be explained by any member of the class."[21] The atomistic fallacy, as we shall see, has wreaked havoc in theology by confounding such issues as the "essence of Christianity" and the unity of scripture.

A first step toward clarifying the concept of paradigm is therefore to recover its original reference to pattern and thus to wholes. The term *paradigm* refers to the constitutive pattern according to which something is organized as a whole-in-parts. The adjective *paradigmatic* could thus be used appropriately to denote pattern-qualities, holistic attributes, features characterizing the whole *as* whole rather than as an aggregate of parts. In this sense of the term, seeing perspective in a painting, hearing a familiar tune, or recognizing a face can be called paradigmatic activities: they cannot be adequately accounted for by cumulative or additive logic; their grammar is holistic, they are essentially patternlike.

The positive principle to which the atomistic fallacy corresponds can be called the hermeneutical priority of the pattern. It is shared implicitly by such apparently diverse enterprises as gestalt psychology, the new philosophy of science, and the views of the later Wittgenstein about language and meaning. All would agree with Hanson's thesis: "Pattern statements are different from detail statements," he claims. "They are not inductive summaries of detail statements."[22] This principle has provoked controversy in all of the disciplines where it has been applied because it goes against the grain of powerful tendencies in modern thought. Kant—to name the most influential modern thinker—might seem to be acknowledging the hermeneutical priority of the pattern in his insistence that knowledge is not the passive accumulation of sense data but an interactive process uniting concept and percept. But despite the importance of the unifying patten for Kant, he sees the problem of knowledge as one of bringing unity to an original multiplicity of sense data (a plural); reason has the job of unifying the manifold of *Erkenntnisse* (a plural: bits of knowledge, individual items of cognition). Despite his view of knowledge as the grasping of a synthetic whole, he always presupposes a movement *from* the (unsynthesized) parts *to* the whole. Kant and the tradition of transcendental philosophy have taught us to see the pattern as prior (a priori), but only in a subjective sense, and to see the parts or sensuous content as given objectively, though in unorganized fashion. In this regard at least, Hegel recognized a weakness in the Enlightenment tradition that Kant did not, whatever one may think of Hegel's own systematic description of *the* whole. His thought begins from the whole and ends there, too; it moves from an empty and abstract notion of the whole to a rich and concrete concept (grasp: *Begriff*) of the Whole. In a sense, then, it is correct to say that Hegel moves *from* the whole *to* its "parts."

The challenge of the recent "holistic" thinkers is to break with the assumption of prior multiplicity, to abandon the prevalent modern presupposition that interpretation or knowledge is achieved by bringing together atomistically conceived bits of data into coherent (best of all, systematic) wholes. Without abandoning the empirical intent of Kant and the Enlightenment, they challenge the assumption that the fundamental units of experience are atomistic "data" or "facts." The hypothesis that experience is essentially "figured" does *not* imply, however, that the various "wholes" we experience necessarily come together in some overarching Whole, as proposed by Hegel and other Idealists. On the contrary, as we shall see shortly, the holistic understanding of science has led to the recognition of apparently irreconcilable discontinuities between incommensurable "wholes."

But paradigms in science, and also in religion, are more than just holistic patterns. Otherwise every coherent theory, every successful experiment, could be called a paradigm. Why are some patterns more "paradigmatic" than other? The question points to the other essential attribute of the true paradigm: its exemplary function. Something serves as a paradigm—that is, as an exemplar or ideal type—because it shows forth a pattern, a coherent nexus of relations, in a simple and straightforward manner. Paradigms function heuristically by revealing the constitutive patterns in more complex aspects of our experience that might otherwise remain recalcitrant, incoherent, or bewildering. Kuhn, in his switch from *paradigm* to *exemplar*, recognized this point while failing to see that the latter term is not an alternative to the former but rather names an essential feature of it. It is precisely the coincidence of organizing pattern and exemplifying function that constitutes the true paradigm. This combination of pattern and example is evident in the ordinary modern usage of the adjective *paradigmatic* to mean not just "patternlike" but "typical, exemplary." To grasp a pattern as paradigmatic means to see it as exemplifying the constitutive organization or essential structure of its object. A paradigm, therefore, is best defined as a normative model for a human endeavor or object of knowledge, the exemplar or privileged analogy that shows us what that object is *like*.

The Logic of Paradigm Change

The characteristic of paradigms that has been at once their most fascinating quality and the source of the greatest controversy in philosophy of science has to do with moving from one paradigm to another. On the simple perceptual level this quality of paradigms is experienced as a gestalt shift—for example, when a person who has been perceiving the duck-rabbit-as-duck suddenly sees it as a rabbit. The suddenness of the experience is an indication of the radical discontinuity between the two aspects: it has an either-or quality suggesting that the different aspects are not only discontinuous but incompatible. Both figures lay claim to precisely the same content; both wholes require the same material for their parts. An observer can become adept at switching rapidly between the two aspects but will never become able to see both at once. Scientific paradigms, according to Kuhn's theory of scientific change, have similar qualities.

Kuhn's view of science has provoked its most vehement opposition at just this point: by its claim that the history of science is punctuated by revolutions that "transformed the scientific imagination in ways that we shall ultimately need to describe as a transformation of the world within which scientific work was done."[23] These "changes of worldview," like the paradigms on which they are based, are discontinuous, incommensurable, irreversible, and highly resistant to verification or falsification. Such claims have attracted charges of irrationality, subjectivism—and even "religion"![24] It is not just coincidental that religion comes up in the debate, since, as we have seen, Kuhn often employs the language of religion in his description of science, calling paradigm changes "conversions" that depend on faith."[25] And neither is it coincidental that the critics who "accuse" Kuhn of "religion" are relying on the common assumption that religion is "subjective" and science "objective"—that is, the very kind of dichotomy that is called into question by holistic theories such as Kuhn's. But our job is not to pass judgment on Kuhn or his critics as philosophers of science but rather to examine that discussion for clues to the nature of paradigms. Whether or not Kuhn is right in his reading of scientific history, his use of the term *paradigm* can be defended against the charge of irrationalism. Again using simple perceptual experiences of gestalt shifts as models, let us examine those features of paradigm shifts that have led to the charge.

The least controversial (but nevertheless interesting) feature of such change is their *irreversible* quality. Hanson refers, for example, to the visual puzzles sometimes found in children's books, where a picture of a tree contains a face "hidden" in its branches. Though it may be difficult to learn to see the face in the first place, once one has recognized it, it is virtually impossible to view the tree without seeing it.[26] A page of text in a language one does not understand appears as a meaningless aggregate of letters and spaces, but after one has learned the language one is unable not to *read* the text, to see words and sentences and "meanings" in it. (Such experiences are indications that "meaning" in language is "paradigmatic" in the general sense: patternlike, logically holistic.) Likewise in science, a convert to Copernican astronomy cannot simply revert to seeing the heavens according to Ptolemaic epicycles. And the case of religious converts is no different: they can no longer see the world apart from the patterns of their newfound faith. To call such changes "irrational" simply on the grounds of their irreversibility is to fall into the atomistic fallacy by failing to grant the priority of the pattern over the elements out of which it is constituted.

A similar logic applies to the *discontinuity* between competing paradigms. Because each is holistic, an organizing pattern, there is no piecemeal or step-by-step transition from one to the other. One cannot, for example, move gradually from the duck-rabbit-as-rabbit to the duck-rabbit-as-duck by learning to see each "duck-part" in turn. When the duck aspect "dawns" (to use Wittgenstein's metaphor), all its "parts" are there at once, whatever the specific occasion of the gestalt switch happens to be. Such experiences also account for the apparently arbitrary nature of the occasion that provokes the change: whatever the last detail to come to our attention may have been, the decisive change occurs in no particular detail but in our perception of the organizing pattern itself. The illusion of "irrationality" in such changes comes from confusing the *psychological* experience of suddenness and surprise that often (but not always) accompanies them with their *logical* features, which can be quite rationally accounted for by the grammar of wholes and parts. The change can be described as irrational only if rationality is assumed to entail a cumulative or associative logic. Kuhn's own defense against the charge of irrationalism in paradigm switches is weakened by his heavy reliance on psychological and sociological accounts of the reasoning process involved.[27] A stronger case can be made: it can be shown not only that scientific communities have in fact come to agree about certain paradigms, but also that such agreement *could only* have come about by a discontinuous "leap" from one way of organizing their world to another.[28] What really deserves to be called irrational is not the claim of discontinuity but rather the opposite view that incremental or piecemeal change from one paradigm to another is possible. The mixing of philosophical and psychological arguments is especially confusing at this point. The philosophical discontinuity between competing paradigms can be accounted for rationally by examining the logical relations of wholes and parts. It is not surprising that such logical discontinuity is often experienced as a psychological discontinuity, but such an experience is neither required nor relevant to the philosophical issue. Psychologically, it may even be possible to appropriate a new paradigm gradually—for example, by first getting "glimmers" of a different pattern; by going through periods of confusion; or by entertaining new possibilities without initially finding them persuasive—but such experiences do not alter the sharp *logical* discontinuity between the two options.

The most controversial claim about competing paradigms is that they are *incommensurable*. Kuhn identifies this part of his theory as the "central constellation of issues which separate me from most of my critics."[29] He had invited charges of subjectivism and mystification in his book by stating, for example, that the "proponents of competing paradigms practice their trades in different worlds." Even more damaging, he went on to claim that before they can hope to communicate fully, one group or the other must experience the conversion that we have been calling a paradigm shift. Just because it is a transition between incommensurables, the transition between competing paradigms cannot be made a step at a time, forced by logic and neutral experience. Like the gestalt switch, it must occur all at once (though not necessarily in an instant) or not at all.[30] Such statements may have been unguarded, but they are not wrong; and their use of religious metaphor, though the kiss of death in the view of the more positivistically minded philosophers of science, is further evidence that Kuhn has stumbled upon an important sense in which religion and science are more like than unlike. Once again, our task here is not to rule on the merits of Kuhn's account of the history of science but to examine the logic of the paradigm changes that he describes. The charges of irrationality and subjectivism stem from a confusion of *incommensurable* with *incomparable,* which is not the same.[31] As before, the key lies in the patterned quality of paradigms, their holistic grammar. To say that two patterns are incommensurable is to say that they involve different schemes of organization that allow no common standard of measurement according to which both could be reduced to the same terms. One pattern cannot, therefore, be explained in terms of the other. Until we agree about the shape of the whole about whose parts we are arguing, we have no common ground for communication, since (as argued above) "parts" are relative to their wholes and hence have no meaning (or a different one) if taken out of the holistic context. In cases where there can be only one "whole"—for example, one way to understand what it means to do microbiology, or to live in conformity to the will of God—no meaningful dialogue can take place about the details until there is substantial agreement about the larger enterprise that constitutes their context.

It is possible to give an account of incommensurable competing paradigms that avoids the appearance of irrational and arbitrary subjectivism by emphasizing that the debate is about wholes and not about parts. To say that alternative paradigms are incommensurable in no way implies that it makes no difference which one a person chooses. On the contrary, such decisions are more momentous than decisions about details precisely because they have more radical and wide-ranging consequences. Neither does the incommensurability of the paradigms imply that the choice between them is arbitrary. As Kuhn has argued against critics like Karl Popper, the incommensurability of paradigms does not imply that they cannot be verified or falsified but only that it is very difficult to do so. For example, Copernican astronomers can argue rationally that the Ptolemaic system, even if it cannot be falsified at any specific point, does not provide the most adequate account of interplanetary relationships. They can make this claim only by describing the state of affairs more adequately—namely, according to the Copernican paradigm. Falsification, in Kuhn's words, "is a subsequent and separate process that might equally well be called verification since it consists in the triumph of a new paradigm over the old one."[32] A good historical example is provided by the discovery of Uranus, which had been sighted at least seventeen times in the previous century but was not recognized as a planet until after the triumph of the Copernican paradigm.[33] Such examples show how paradigm changes can be discontinuous and incommensurable without therefore being arbitrary or subjective. Religious differences—to anticipate the parallel that will be developed more fully in the next chapter—have a similar logic: they do make meaningful assertions about the world insofar as they claim to explain the world in the most adequate fashion. The fact that they cannot be falsified by pointing to anomalous details does not entail their meaninglessness but shows rather that they involve paradigm choices and are therefore subject to verification or falsification not on the basis of details but only on holistic grounds.

Finally, it should be emphasized that the mutual incommensurability of paradigms does not necessarily imply their incompatibility. The duck-rabbit, to take the simple visual example, demonstrates both the incommensurability of the aspects (because they depend on different configurations of the whole) and their compatibility (the fact that it can be seen as a duck does not preclude the possibility of seeing it as a rabbit). Paradigms *may* be incompatible (the face across the room is either my next-door neighbor's or it is not), but nothing about their grammar entails that they *must* be (it is no truer to call it a duck than a rabbit). One of the characteristics of patterns (as opposed, for example, to atoms, or substances, or essences) is that they can share elements with other patterns. In much of our everyday experience, patterns dovetail with other patterns continually and unproblematically. Things can be organized in one way for one purpose and then in another way for another purpose. As an example, consider the activity of "listening for." We can listen to a speaker for traces of a German accent, or we can listen for the subject of his speech. We might even listen psychoanalytically, gathering evidence from his diction or slips of the tongue for his psychic and emotional makeup. How foolish it would be to ask, "Did she speak in French or about tax reform?" Paradigms, because they are patterns, share this quality; there is no a priori way to know whether one is compatible with another. A great deal of confusion in the debates about paradigms in science could have been avoided by attending to this characteristic of paradigms. A corresponding religious confusion shows up in debates about the "essence of religion," Christianity and other religions, and similar themes. The important point to note is that the compatibility or incompatibility of incommensurable paradigms can only be decided on a case-by-case basis. The fact that such issues often *can* be adjudicated is evidence against the alleged irrationality of paradigm choices.

In addition to the compatibility of alternative paradigms—what might be called "horizontal" compatibility—there is another way in which incommensurable paradigms may be compatible, namely, at different organizational levels of a complex process. This "vertical" compatibility of paradigms has not, so far as I am aware, received as much attention from philosophers of science. Put most simply, the point is that patterns may be components of other patterns. What counts as a "whole" or a "part" is relative to the organizational level. An example is provided by the history of the modern physical sciences in their search for the ultimate building blocks of nature. Modern chemistry had its origins in the discovery that most familiar substances are compounds—that is, complex patterns whose properties are determined by a unique arrangement of elements. In time it was discovered that these elements were not so "elemental" after all but rather consisted in turn of a complex of interrelated parts, for which new names (proton, neutron, electron, etc.) had to be devised. But the search did not end there, for these "protoelements" are likewise susceptible to further analysis into components that can no longer be adequately described even as particles. It appears (so far as a layman is able to understand such highly specialized theory) that the deeper science penetrates into physical reality, the more nearly the "parts" are describable only in terms of pure mathematical pattern. The hierarchy can also be extended at the other end, since compounds can function as the elements of larger wholes—and so on. Each level has its own paradigmatic organization of wholes and parts, and what counts as a whole at one level may function as a part at the next.

The structure of organizational levels shows another way in which patterns have priority over the elements of which they are composed, and therefore another reason why paradigms, the exemplars of pattern, are so important. Each level retains its "paradigmatic" integrity, even when it is considered in relation to a more complex hierarchy. This feature can be demonstrated by examples that try to ignore intervening organizational levels. A chemist would find it absurd—and probably impossible—to describe even so simple a compound as table salt, for example, in terms of the interactions of protons, neutrons, and electrons. These are not parts of salt, but rather parts of sodium and of chlorine, which in turn—at another level—are parts of sodium chloride. The only thing more incomprehensible than a recipe for bread listing various atoms as the ingredients would be one listing subatomic particles. "There is no justification for checking generalization at any particular stage," wrote Whitehead. "Each phase of generalization exhibits its own peculiar simplicities which stand out just at that stage, and at no other stage."[34]

Whitehead also argues that greater generalization (the aim of philosophy, he believes) always requires what he calls a "leap of imagination," not directly obtainable from the facts. The recurrence of the "leap" as a metaphor for paradigmatic change is a reminder that the similarities between science and religion have to do with the holistic grammar of both enterprises and therefore with the important role played by paradigms and paradigm changes in both. But Whitehead's linking of the leap to the imagination is a reminder of the thesis toward which our whole discussion of science and religion has been aimed: that there is a close relation between the role of paradigms and the imagination. Precisely what that link is, and how it clarifies the nature of religious imagination, are the issues to which we now must turn.

CHAPTER 4

Religion and the Paradigmatic Imagination

In exploring the meaning of revelation in relation to reason and imagination, H. Richard Niebuhr employs a metaphor taken from the experience of understanding a text: he likens revelation to a "luminous sentence" that we encounter in reading a book, "from which we can go forward and backward and so attain some understanding of the whole."[1] A related metaphor is used by the literary critic George Whalley to explain the genesis of a poem in the imagination of the poet: he speaks of the "poetic germ," whose "function is to crystallize, to 'seed' the images of memory into a pattern which is felt to be significant even though the significance cannot be known until the poem has been fully extricated."[2] Both metaphors, one from the reading of a text and the other from the chemistry of crystals, have to do with the constellation of a pattern out of a chaos of potential "parts." The events being metaphorically described, the experience of revelation and the making of a poem, are in this way reminiscent of other events, discussed in the previous chapter: the gestalt quality of perception and the role of paradigms in scientific discovery. All have in common that "paradigmatic" logic, according to which the whole emerges from the parts not by cumulation but by a discontinuous "leap."

Another similarity between the metaphors of Niebuhr and Whalley brings into focus the specific task of the present chapter: both the theologian and the literary critic attribute the events described by their metaphors to the operation of imagination. Philosophers of science and gestalt psychologists also speak sometimes of imagination in connection with paradigmatic phenomena in their fields of inquiry, though usually without developing it explicitly as a technical term. I am convinced that it is the right term to use in bringing conceptual clarity to these puzzling but tantalizing parallels between diverse areas of thought and experience. In particular I believe that a well-crafted concept of imagination can do service in theology by permitting an anthropological account of the revelatory *Anknüpfungspunkt* that brings the religious event of revelation into comparative relationship with other human experience without thereby succumbing to the seduction of "natural theology."

One of the chief attractions of the term *imagination* is its firm rootedness in a variety of everyday linguistic contexts. The corresponding difficulty is the wide range of meanings it encompasses, which poses the threat of vagueness or ambiguity if the word is introduced carelessly into theological discourse. A good way to approach such a concept is to follow the recommendation of ordinary-language philosophy and pay particular attention to the range and pattern of meanings of *imagination* and its family of related terms in typical nontechnical usages. Further development of the concept as a technical term for theology ought at least to remain consistent with ordinary usage.

What is required, therefore, is an examination of the term *imagination* to discover its implicit logic or "grammar" (in Wittgenstein's useful metaphor). Such an exercise can legitimately be called philosophical in the modestly nonfoundational sense of the word. As such, it properly precedes a specifically theological consideration of imagination, not for any weighty "systematic" reasons, but simply because theological discussion (like any other) is more fruitful when it is clear in advance how key words are being used.

The Grammar of Imagination

Common to the various uses of *imagination* (including the family of related terms like *fantasy, fanciful, image, imaginary*) is an image or picture representing some object that is not directly accessible to the imagining subject. Kant offers a surprisingly simple definition: "*Imagination* is the faculty of representing in intuition an object that is *not itself present*."[3] Imagination re-presents what is absent; it makes present through images what is inaccessible to direct experience. As a point of departure for a conceptual grammar of *imagination* in ordinary usage, Kant's straightforward definition is useful, as long as his emphasis on representation is not taken too literally. The point is that imagination makes accessible what would otherwise be unavailable to us; whether *representation* is the best way to express this function is open to question.

As soon as this very general description is made more specific, we encounter a systematic ambiguity that appears regularly in ordinary language: objects of imagination may be either real or illusory. I must imagine the table in the next room because I cannot perceive it directly, but I can also imagine a quite different table from the one that is in fact there. Certain words in the imagination family call attention to this ambiguity. The table that I only imagine to be there is called an *imaginary* table. Other terms, such as the attribute *imaginative,* imply a realistic use of imagination. When we seek "imaginative leadership," we are not looking for a leader who tells tales or sees things that aren't there, but rather for one who is especially gifted at seeing what *is* there and able to envision new possibilities for realistic action. The word *imagination* itself moves between these two poles. It is one thing to say, "It's all in his imagination," and quite another to say, "He demonstrates insight and imagination." The distinction between realistic and illusory uses of imagination is a fundamental feature of the concept, which not only accounts for the slipperiness of the term but also makes it uniquely appropriate for theological anthropology.

Because this inherent ambiguity is so important a feature of imagination, it will be useful to look more closely at the various ways in which we imagine reality and unreality. The illusory side requires less attention, both because it is less problematic and because it is less directly pertinent to theological applications of imagination. Two such uses of imagination can be distinguished. The first can be called *fantastic,* since it produces what is commonly known as fantasy and includes the various fanciful and imaginary activities of the human spirit—for example, in art, in play, or in daydreaming. What is common to these uses of imagination is that they are deliberately fanciful, acknowledged departures from the real world, whether of science or of everyday experience. A second variety of illusory imagination can be called *deceitful* and includes all attempts to falsify, distort, or misrepresent reality for the purpose of misleading oneself or others. Lies depend on the ability of the liar to manipulate the hearer to imagine as real what in fact is illusory— and vice versa. Deceit, like other forms of imagination, need not be either deliberate or conscious. One type of atheism, for instance, explains religion as a variety of unconscious deceitful imagination.

But imagination is by no means limited to the illusionary purposes of fantasy and deceit. On the contrary, our language is full of implicit acknowledgments that imagination is related to truth and discovery as well. In general, realistic imagination comes into play when we have to do with real objects that are not directly accessible to us. The most obvious examples involve objects that are not present but that could be directly apprehended if they were. (Kant's definition cited above assumes

this kind of object.) But there are other real objects—including religiously significant ones—whose inaccessibility is not due simply to physical
nonnpresence. We need to examine each of these cases in turn.

There are two chief modes of physical nonpresence, temporal and
spatial, and it will help to clarify the meaning of imagination if they are
treated separately. The clearest case of *temporal* absence is past reality,
and it has long been recognized—at least since Augustine's *Confes-
sions*—that memory requires an act of imagination. Not quite so obvious
but surely undeniable is the role of imagination in recalling the social or
collective past: in history. Out of the wealth of past occurrence the historian selects a small portion, which he must integrate in only one of
many conceivable ways in order to mediate between his present readers
and past reality. Much more obvious is the role of imagination in the
case of future reality, which can be presented by means of extrapolations
from past experience, anticipations of new developments, and hypoth-
eses about future states of affairs. This anticipatory use of the realistic
imagination merges at some point into fantasy, but the distinction is
nevertheless significant, at least at the level of intent. We commonly distinguish, for example, between scientific projections of the future and
science fiction.

The other realistic use of imagination involving empirical objects can
be called *spatial,* since it comes into play in situations where a real object
is not directly accessible because of its spatial relationship to the observer. The obvious cases are the ones in which I as the observer happen not
to be in proximity to an object that I could perceive directly if I were: as
long as I stay where I am, I can only imagine the table in the next room,
or the Taj Mahal. More interesting are cases in which the spatial relationship of the observer to the object precludes direct observation under
any circumstances. This occurs with regard to the realm of the very
small—what we might call *microcosmic* reality. The study of subatomic
structures in physics has led to a descriptive language that can no longer
operate on the assumption that reality is "picturable," where analogies
to the particles and waves of classical physics and everyday experience
become increasingly indirect.[4] But there is a corresponding state of affairs at the opposite pole, the *macrocosmic* realm of astrophysics and cos-
mology. Here, too, scientists must increasingly employ imagination in
new and "unpicturable" ways in order to describe the character of the
universe as a whole, appealing to schemes of space-time involving four
or more dimensions in order to do justice to their data.

In addition to objects not present to us because of their temporal or
spatial remoteness, there remains a class of real objects whose inaccessi-

bility can be called *logical*.[5] People who speak, for example, of "souls," or "Satan," or "gods," often assume both that these objects are real and that they *could* not be directly present to us in such a way as to render imagination superfluous. Their intangibility is not just a matter of size or distance. This kind of inaccessibility is logical, rather than spatial or temporal, because *in principle* the objects are not subject to direct observation. Nevertheless, such objects are frequently imagined in spatial or temporal metaphors. God may be worshiped as one "exalted above the heavens" in poetry or liturgy, and even the more philosophical language about God's eternity or infinity trades on spatiotemporal analogies.

This cursory overview of imagination is intended to offer a preliminary "grammatical" orientation, a kind of conceptual map for charting possible theological applications of the term. Common to the various uses of imagination are selective and integrating images that serve to present—whether as illusion or reality—something that would otherwise remain inaccessible. Historical or anticipatory, microcosmic or macrocosmic—all realistic use of imagination aims at mediating aspects of reality that are incapable of nonimaginative presentation.

In order to locate more precisely the sense in which imagination is theologically relevant, it will be useful to distinguish three levels of inquiry into imagination, only one of which is directly pertinent to theology. At the most basic level it is possible to speak of imagination in the context of a *transcendental* inquiry into the a priori structures of experience. Here imagination refers not to any part or aspect of experience itself but rather to the conditions necessary for there to be any experience in the first place. Kant's transcendental analysis of imagination is the classic case, which firmly established the term in the vocabulary of modern philosophy. At this a priori level imagination also selects, integrates, and mediates—not the contents of our experience but rather its sensuous preconditions.

Philosophers are also accustomed to consider imagination at the level of *perception*, and here they are joined by psychologists as well. The experiments of the gestalt psychologists, mentioned in the previous chapter, showed that we perceive not by the cumulative association of atomistic sense data but rather by grasping a whole pattern (*Gestalt*) in a single perceptual act. The simple visual figures used to demonstrate perceptual gestalt-qualities, such as the Necker cube and the duck-rabbit, attracted the attention of Ludwig Wittgenstein, whose fragmentary discussion of the seeing of "aspects" and other functions of visual imagination[6] inaugurated an ongoing philosophical debate about "seeing and seeing as," which has found its way into recent philosophy of religion and will be considered below. The role of imagination in perception has an indirect heuristic value for the philosophy of religion and thus for theology, just as it has had for recent philosophy of science. Examples of perceptual imagination, such as those provided by shifting-gestalt figures, can function as models to suggest the logic of imagination in thinking, knowing, and interpreting experience.

It is only at this third and highest level,[7] which can be termed *interpretation*, that imagination is directly pertinent to theology. The term is deliberately broad, intended to cover the kinds of explanation found in the natural sciences as well as the hermeneutical procedures of the humanities and social sciences.[8] In all of the activities involving interpretive imagination, sense perception is simply taken for granted, just as in perceptual imagination the transcendental imagination is presupposed. Interpretive imagination is what we usually mean by imagination (at least in its realistic use) in ordinary language. But since imagination occurs so frequently in philosophical contexts in its transcendental and perceptual senses, it is important to emphasize that it is at the interpretive level that the term shows theological promise. In all interpretive imagination a subject matter that is not available to direct observation is mediated by selective and integrating images, which are themselves of necessity drawn from our experience of reality that *is* immediately accessible, that is, from the "mesocosmic" world of present, everyday experience—what can be directly seen, heard, handled, felt.[9]

Imagination as Paradigmatic

The concept of paradigm, suggested by recent philosophy of science and developed in the previous chapter, provides a key to the nature of imagination and offers a way of gaining control over this unwieldy concept. Briefly stated, my proposal is to regard the imagination as the paradigmatic faculty, the ability of human beings to recognize in accessible exemplars the constitutive organizing patterns of other, less accessible and more complex objects of cognition. The grammar of imagination as it occurs in ordinary usage encompasses both illusionary and realistic senses. This systematic ambiguity in the concept accounts for much of the confusion about its use in connection with religion. Imagination is the means by which we are able to represent anything not directly accessible, including *both* the world of the imaginary *and* recalcitrant aspects of the real world; it is the medium of fiction as well as of fact. This feature of the concept accounts for the suspicion it arouses among the theologically orthodox, but it also precludes any liberal temptation toward a "natural theology of the imagination."

A paradigm, as the concept was developed in chapter 3, can be concisely defined as a normative exemplar of constitutive structure. Something serves as a paradigm by exhibiting a pattern, a coherent nexus of relations, in a simple and obvious way. Paradigms have a heuristic function, serving to reveal the larger patterns in broad areas of experience that might otherwise remain inaccessible because they appear incoherent or bewildering in their complexity. It is important to note that "paradigm" is defined *functionally*: anything can become a paradigm if it functions paradigmatically. The corollary is that something may serve as a paradigm in one context or for one purpose and not in another; it all depends on the use to which it is put. In science a paradigm is characteristically a model—think, for example, of the Bohr model of the atom as a kind of mini–solar system—or a theory, such as Darwin's theory of evolution.

In religion a similar function is often performed by normative texts, rituals, and dogmas. An example of a religious paradigm in Christianity is the Apostles' Creed, which sketches the grammar of Christian belief in capsule narrative form. Employing the trinitarian formula as its basic structure, it frames all reality between an absolute Beginning and a final End. Its central section is a terse narrative summary of the career of Jesus Christ: "... was conceived ... born ... suffered ... crucified ... descended ... rose ... ascended ... sitteth ... will come again ..." The paradigmatic function of the creed is evidenced not only by its high status as normative dogma but also by its ritual centrality in Christian worship. For centuries Christians have read the Bible and viewed the world according to the pattern internalized by repetition of the creed. We can make the same point, employing the concept of paradigmatic imagination, by saying that Christians have *imagined* the world according to the paradigm exemplified by the creed.[10] This description can be endorsed without prejudicing the question of the truth of Christian assertions, since it remains accurate whether or not such Christian use of imagination is regarded as realistic or illusory. This ambiguity has important implications for theology that will be developed in the final chapter. The present task is to describe the paradigmatic imagination in terms that include its religious use but also encompass its uses in other fields like the natural sciences and literature.

An important and surprising feature of paradigms is what Margaret Masterman, commenting on Kuhn's theory, calls their "concreteness or 'crudeness.' "[11] The basic "construct-paradigm" or "artifact" operates as an analogy to induce a "new way of seeing." What is surprising about these paradigms is the fact that they may not even be fully accurate in the light of subsequent developments. An example from the history of science is Copernicus's model of the solar system, which assumed circular planetary orbits. Not until Kepler worked out the mathematics of elliptical orbits did a satisfactory theory of planetary motion become possible. And yet the revolution is rightly called Copernican, for it was the crude and overly simple original model that performed the decisive paradigmatic function by providing an accessible model exemplifying the essential pattern of the planets. It was Copernicus who "seeded" the imagination of scientists, including Kepler, and thereby gave birth to a "new way of seeing." One finds theological parallels in the relation between the simple and "crude" narratives of scripture, which nevertheless become the means of capturing the religious imagination of believers, even though the narratives themselves may not measure up to the precision of later dogmatic standards. A classic example is the doctrine of the Trinity, which is not found explicitly in scripture (and is in fact difficult to reconcile with certain passages) but whose legitimacy nevertheless rests on its claim to articulate the implicit grammar of scripture.

The fact that paradigms are based ultimately on concrete models also helps to explain the misuse of imagination and thus to clarify what is at stake in paradigm disputes. The root of paradigm error is false analogy, the mistaken, misleading, or inappropriate application of a model. Paradigm disputes—whether in science, religion, or other areas—are disagreements about what the world is *like*; in other words, they involve decisions about which models are to be taken as the typical and therefore normative exemplars. The most serious errors, and the ones most difficult to eradicate, are those that involve the "misimagining" of the world.[12] The "Feuerbachian" type of modern atheism, for example, can be summarized in the thesis that religion is a species of "bad imagination."[13] Every such critique is necessarily paradigm dependent, the mirror image of an alternative vision of the world. The persuasive force of Feuerbach's critique of the religious world as illusory depends on the persuasive force of his own anthropological model of reality. The same is even more obviously true of Marx, whose paradigmatic vision has strongly "theological" features. The bad imagination is for him the alienated imagination—alienated from the *true* human condition, imagined according to the grammar of dialectical materialism. Such choices, as H. Richard Niebuhr recognized, are never "between reason and imagination but only between reasoning on the basis of adequate images and thinking with the aid of evil imaginations."[14]

The realistic imagination thus depends entirely on paradigms to gain access to the "transcendent," taken here in its literal sense as the "world beyond"—any aspect of reality outside the "mescocosm" of familiar experience. In order to avoid any mystification of "the imagination" as some kind of arcane faculty or sixth sense, it would be clearer to say that imagination *is* the taking of paradigms to explore the patterns of the larger world. For the purpose of this discussion, therefore, "imagination" always refers to this patterning and exemplifying activity, which I have called the paradigmatic imagination. Whether or not *all* imagination is paradigmatic is a question that can be left open. The term is very old and very broad and has many legitimate uses that need not be forced under a single definition. I am nevertheless persuaded that all of the uses of imagination pertinent to religion and theology—including both realistic and illusionary varieties—are encompassed by the paradigmatic imagination.

The centrality of paradigms to the imagination clarifies the relationship between religion and two very different fields with which it is often compared: on the one hand, the natural sciences with their disciplined employment of the realistic imagination; and on the other hand, the arts, and especially literature, with their creative use of imaginative illusion and fantasy. By taking the imagination as our point of reference, we can bring under one conceptual roof the concerns of "religion and science" and those of "religion and literature." Such a move should not be misunderstood as "foundational" in the sense criticized in chapter 2. Rather, the choice of imagination is pragmatic and avowedly relativistic; it is chosen because of its ability to bring the diverse patterns of religion, science, and literature into meaningful comparative relationships—a method inspired in part by functional systems theory.[15]

At the heart of the similarities among religion, science, and literature is their common use of analogy. Paradigms serve the imagination analogically: by their likeness to the objects they exemplify. In the natural sciences, analogies are frequently embodied in models, which can be articulated in theories. In literature, metaphor is the typical analogical structure, the means by which the poet or novelist creates an imaginative world using the same words ordinarily employed to describe the everyday world.[16] The most important quality shared by all these analogical terms—*paradigm, model, metaphor, myth,* and so on—is their open-endedness. A true metaphor, as distinguished, for example, from allegory, proposes an analogy without foreclosing on its possible application. "No limits can be set as to how far the comparison might be extended," in Barbour's words; "it cannot be paraphrased because it has an unspecifiable number of potentialities for articulation."[17] I would prefer to say that it cannot be *exhaustively* paraphrased, in order to guard against the temptation—rampant among theological enthusiasts for metaphor—of mystifying metaphor into an ineffable enigma heavy with "religious" significance. For, as I will argue more extensively in chapter 7, the primary job of theology (like its counterparts in science and literary criticism) is precisely the systematic articulation of the analogical metaphors, myths, and paradigms that constitute the primary "data" of the enterprise. Theology is in just this sense a hermeneutical inquiry, a disciplined interpretation of imaginative texts.

Imagination and Interpretation

The important distinction between imaginative discourse and its interpretation raises the issue of the relation of image to concept. At least since Hegel distinguished *Vorstellung* from *Begriff*, versions of the duality have played a key role in philosophy of religion and theology.[18] Increasing recognition of the centrality of metaphor in all language has made it more difficult to maintain a distinction between metaphoric image and nonmetaphoric concept. It can even be argued that language *is* a complex network of metaphor, a history of perceived likeness between the familiar and the novel, embodied in images. Eberhard Jüngel, for example, reworks Nietzsche's cynical thesis that truth is nothing but a "moving army of metaphors, metonymies, and anthropomorphisms" into a plausible account of language as the history of metaphor.[19] As the etymology of most words testifies, even the most abstract and technical concepts had their origins in metaphoric insight, and the historical evidence is corroborated by our ongoing experience of the transformation of once-fresh metaphors into stable and conventional concepts.[20] Language appears to grow by means of the "cooling" of metaphoric image into stable concept. Metaphors are potential concepts; concepts are petrified metaphors. This movement from implicit image to explicit concept is balanced by a countervailing process of continuing metaphoric creativity: language moves in both directions.

The clearest way to represent the relation of image to concept, therefore, is not as a dichotomy but a spectrum, extending from the pregnant image, full of implicit or potential application, to the developed concept, in which the underlying analogy has been articulated and delimited. In the concept, the image has become transparent, unambiguous, precise. This process explains why concepts can be traced back to original metaphors but also why etymology is not very useful (even misleading) in getting at the meaning of concepts. In conceptual language, the images have been fixed clearly and shorn of their associations, implications, and ambiguities. Most of our language moves somewhere on the spectrum between these extremes: its metaphors are to a greater or lesser extent "frozen." It is important to acknowledge the need for the full linguistic range, against the tendency of some (especially when speaking about religion) to romanticize the metaphoric at the expense of the conceptual.[21] The scientist, for example, depends on the precise delimitation of concepts, shorn of their metaphoric associations, just as the poet depends on the open-endedness of the unexplored image. Diversity is likewise essential at the level of everyday life: we desire neither purely conceptual expressions of human sentiment nor metaphoric instructions for the operation of machinery.

The spectrum from image to concept also clarifies the relationship between religion and theology. The world of religion is imaginative, pregnant with metaphoric images. The task of theology is conceptual, the articulation and interpretation of the religious imagination. In Christian terms, the progression Christ–scripture–dogma–theology is a movement along the spectrum to the "right." Yet the progression, though necessary and inevitable, is not a progress, for authority remains anchored on the "left," to which the theologian like every believer must continually return, lest conceptual language become dry, empty, and "abstract" in the rightly pejorative sense. The aim of the remaining chapters will be to explore this movement and in so doing to clarify the nature, warrants, and task of Christian theology.

Before taking up these explicitly theological matters, we need to look more closely at the general relation between paradigmatic imagination and its interpretation. An ongoing debate among philosophers about the meaning of figures like the duck-rabbit has taken place under the rubric "seeing and seeing as."[22] Wittgenstein called attention to the fact that seeing something means seeing it *as* a particular object. John Hick prefers the phrase "experiencing as," and Ian Barbour argues that "interpreting as" is still better. But surely the main point is lost in these translations, for what is striking about the shifting-gestalt figures is that we simply *see* them, quite apart from any deliberate cognitive effort. Hanson argues that differences of visual aspect are *not* different interpretations. If one insists on so describing these experiences, one is driven finally to the absurdity of positing instantaneous and unconscious interpretation.[23] Undeniably something rather *like* interpretation is a quality of perception itself, but it is also quite unlike those acts that we normally mean by interpretation. Interpreting is a deliberate activity, something that we do intentionally and subsequently to an experience. For this reason, it will help to keep our categories straight if we adhere to the earlier distinction between perceptual and interpretive imagination. The fascination of the duck-rabbit is that something happens *without interpretation* that causes us to see one object rather than another. The hermeneutical implications of this fact become apparent only if we maintain the distinction.

The philosophical interest of the duck-rabbit lies in its ability to demonstrate that imagination plays a necessary role in perception. It is not the case that a physical event (called "seeing") must first occur, after which a mental event (called "interpretation") takes place. Rather, there is only one event, and it cannot be adequately analyzed into dichotomous "physical" and "mental" stages. The shifting-gestalt figures are useful, not because they are typical of seeing, but rather because they embody limit-conditions that reveal qualities of all seeing. We are normally unaware of the "figured" nature of perception because most of our sense experiences are unambiguous. The duck-rabbit is deliberately constructed so as to balance two figures that happen to share precisely the same sensory material, thereby making it obvious that seeing a particular figure is something distinct from the receiving of certain sense data. Hanson puts the point simply: "People," he says, "not their eyes, see." The obverse is likewise valid: "Cameras, and eye-balls, are blind."[24]

Seeing a rabbit, or seeing a duck, is an ability that depends not only on the reception of sense data but also on prior experience and context. A person who has never seen a rabbit but is familiar with ducks will surely see a duck. Someone seeing the duck-rabbit drawing for the first time on a page surrounded by unambiguous pictures of rabbits is more likely to see a rabbit. Further examples are easy to imagine and to verify. If the figure is shown to a person embroiled in a discussion of the behavior of ducks, it is likely that he or she will see the duck-rabbit as a duck. But if you show someone the figure and ask at the same time, "Does this look like a rabbit?" the chances are good that that person will see a rabbit. We see something by recognizing that it is *like* something else; that is, we always see according to some paradigm.

The difference between seeing visual aspects and interpreting them can be demonstrated by showing figures such as the duck-rabbit or the Necker cube to a group of people who are unfamiliar with them.[25] Some will see one aspect, others another; some people may discover right away the various perceptual possibilities, while others will be unable to see the alternatives despite the help offered by those who do. The instructive part of the experiment is the dialogue between those who see a particular aspect (say, a rabbit) and those who do not:

"Just look at those long ears—it's obvious!"
"What ears?"
"These . . . right here" (pointing).
"But that's the duck's bill!"
"Well, try looking at this spot here as the rabbit's nose seen from the side and imagine your 'bill' as its ears."
". . . Aha! Now I see it! Why didn't I see it before?"

It becomes apparent in such a dialogue that the word *as* in an expression like "seeing *X* as" is a signal indicating the speaker's awareness of more than one perceptual possibility for *X*. The argument between Hick and Barbour revolves around Hick's example of someone saying, "In the twilight I experienced the tuft of grass as a rabbit." Barbour wants to substitute "interpreted" for "experienced." But only philosophers in textbooks talk like that; surely most people would report, "In the twilight I *saw* the tuft of grass as a rabbit." Moreover, until the person has learned to see differently he will report only that he "saw a rabbit." The introduction of the signal word *as* communicates to us the speaker's awareness of some *other* possibility, an alternative paradigm by which to imagine the situation. The paradigmatic imagination is the ability to see one thing *as* another. Kant called "is" the copula of judgment; I take "as" to be the "copula of imagination."[26] Defining imagination in this way avoids some of the problems of the "re-presentation" view, which seems to imply that the image is a duplication of some elusive "original." Put informally, this definition states that imagination is the ability to say what something is *like*. The act of interpretation did not occur when the speaker saw a rabbit but only when he *thought about* the experience in the light of further investigation and became aware of other possibilities. Imagination was involved in both acts: perceptual imagination in the experience and interpretive imagination in the subsequent interpretation. At both levels paradigms—implicit in the perception and explicit in the interpretation—played the key role.

Though it is misleading to call the perception of a new aspect an interpretation, since interpreting follows perceiving and depends upon it, it is sometimes the case that interpretation gives rise to new perception. In the dialogue about the duck-rabbit, the speaker who could see both aspects *interpreted* the figure to the one who could see only the duck and in so doing enabled him to see something new. Comparable examples can be found in discussions among scientists and in religious dialogue. Interpretation has the form, "Look at it *this* way . . ." In other words, interpretation has an *ostensive* aspect. In trying to explain something we find ourselves pointing, literally or figuratively, to something else. In the case of the group looking at the shifting-perspective figures, the discussion invariably involves the pointing of fingers to this or that feature of the drawing. Interpreters who are denied the freedom to point feel inhibited in their effort to "convert" others to their way of seeing. In the case of the drawings, the pointing is physical because the experience is perceptual, but something analogous takes place at the level of interpretation and knowledge. The ostensive dimension of interpretation is another indication that paradigms are the key and are always concrete—"artifacts" in Masterman's term. We point to the concrete paradigm as if to say, "Look here—don't you see the likeness?"

Overcoming "Mesocosmic Parochialism"

Developments in the natural sciences since the end of the nineteenth century have allowed us to become increasingly aware of the unique cultural role played by "modern science"—that is, by the "new science" that began in the seventeenth century with the overthrow of the old Aristotelian natural philosophy and accumulated so impressive a list of accomplishments in the following two centuries. Because modern science has been surpassed and is now passing rapidly into history, its cultural significance has become more apparent. Only now does the Owl of Minerva begin her flight. What she sees is an intellectual movement that enabled us to achieve a remarkable understanding of the physical world around us—what I earlier termed the "mesocosmic" realm. The objects of the "new science" were primarily those aspects of our world with which we had direct sensory contact. Galileo, for example, employing the new technology of lenses, extended our sensory contact sufficiently to prove that the physical rules that obtain "up there" (e.g., in the moons of Jupiter) are the same ones to which things conform "down here" (e.g., in the movement of a pendulum). Darwin's revolution in the life sciences played a corresponding role; for the persuasive force of the theory of evolution has much to do with the fossils we can see and touch, not to mention the living "fossils" of the Galapagos Islands and the Amazon Basin. Modern science has taught us to see more clearly the things in the world around us.

What makes this world distinctive is the fact that it is populated by "middle-sized" things—objects roughly the same size as ourselves, like microbes and rocks and planets. In the past century the natural sciences have increasingly probed beyond this world. On the one hand, particle physicists have penetrated into the atoms that are too small for us to see, not because we lack the technology but because they are smaller than the units of light by which "seeing" itself is defined. On the other hand, the astrophysicists have pushed our horizons beyond the largest objects that we could see even in principle, directing their attention to the shape of the universe itself. As a result of these scientific advances we are now in a position to recognize the uniqueness and relativity of that middle-sized world that modern science had taught us to call "reality." To make this point is not to engage in "God-of-the-gaps" apologetics, for we can expect neither positive nor negative "evidences" for God from the findings of scientists. The contribution of natural science to theology is not direct but only indirect, not by virtue of its content but by the example of its method. Natural scientific and theological methodologies are comparable because of an important, though negative, parallel between their objects: both nature and God transcend the mesocosmic world, the knowledge of which is the specialty of both common sense and modern science. But this negative analogy can also be expressed positively in the thesis that both the natural scientist and the theologian depend in crucial respects on the paradigmatic imagination.

The growth of the natural sciences beyond mesocosmic experience has generated a philosophical discussion about the "picturability" of scientific theories, a discussion that has particularly interesting implications for theology. If objects of unusual scope produce unusual problems in science, we can expect the same to be true a fortiori in religion. Scientists and philosophers of science now speak routinely of the "unpicturability" of theories, especially in microphysics. The situation they describe has suggestive formal affinities to theological attempts to describe the nature of God, affinities that bring out with particular clarity the operation of imagination in both science and religion. Hanson draws attention to the confusion that has resulted from insisting that theories must be picturable in order to explain microcosmic phenomena. He argues that "atomic particles *must* lack certain properties," that they "could not be other than unpicturable."[27] The much-discussed example of wave-particle duality leads to the same conclusion: in order to account for the behavior of certain subatomic entities, physicists must attribute properties of both waves and particles to them, properties that cannot be harmonized in any picturable manner. An example of an unpicturable theory is the postulation of the existence of the neutrino to explain the apparent violation of the conservation of energy in beta disintegrations, for the neutrino combines a set of properties incapable of being visualized together in terms of classical physics. "The neutrino idea," Hanson says, " . . . is a retroductive conceptual construction out of what we observe in the large."[28] But such a description is admirably suited to theological theories as well—for example, the Nicene definition of the divine Trinity. The church fathers of the fourth century also found it necessary to combine a set of properties not capable of being pictured in terms of the created world in order to provide a satisfactory description of the Creator revealed in scripture and confessed by the church. In order to give adequate theoretical articulation to their data, to the "facts" that they recognized on the basis of the constitutive paradigmatic commitment of their community, they had recourse to a "retroductive conceptual construction" of unpicturable reality: the triune God uniting in one *ousia* the distinct but inseparable hypostases called Father, Son, and Spirit. Yet the theologian's hypostases, like the scientist's particles, in spite of their unpicturability, "are not logical fictions."[29]

But the implications of unpicturability for the concept of imagination are not readily apparent and have sometimes been obscured in the course of the debate. Hanson, for example, rightly claims that "to picture particles is to rob oneself of what is needed to explain ordinary physical objectives." But he continues, "Though intrinsically unpicturable *and unimaginable*, these mathematically described particles can explain matter in the most powerful manner known to physics."[30] By equating picturability and imaginability Hanson confounds the issue. What could it mean to know something but to be unable to imagine it? Hanson's own inadvertent use of language offers some hints of a more adequate view. In the passage just cited he notes that the particles are "mathematically described." Mathematics, however, is a set of coherent patterns—a form of imagination. To know that certain particles behave according to the paradigm embodied in a mathematical formula is to be able to imagine them, to know what they are *like*. Hanson shows implicitly that he recognizes this truth by a quite different reference to imagination. Progress in nuclear physics only became possible, he notes, when scientists abandoned the assumption that the atomic world must be a miniature version of the Newtonian, Euclidean space hitherto assumed by modern physics—the assumption, that is, that the world of the atom must be picturable. Such an assumption, he writes, "no longer *serves the imagination*."[31] But this comment rightly implies that theories, though unpicturable, can nevertheless serve the imagination. Something is picturable if it can be visualized, which is to say if it can be modeled after something in the mesocosmic world. "Imaginable" is a broader term, including "picturable" but going beyond it to encompass other sorts of paradigms as well.[32] The fact that the behavior of elementary particles is unpicturable in terms of Newtonian space-time does not mean that it is unimaginable; on the contrary, it requires *more* imagination to be understood because it is further from everyday experience.

The logical parallels between scientific and religious imagination, of course, in no way compel belief in either the neutrino or the Trinity. The point is rather that both depend, in philosophically significant ways, on imaginative constructs rooted in paradigmatic commitments. At most one might draw the negative apologetic conclusion that unpicturability is no more a valid ground for disbelief in God than it is for disbelief in atomic particles. One of the most debilitating consequences of the bondage of the modern imagination to the mesocosmic paradigms of modern science has been a narrowing of attention to those aspects of reality that can be visualized in terms of Newtonian space and time, and the corresponding illusion that anything requiring imagination must be imaginary. By demythologizing this restrictive view of science, philosophers of science have brought to light the essential role of imagination in the scientific understanding of nature and thereby enabled us to see significant parallels between religious and scientific thought. As soon as one probes beyond the middle-sized world of familiar objects, whether in natural science, in poetry, or in theology, imagination becomes increasingly indispensable. At the same time, the relation between its factual and fictive aspects becomes increasingly ambiguous—a turn of events that is of even greater importance in theology than in science.

Religious Imagination

A remark by the philosopher John Wisdom about the notion of "seeing as" suggests that it has special relevance to the definition of religion. "It seems to me," he writes, "that some belief as to what the world is *like* is of the essence of religion."[33] Theologians and philosophers in recent times have found great difficulty with the notion of an "essence," conceived as the irreducible core of some phenomenon. Especially influential has been Wittgenstein's exposé of this notion as one of the habits of language by which we confuse ourselves. Attempts to identify the "essence of Christianity"[34] have found little favor with recent theologians, and surely no account of the "essence of religion" would find widespread acceptance in religious studies today. The superficiality of such proposals, and the confusion they generate, results from their failure to take account of the paradigmatic character of religious commitment.

Understanding religion in terms of paradigmatic imagination offers a way of identifying the "essence" that avoids this confusion. To seek a paradigm is not to look for some favored *part* of the object that is its irreducible kernel but rather to look for the pattern by which the object is constituted as a *whole*. Understood in this way, the question of the essence of religion or of a particular religion like Christianity can be appropriately addressed. One of the difficulties with the earlier search for an essence was the implication that the rest was nonessential, a mere "vehicle" for the true content (such as the Bible and the church in Kant's interpretation of Christianity) or a "husk" that had no value except to contain the kernel of truth (such as dogma in Harnack's view of the gospel).

If the definitive feature of a religion is not an abstract and general "essence" but rather a concrete paradigm that embodies its unique structure, another peculiarly modern problem also appears in a different light. Many thinkers since the eighteenth century have been troubled by the "positivity" of religious belief—that is, by its stubborn involvement with particular historical occurrences and personalities and its corresponding irreducibility to generally recognized criteria of rationality and truth.[35] (It is no accident that Barth's theology, which takes such pains to avoid reductionism, should be accused of perpetrating a *"positivism* of revelation": it is the seeming arbitrariness of the position that gives offense, its refusal to be judged by any external standards.) Hegel used the term in his early essay "The Positivity of the Christian Religion," and it received considerable attention from the German Idealists before fading into disuse later in the nineteenth century. It has since been revived periodically, most recently by Wolfhart Pannenberg.[36] Positivity has been defined as "what is factually given in contrast to what is derived from general concepts or principles . . . ; thus *positive religions* are the actual, historical religions appealing to divine revelation in contrast to 'natural religion.' "[37] Adapting a traditional distinction in legal theory between natural law and positive law (i.e., legislation laid down or "posited" by divine or human authority), thinkers of the European Enlightenment developed their well-known theory of natural, or rational, religion as the alternative to the "positive" religions that appeal to historical revelation and arbitrary authority. The desire to "depositivize" religion (which has usually meant historical Christianity) survived the demise of eighteenth-century rationalism and has remained one of the strongest underlying motives in religious thought from Kant to the present.

The issue of positivity, reconsidered from the vantage point of the paradigmatic imagination, turns out to be a reflection of the discontinuity between paradigms. *Every* paradigm appears "positive" or arbitrary to one whose imagination is patterned by a competing paradigm. Major advances in science are typically accompanied by charges of irrationality and "unscientific" procedures for precisely this reason: because the paradigm—the model from which the standards of rationality and methodological rules are themselves derived—has been called into question. It is naive to expect that neutral criteria can be adduced by which to establish the "reasonableness" of a religious conviction, just as it is naive to expect paradigm disputes in science to be settled by appeal to paradigm-independent criteria. This state of affairs exempts neither scientists nor theologians from responsibility for the *truth* of their assertions, as critics have sometimes charged, but it does make more difficult the adjudication of disputes about their truth. There is a formal analogy between paradigm-based conflict in the sciences and disagreements among divergent religious traditions. In both cases the issues are so difficult to resolve because the disagreement involves clashes between incommensurable, positive images, each taken by its adherents to be the key to a pattern of ultimate significance—and thus to the very criteria according to which conflicts can be adjudicated. In other words, the matter at stake is the appropriate paradigm for the endeavor itself. What kind of an enterprise is it, and what rules, methods, and criteria does it entail? The simplest form of this question is, What is it *like*?—for example, to do astronomy, or to believe in God.

Adopting the relative standpoint of comparative imagination has put us in a position to recognize and account for some significant parallels between religion, on the one hand, and the natural sciences and the arts, on the other. Implicit in these comparisons is a definition of religion itself. Without claiming any privileged "foundational" role for this definition, I want to make it explicit and defend it as a useful conceptual tool. Religion has been and can be defined in other ways for other purposes—one of the benefits gained by freedom from foundationalist thinking. The present definition is formally functional, taking religion to be something that human beings do and identifying its essence with the functional aim of that activity. The material aspect of the definition is provided by the paradigmatic imagination. The employment of this particular ability for a particular function or purpose constitutes the "essence" of religion. Put most simply, the function of religious imagination is to tell us "what the world is like" in its broadest and deepest sense. In more formal terms, if imagination is the human ability to perceive and represent likenesses (the paradigmatic faculty), religions employ that ability in the service of cosmic orientation, rendering the world accessible to the imagination of their adherents in such a way that its ultimate nature, value, and destiny are made manifest.

This view of religion has advantages over the widely held theory of religious language as "limit-language," proposed by David Tracy and others, which leaves religion apparently relevant only at the edges of life, only to life *in extremis*.[38] But if religious language functions paradigmatically—to pattern life—it is truly related at *all* points to experience without being simply identical to all experience or to any particular experience. This way of conceiving religion also avoids the weakness of many "essentialist" definitions, which founder on the dilemma of having either to exclude nontraditional "quasi-religions" (such as Marxism or some forms of therapeutic psychology) or to include them all at the price of so diluting the meaning of "religion" that it is rendered useless.[39] A major advantage of functional definitions is their ability to identify functional equivalents, other cultural systems that may on occasion fulfill a task normally performed by another social institution. A movement such as Marxism-Leninism can be understood accordingly as a functional equivalent of traditional religion in particular historical situations without our having to decide whether it qualifies as "a religion" or something else.

Given these definitions of religion and the religious imagination, theology will necessarily be an interpretive discipline, more akin to literary criticism than to poetry. Theologians, that is, are in the business of identifying and elucidating religious paradigms and developing their implications for the theory and practice of the faith. Just as there is no *one* "scientific method" that can be applied indiscriminately by botanists, astrophysicists, and microeconomists alike, so there are no rules for theology that transcend the paradigmatic commitments of actual religious communities. In the chapters that follow I want to show, for the Christian case, how such a theology works. I am persuaded—though I cannot attempt to prove it here—that the argument up to this point has broad application to many, perhaps all, religious traditions.[40] But given the conclusions of that very argument—that religions are inherently "positive" because they spring from unique, incommensurable paradigms—no *general* proof of the thesis is possible without contradiction. I will therefore do the only thing I can do: make the best argument possible for the place of imagination in Christian theology. If that case has merit, others will not fail to see in it analogies to their own traditions.

Part II.

THE CHRISTIAN IMAGINATION

CHAPTER 5

The Image of God: The Meaning of Revelation

We are now in a position to understand more clearly both why nineteenth-century interpretations of religion as imagination so often led to reductionistic conclusions and why those conclusions now appear to be unwarranted. Two centuries of dramatic progress in modern science had lured leading Western intellectuals into a positivism that simply identified truth with scientific knowledge and rejected all other truth claims, including those of religion, as illusory. Even thinkers sympathetic to religion, defensive and apologetic, implicitly accepted versions of this dichotomy while insisting that religion possessed its own kind of truth. As the positivistic view of science that produced and supported this dualism of "real" versus "imaginary" has been replaced by a more adequate and complex philosophy of science, the appeal of the dualism in its various guises has weakened accordingly. Analysis of the paradigmatic imagination in the previous two chapters has shown that such widely divergent human activities as religious belief and practice, the scientific investigation of nature, and artistic endeavors of various kinds all employ imagination in comparable ways. Imagination turns out to be not the opposite of reality but rather the means by which manifold forms of both reality and illusion are mediated to us. Religions characteristically employ this power of imagination in order to make accessible the ultimate "shape," the organizing pattern, of reality itself, thereby illumining the meaning and value of human life.

These final three chapters will apply the theory of paradigmatic imagination, and the corresponding understanding of religion, to the Christian tradition. The argument will aim in particular at clarifying the nature and task of theology. This goal cannot be achieved through further investigation of the imagination itself—a conclusion that follows from the very nature of imagination as the paradigmatic faculty. In theological terms the point can be stated this way: whereas imagination designates the human locus of revelation, it implies nothing about the source or content of revelation. The key to theological imagination will therefore not be found by philosophical or psychological examination of mental processes. Paradigmatic imagination is the form, one could say, of revelation; its material content, on the other hand, depends entirely on the paradigms that give shape to each particular embodiment of religious imagination. The "positivity" of Christian revelation—its dependence on certain concrete paradigms—precludes the possibility of a "natural theology of imagination." The specifically Christian content derives not from the fact *that* we imagine but rather from *what* it is we are imagining. Christian imagination, like all human imagining, is dependent on the paradigms that make it possible by giving it shape and substance.

For the same reason it should now be clear why imagination as a subjective experience contains no clue to the *truth* of what is imagined, since imagination can serve also as the organ of fiction and deceit. It is an important step to see that whatever truth we may come to know is mediated imaginatively; but the mediation itself remains neutral—perhaps it would be better to say ambiguous—with regard to reality or illusion. It is, then, the "objective" content of the Christian imagination, the paradigmatic images themselves, to which we must turn our attention.

Imagination and the "Image of God"

The biblical metaphor of the *imago Dei* has long focused the attention of Christian theologians on the intertwined issues of human nature and the knowledge of God, beginning in the New Testament itself and continuing throughout the entire history of Christian doctrine. Since God created the original human beings in his own image (Gen. 1:26–27), that image is surely both the key to human nature and the link between man and God. It is therefore the clue to the whole question of human knowledge of God. "The doctrine of the *imago Dei*," Emil Brunner wrote even before his notorious debate with Karl Barth, "determines the fate of every theology. The whole opposition of Catholicism and Protestantism originates here."[1] The opposition between Brunner and Barth likewise originated here, for the first thesis in their 1934 nature and grace debate concerns the character of the original divine image and its fate in the fall.[2] The doctrine has traditionally dealt with the creation of man in the image of God, the loss or impairment of the image in the fall, and its restoration in Christ. The *imago* thus represents at once the essence of human nature and the *Anknüpfungspunkt* for revelation. It also raises a number of difficult questions, such as the anthropological nature and location of the image, how and to what extent it was damaged by the fall into sin, and the relation between the image of God in all people and in Jesus Christ.

The connection between the issue of the *Anknüpfungspunkt* of revelation and the doctrine of the *imago Dei* is thus no novelty. Yet despite the prominence of a Christian doctrine of the image, little theological attention has been paid to imagination. The theory of the paradigmatic imagination is especially well suited to the task, since its focus is the paradigm, or exemplary image. I propose to develop the traditional doctrinal locus of the *imago Dei* into a Christian doctrine of imagination. The central thesis can be stated briefly in this way: the point of contact for revelation is formally the paradigmatic imagination and materially the image of God. This approach retains Brunner's distinction between the form and content of revelation without the problematic consequences of a natural theology, for which he was so vigorously opposed by Barth.

The doctrine of the *imago Dei* as it has traditionally been formulated identifies the human essence with the created image of God, describes the consequences of sin as the loss or impairment of that image (the point of greatest controversy), and interprets salvation in Christ as the restoration of the true image of God. The key issues addressed by the doctrine can be most simply stated as follows: (1) What is the image of God? (2) What happens to it as a result of sin? (3) How is it restored? (4) What does the restored image do? The first of these issues will occupy the remainder of this section, and the others will be taken up in the following sections. In each case we will be concerned first to discover what is at stake in the traditional formulations and controversies, and then to show how the issues can be clarified by reformulating them in terms of paradigmatic imagination. Valuable insights from the history of this doctrine need to be retrieved from the metaphysical thought forms in which they have traditionally been expressed. An effective way of doing so is to translate the metaphysical conceptuality into functional and relational terms, which are not only more attuned to contemporary thought forms but also more appropriate to interpretation of the underlying biblical narrative. Instead of the metaphysical question, What is its nature? we will be asking the functional question, What does it do? and the relational question, How does it fit into the larger pattern?

The first matter in need of such translation is one of the oldest and most divisive issues in theological anthropology: the proper identification of the divine image in human nature. The dominant strain in the ancient and medieval church identified the *imago* with the reason or rational soul.[3] Augustine is typical in his view of the divine image as a "soul endowed with reason and intelligence," by which man is distinguished from the lesser creatures.[4] Also influential were his several attempts to discover traces of the triune God in human nature, *vestigia trinitatis*. Thomas Aquinas specifically limits the *imago* to mental attributes, concluding that "being in God's image has reference solely to the mind."[5] In general, the doctrinal tradition has identified the *imago* with the soul, especially with its intellectual powers, specifically rejecting any participation of human physical attributes. Not only does this interpretation depend on an antiquated metaphysical dualism, but it also fails to do justice to the biblical materials that it purports to explicate.

A more promising strand—relational rather than metaphysical—in the traditional treatment of the doctrine is the view that the *imago Dei* denotes the *relationship* between God and his human creature. The original man, because he was in a right relationship with God, was also in harmony with himself: his will remained subject to his reason, which in turn had a right knowledge of God's will. Luther—a prime exponent of this tradition—allows himself to speculate about the superlative qualities that Adam must therefore have possessed. "His intellect was the clearest, his memory was the best, and his will was the most straightforward," Luther comments on Gen. 1:26, "all in the most beautiful tranquility of mind, without any fear of death and without any anxiety." He extends such speculation even to "those most beautiful and superb qualities of body and of all the limbs," by which Adam surpassed the other creatures. "Moreover," Luther imagines, "he had greater strength and keener senses than the rest of the living beings."[6] Luther's treatment reflects the fact that the image of God had come to be identified in medieval theology with the "original righteousness" of the first parents before the fall. The doctrine had thereby become a teaching about the *status integritatis*, the human condition before (hence in abstraction from) the disruption of sin. Despite the abuses to which such speculation sometimes led, its basic thrust is in harmony with the clear intentions of the Genesis narrative itself. One way to shed light on the present human condition is to imagine it as it ought to have been— or, expressed in the narrative terms of the biblical account, as it once actually was. Here the religious imagination is doing its characteristic work of providing a framework of meaning for human life by viewing it within a broader, an ultimate, imaginative context. Interpreting the *imago* relationally avoids the long-disputed issue of its content. Whatever its "nature" may be, the text is telling us, the *imago* represents the original *relationship* between divine and human: man is *like* God in some basic and definitive way. There is a "family resemblance" between God and human beings. It would be only a slight exaggeration to say that according to Genesis the content of the image *is* the relationship it posits between God and man.

Looking at the doctrine functionally leads to similar conclusions.[7] By asking, not How is the image of God constituted? or Where is it located in human nature? but rather What does it enable human beings to do? we gain further insight into the point of the *imago Dei*. In the Priestly creation narrative of Genesis 1 the *imago* functions quite literally as the *Anknüpfungspunkt*, the point at which human and divine touch. Michelangelo's interpretation of this story on the ceiling of the Sistine Chapel captures this point graphically: the touch of the fingers is the focus of the entire scene, and the figures of God and Adam seem to mirror each other. The art historian would note the robust humanity of Michelangelo's God, but the theological point is just the reverse: not the anthropomorphic rendering of God but the theomorphic rendering of man. This angle on the creation story also brings into view an unexpected similarity between the two accounts of creation in Genesis. The Yahwist creation narrative of Genesis 2, though never employing the words *image* or *likeness*, in fact makes the same point graphically by imagining the Creator molding a human figurine out of mud and endowing it with life.[8] By placing this story in the context of the Priestly account, the redactor enables us to envision the man as receiving his form—his actual shape—from God, while his material substance is taken from the earth. It is important to note that this dualism is quite different from the traditional metaphysical one that turns the God-given breath of life (the *nephesh* of Gen. 2:7) into a substantial but immaterial "soul" residing "in" a fleshly body.

The theological importance of the *imago Dei* is thus the original relationship that it posits, and the point of the relationship lies in its function. As the point of similarity between Creator and creature, the original *Anknüpfungspunkt*, the *imago Dei* made God accessible to the human imagination: Adam in the garden could imagine God as he truly is. Whatever may be its "nature," its function is to enable us to imagine God. And since the divine image according to which we were created is the true image of God, it enables us to imagine God *rightly*, in other words, to have real knowledge of God. But before we can make any further progress in interpreting the *imago*, we must return to the story. For whatever the image of God may have enabled human beings to do once upon a time, the scriptural narrative makes abundantly clear that it is no longer an available option in a fallen world.

Sin and the Image of God

Historically the focal point of controversy about the image of God has been its fate in the fall. Just as the original human creature bore an analogy to the Creator, so the original temptation begins with an appeal to a false analogy ("you will be *like* God," Gen. 3:5) and ends in the destruction of the true analogy. There is a bitter irony in the serpent's message, for the very creature who has just been formed "in the image of God" is now lured into destruction by the promise of becoming "like God"! The story thus captures at the outset the essentially irrational and self-destructive nature of sin.

The doctrinal and theological implications of this narrative have been a source of debate from the early church to the present. Medieval theology distinguished between the "image" and the "likeness" in Gen. 1:26, identifying the latter with Adam's "original righteousness" while reserving the former for the less important but more basic substratum of human nature. The *similitudo* with God, man's original virtuous state, was lost in the fall and can only be restored by grace. The *imago*, on the other hand, because it was understood to be the sine qua non of human nature as such, could not be lost through sin—though it was "wounded." The Protestant Reformers, finding this distinction both exegetically dubious and theologically misguided, reasserted the unity of the *imago Dei*[9] and concluded that it must have been—for all practical purposes, at least—lost or destroyed by sin, since both the image of God and human sinfulness affect the entire human being. The point of the much-maligned Calvinist doctrine of "total depravity" was not to heap scorn upon humanity but rather to emphasize just this point. Sin is total, one could say, not in degree but extent: there is no protected island, no last, "natural" refuge of virtue to which the sinner can retreat.

The issue of the corruption of the image in the fall likewise appears in a new light when viewed in functional and relational terms. What is impaired is not some*thing*, some "faculty" in the old psychological sense, but rather a faculty in the verbal sense, that is, an ability. According to the biblical narrative, the first parents initiated a chain of events that resulted in the loss of an ability they had previously enjoyed: to live in a state of blessedness, with immediate access to their Creator. Expressed theologically, this story is saying that human beings characteristically behave in such a way that they are unable to enjoy the direct access to God that is theirs in principle. In short, they find themselves unable to imagine God rightly, because their thoughts and actions—which is to say their essential selves—no longer conform to God. Their original likeness to God has become distorted by their own doing, so that they no longer possess that ability to know God that was based on the original analogy between Creator and creature. Viewed in this way, the doctrine no longer appears to involve the loss or corruption of some "substance," some intellectual or moral attribute. Rather, it articulates in theological terms what the story tells: a set of events, the specific interaction of character and circumstance depicted in the narrative. The divine image, the God-like form of the human creature, is thus his "narrative shape"—the conformity to God of the pattern of his lived life. It is *this* "image," this likeness to God, that is disrupted by sin. By not behaving like a creature of God, he obliterates his essential likeness to God. One consequence is the loss of the ability to imagine what God is like, since there is no longer a positive analogy between himself and God.[10]

Human possibilities are limited by human imagination. Sinners are unfree, at the mercy of the *servum arbitrium*, because (quite literally) they cannot imagine what it would be like to live in conformity to the will of God. The image of God, the possibility of imagining God and therefore of imagining themselves in a right relation to God, has been obliterated by their own doing, by the "evil imaginations" of their hearts. Medieval theology was right to insist that the human nature created according to the image of God must in some sense survive even in the most hardened sinner. In this sense, the *imago Dei* is the human imagination itself. But if it survives, it does so only in the most "formal" sense, as the bare ability to imagine. Materially, sinners have lost the image of God, the paradigm of God in themselves. For this reason the Reformers were right in a more important way in their insistence that nothing whatever remains of the likeness to God in the life of the sinner. The appearance of contradiction—that the *imago* both survives and has been destroyed—is rooted in the substantialist conceptuality shared by both sides in the sixteenth-century debates. Expressed in terms of a functional theory of imagination, the paradox vanishes. Human beings are indeed like God in their formal ability to imagine. But for the creature, unlike the Creator, this ability is limited by the material at hand—that is, by the available images. This material, the paradigm according to which the imagination imagines, is just what sin has disfigured. The sinner, in other words, while retaining the ability to imagine, has forfeited the basis on which to imagine *God*. Here is the point that has always been the backbone of

Protestant theology: God saves sinners solely by grace, and any teaching that implies an exception to this rule, by attributing any natural human ability to turn to God, denies the very heart of the gospel message. Expressed in terms of the imagination, the point is this: the human creature is most God-like in his ability to imagine, to make present to his "mind's eye" what is absent or even unreal. But this ability, like all human abilities, does not constitute an exception to sin but is co-opted by it. The sinful imagination, far from being a source of deliverance, becomes the most destructive weapon in the arsenal of human enmity toward God. The *servum arbitrium* entails the *serva imaginatio*. Salvation must therefore take the form of something that can release the imagination from its bondage to false images. Once again it becomes clear that the theologically decisive point is not the imagination in the formal sense as a human ability but its concrete content.

As we have seen, the historical controversy about whether the image of God is lost or merely damaged by sin derives in large part from conceptual confusion. By treating the *imago* as a substance, theologians on both sides were drawn into the misleading question of how much of it remains after the fall. If the image of God is thought of as a pattern, however, the appearance of contradiction between the classical Roman Catholic and Protestant teachings becomes at most a question of relative emphasis. When does a pattern cease to be the same pattern and become a different one? The "catholic" position emphasizes that the elements of the image are still there after the fall, while the "protestant" view stresses that their relations have been so severely disrupted that the pattern is no longer recognizable. Irenaeus, writing against heresy in the second century, likens the Gnostic use of scripture to the work of a fraudulent artist who misuses a mosaic portrait, a "beautiful image of a king . . . constructed by some skilful artist out of precious jewels." Suppose, Irenaeus writes, that the forger "should then take this likeness of the man all to pieces, should re-arrange the gems, and so fit them together as to make them into the form of a dog or of a fox . . . ; and should then maintain and declare that *this* was the beautiful image of the king which the skillful artist constructed."[11] Sin removes nothing of the human "substance," yet it is able to destroy the image of God. Everything depends on the organization, the pattern, the gestalt. Sin, like heresy, is a "paradigmatic" disorder: it appropriates the "parts" to misrepresent the "whole." Like the face hidden in the leaves of the tree in children's puzzle books, all of the elements may be present without our being able to see the proper "aspect." The decisive point theologically is that the image of true human nature in its relation to God is so distorted by sin that the resulting pattern ceases to mediate God to the human imagination.

Idols, Icons, and Images: An Excursus

The foregoing discussion suggests that sin, understood in the context of a Christian doctrine of imagination, can be accurately described as "bad imagination." Another Old Testament word, *idolatry*, is the corresponding term for sin in the specifically religious mode (i.e., bad religious imagination). The idol is the precise negative counterpart of the *imago Dei*. Since *idolatry* has also been a favorite term for a number of recent Christian theologians, it is important to examine it more closely before proceeding to the restoration of the image of God.

Ever since its early encounter with Hellenistic philosophy, Christian theology has flirted with dualistic schemes that exalt the spiritual at the expense of the material. Though the dominant orthodoxy rejected the most blatant dualisms of the ancient world, such as Marcion's bifurcation of the biblical God and the speculations of the Valentinian Gnostics, a love-hate relationship between Christian thought and the Platonic tradition has continued into modern times. Theologians sympathetic to spirit-matter dualism have interpreted the biblical polemic against idolatry as a rejection of all finite representations of divinity. Thinkers from Origen to Tillich have assumed the defining characteristic of idolatry to be its subjection of the infinite God to the forms of finitude, and religious purifiers from the iconoclasts of the eighth century to the feminists of the twentieth have taken offense at the concrete specificity of the Christian imagination, for which the favorite pejorative is idolatry.

The biblical texts to which these theologians appeal, however, do not support this reading of idolatry. One major strand of Old Testament tradition (expressed preeminently in the commandment "You shall have no other gods before me") rejects the worship of images not because they are physical but because they represent other gods than Yahweh. The other main strand ("You shall not make for yourself a graven image") does reject images of Israel's God.[12] But the reason for the prohibition is not the material or finite *nature* of the images per se but rather their religious *function* of allowing human worshipers to manipulate the deity to their own ends. Idolatry compromises not the immaterial nature of God so much as his sovereign freedom. The fundamental objection to idolatry is its confusion of creature and Creator, objects "made with hands" with the divinely created image. There can be no *graven* image of

God, not because God has no image but because he has already established his own, *human* image of himself.

The concept of paradigmatic imagination offers a way of interpreting
idolatry that helps to account for its importance in scripture and tradition while overcoming some long-standing difficulties. Idolatry, on
this reading, is the misuse of the religious imagination; the idol, a false
paradigm of deity. Once again the central issue is most coherently understood not as a metaphysical problem (material idol versus spiritual
God) but in relational and functional terms. Idols present so great a religious danger because the religious imagination depends totally on
having at hand a suitable image of God. Expressed in relational terms, a
valid image of God must protect God's freedom—which is also the
foundation of freedom for the human worshiper. The same point can
be expressed functionally by saying that the true image of God communicates God's own gracious—and therefore free—giving of himself,
while the idol futilely attempts to subject the divine will to human
control, thereby enslaving the human imagination to a false model and
a hopeless quest.

The debate about idolatry raises issues central to a Christian doctrine of imagination and suggests an area of potential confusion that
needs to be clarified before we turn to the positive side of the theology
of the *imago Dei*, the restoration of the true image and the reformation
of human life and imagination. This problem invites confusion because it has to do with what might be called "imagining imagination":
second-order reflection on the first-order activity of imagination. This
second-order analysis examines the images and metaphors through
which we think about the human imagination itself; it seeks to articulate the paradigm of the paradigmatic imagination. The problem is
rooted in the fact (obvious when we reflect on it but insidious if we
ignore it) that we can no more think about imagination than about any
other complex aspect of human experience without the medium of
metaphors and paradigms. In order to avoid becoming confused by our
own metaphors, it is important to examine them critically. The doctrine of the *imago Dei* lends itself naturally to the issue of imagination
because both depend on a similar set of images.

Most of the terms belonging to the "imagination family" can be
traced back etymologically to the common experience of seeing one
thing as a picture of another. *Imaginatio* clearly depends originally on
the analogy of seeing a picture of something that is not present. In the
German *Einbildung* this model is especially obvious; *Einbildungskraft* is
the power that derives from having an internal picture to which one

can refer. *Vorstellung* suggests the same model seen from a slightly different perspective: now the image appears as something "placed before" the mind's eye. The other main branch of the imagination family is the fantasy group—words like *fantastic, fancy, Phantasie*—which can be traced back through Greek *phainein*, "to show," to *phos*, "light." Again the primitive experience is visual: the imagination is imagined as a kind of inner sight, modeled on the analogy of sensual vision.

The potential confusion inherent in the use of this imagination language is that we may forget that its own imagery is metaphorical and begin to believe that imagination is really a matter of viewing mental pictures. Thomas F. Torrance warns against the tendency in the Western tradition, going back to the ancient Greeks, "to take vision not only as the model of all sense-experience but of all knowledge."[13] This prejudice is doubly distorting for theology because of the biblical priority of hearing over seeing. But when Torrance criticizes Austin Farrer for claiming that "we cannot by-pass the images to seize an imageless truth," he falls into his own confusion about the nature of imagination. He counters Farrer with a question: "Do the images signify by *imaging* the reality, and does this mean that the reality is imageable in its nature?" He is worried about that old bugaboo, idolatry: "If we can think of God only in images, . . . is this not essentially a form of idolatry?"[14] The problem, however, lies not in Farrer's conception of theological knowledge but rather in Torrance's "image of imagination." The religious imagination does not "image" God (i.e., construct some kind of picture of God) but *imagines* God (i.e., thinks of God according to a paradigm). The paradigmatic imagination is not mimetic but analogical; it shows us not what God *is* but what God is *like*. (Idolatry, reduced to an epigram, confuses the "is" with the "as.")[15]

The elusive but all-important distinction between the first-order images of imagination and the second-order concept of imagination may be brought into clearer focus by distinguishing carefully between *picture* and *image*. These originally equivalent words manifest in some everyday contexts a subtle but significant difference. Talking about a "picture of God," for example, strikes us as naive or blasphemous, while the notion of an "image of God," though it may be controversial, is taken seriously. The key lies in the use or function: a picture reproduces; an image exemplifies. An image is a picture in which nonessential features have been suppressed and essential ones highlighted. A picture, we might say, represents features indiscriminately; an image, by contrast, represents selectively. An image is both more and less than a picture: more insofar as it makes a claim about what is definitive or essential to the object; less insofar as it may be less complete or "literal." A picture shows us something; an image seeks to show us what that something *really* is.[16]

Most of our imagination language relies on the visual model of seeing an image—that is, on the paradigm of having available a picture of something that is able to function as its image, thereby shedding light (metaphors are unavoidable even in second-order discourse) on the object being imagined. The important point of the second-order reflection is that such visual imagery is itself being used analogically. Imagination *is* not inner sight though it is *like* inner sight. (The same point might be expressed as follows: imagination is not inner sight; rather, it is "inner sight.") It is thus no contradiction to speak, for example, of the aural imagination of the Hebrew prophets. Neither is visual imagery granted any privileged status in a doctrine of the Christian imagination. In fact, as we shall see in the next chapter, visual metaphor is generally reserved for eschatological contexts in Christian imagination.

The confusion inherent in the visual imagery built into our language of imagination can be further reduced by moving a notch farther along the spectrum from image toward concept. *Pattern*, though generally connoting visual experience, is more abstract than *image* and less dependent on visual metaphor. It is less metaphorical, for example, to speak of a "musical pattern" than a "musical image." If "mathematical" is substituted for "musical," the distinction becomes even stronger. A pattern is an arrangement of elements in any medium.[17] For this reason, I have preferred to describe imagination, not as the image-making faculty, but rather as the paradigmatic (pattern-making and pattern-recognizing) faculty.

The rampant theological confusion about idolatry is rooted, I believe, in a long-standing failure to distinguish clearly between the paradigmatic *activity* of the religious imagination and the visually oriented *conceptuality* of imagination. Idolatry cannot be simply equated with imagining God; rather, it is the error of representing God visually—that is, *picturing* God. The situation is further complicated by the fact that the term *imagination* has generally been used (in religion and elsewhere) to include the act of mental picturing as well as the analogical use of images as models, metaphors, and paradigms. A Christian theological doctrine of imagination needs to distinguish between the pictorial imagination, the act of representing God mimetically, whether in thought, paint, or marble, and the paradigmatic imagination, which uses "mesocosmic" images of God analogically for purposes of thinking about, praying to, or worshiping God. The alternative to idolatry is therefore not an iconoclastic *via negativa* that eschews all images of deity but rather a critical theology that sets about to distinguish between appropriate and inappropriate paradigms of deity. An especially destructive tendency unleashed by the iconoclastic bias in theology is the assumption that the least metaphoric concept of God is the best.[18]

The most renowned battle about idolatry in the history of the church was the iconoclastic controversy of the eighth and ninth centuries, whose orthodox outcome is preserved authoritatively in the documents of the seventh general council, held in Nicaea in 787. A closer look at the orthodox doctrine of icons—which "remains the most distinctive feature of Eastern Christian doctrine and practice"[19]—and the arguments of its critics will help us to sort out the genuine theological issues raised by idolatry from a host of pseudo-issues. As spokesman for the orthodox "Iconodule" position, I will take John of Damascus,[20] who, along with Theodore of Studios and Patriarch Nicephorus of Constantinople, ranks as one of its three classical exponents. Within the major "orthodoxies" of the Christian church, no thinker raises more serious questions about the use of images than John Calvin,[21] whose austere theological aesthetic has left an indelible mark on the Reformed tradition.[22]

One ancient and simple argument—Calvin called it an "old saw" in the sixteenth century (105)—can be dealt with quickly, namely, the "pedagogical" apologetic that "images are the books of the uneducated." Not only does it imply a religious aristocracy of the learned very difficult to square with the gospel, but it also rests on the questionable assumption that pictures communicate more readily than stories. It does nevertheless suggest a theological criterion for the Christian use of art. If, as will be argued in the next chapter, God is rendered authoritatively for the Christian imagination in scriptural narrative, visual images can be judged according to their power to interpret scripture. By this test, even the portrayal of God the Father by Michelangelo has its place in the exegesis of Gen. 1:26–27.

A weightier argument, also with pedagogical implications, is the claim of John of Damascus that "visible things are corporeal models which provide a vague understanding of intangible things." Some of his language, in fact, comes very close to the description above (chap. 4) of the paradigmatic imagination making use of "mesocosmic" images to understand intrinsically unpicturable reality. He says, for example, that "our inability immediately to direct our thoughts to contemplation of higher things makes it necessary that familiar everyday media be utilized to give suitable form to what is formless, and make visible what cannot be depicted" by constructing "understandable analogies" (20).

The controversial point, however, is the identification of the appropriate "everyday media." Calvin consistently opposes, not analogical *images* of God, but visible *pictures*.[23] Here once again we encounter the subtle but crucial ambiguity between analogical image and representational picture. In terms of the distinction made above between "image" and "picture," the Iconodules were apparently promoting the use of *pictures* in worship, which is why the debate was so intense. The use of images in the analogical sense—that is, of verbal imagery—was never in dispute in the ancient church.

What, then, is really at stake in the theological debate about idolatry, sparked by the use of images in worship? John of Damascus and John Calvin, in fact, agree on the answer even though they differ about its liturgical consequences. The crux of the matter is not whether but *how* God is to be represented and the use to which the image is put. Both of these questions depend on a more fundamental one: how does God make himself accessible to us? The difference between the genuine *imago Dei* and the idol is that God is the creator of the former while the latter is "made by hands."[24] Calvin has a surprisingly sophisticated understanding of religious image-worship, acknowledging that no one worships an image as such but rather the god represented by the image. But "there is no difference whether they simply worship an idol, or God in the idol," he claims, since "as soon as a visible form has been fashioned for God, his power is also bound to it" (109). The idol is by definition the humanly crafted image of God, whose function is to bring divine power under human control. "Man tries to express in his work the sort of God he has inwardly conceived," Calvin writes. This is the context for his famous dictum that "man's nature, so to speak, is a perpetual factory of idols" (108). There are passages in John of Damascus that sound a similar note: "If we attempted to make an image of the invisible God, this would be sinful indeed," he writes. "It is impossible to portray one who is without body: invisible, uncircumscribed, and without form" (52). But the icon is not such an image but rather a "dark glass, fashioned according to the limitations of our physical nature" (53).

The real key to the orthodox position on icons, however, is the reason that such portrayal according to our physical limitations is both possible and permissible. "In former times," John writes, "God, who is without form or body, could never be depicted" (23). But times have changed: "I adore the one who became a creature, who was formed as I was, who clothed Himself in creation without weakening or departing from His divinity, that He might raise our nature in glory and make us partakers of His divine nature" (15–16). The heart of the matter is thus christological: since the "flesh assumed by Him is made divine and endures after its assumption," John concludes: "Therefore I boldly draw an image of the invisible God, not as invisible, but as having become visible for our sakes by partaking of flesh and blood" (16).

The issue that emerges from the juxtaposition of these two theologians from different ages and traditions centers finally on the implications of the incarnation. On the one hand, the Eastern Orthodox Christology of the icon points up the danger that the Reformed rejection of visual representation may lapse into Gnostic denial of the real, fleshly humanity of Christ. On the other hand, the anthropological realism of Calvin and his tradition about the ever-present human tendency to idolatry raises a valid question about the appropriate way of representing God incarnate. Does the real humanity of Jesus justify the preoccupation of Eastern Orthodoxy with his *physical* appearance—especially in view of the remarkable silence about it among the eyewitnesses? The comparison has also clarified the relation of imagination to idolatry by showing that the properly theological issue is not whether to use images of God but rather which ones to use and how to use them.[25]

This excursion into the issues of idolatry and iconoclasm in Christian theology has brought us back in the end to the crucial—that is, the christological—point of the *imago Dei* and the Christian use of imagination: how the image of God, having been disfigured by sin, is restored and renewed.

Christ as the Image of God

Christian doctrine has long taught that the image of God, damaged or lost in the fall, is restored in Christ. The Letter to the Colossians declares Christ to be the "image of the invisible God," apparently recalling the *imago Dei* of Genesis in the following phrase, "the first-born of all creation" (Col. 1:15). Other Pauline passages draw an explicit contrast between the two images. In his discussion of the resurrection body in 1 Corinthians 15, Paul makes use of the creation narrative of Genesis 2 to develop a contrast between the "first Adam," described as *psychikos* ("psychic," unspiritual, physical), and the "last Adam," who is *pneumatikos* (spiritual). Then, using the term *eikon* (the "image" of Gen. 1:26), he elaborates the distinction as one between the "image of the man of dust" and the "image of the man of heaven," both of which are borne by human beings. In the "kenotic" hymn of Phil. 2:6-7, a similar duality appears, when Christ is described as being *en morphe theou*, which is contrasted with his taking the form of a servant (*morphe doulou*). The latter "form" is then immediately identified with his birth *en homoiomati anthropon*—that is, in human "likeness"—the second term used of the *imago Dei* in Gen. 1:26. Just as the original man was created in the likeness of God, so now the incarnate God assumes the likeness of man.

The predominant imagery of these passages is plastic—shaping, forming, molding—undoubtedly reflecting the language of the original *imago* passages in Genesis. (Much of this imagery has also found its way into Christian tradition, especially in the various terms deriving from the Latin root *form:* we speak of Christian formation, of the deformity of sin, and we seek the reformation of the church.) Central to the New Testament as to the Old, however, is the language of hearing: Christ is above all else the *Word* of God (John 1:1 is only the most prominent example), and our response is therefore a matter of *hearing.*[26] But the metaphors of seeing and hearing are not simply parallel and interchangeable. The subtle but significant relation of hearing to seeing that runs through much of the New Testament can be formulated in terms of imagination, which is the ability to *hear* of something not seen and to "picture" it. Hearing the Word of God enables us to imagine God—that is, to "see" him without *seeing* him. The ear is the organ of faith; the eye is reserved for the Eschaton. In this life "we walk by faith, not by sight" (2 Cor. 5:7), since "faith is the assurance of things hoped for, the conviction of things not seen" (Heb. 11:1).

Just as the Christian doctrine of sin is influenced by the interpretation of the image of God at creation, so the doctrine of salvation from sin depends on how the new image in Christ is understood. The traditional identification of the *imago Dei* with human reason, for example, leads naturally to an emphasis on ideas and right doctrine. Virtually all theological treatments of the doctrine from the church fathers to the Enlightenment assumed the creation, fall, and restoration of the image of God to be something affecting the soul. The philosophical revolution of modern times has left this doctrine, like so many others, an intellectual orphan. With the demise of the metaphysics in terms of which the doctrine had traditionally been explicated—for example, the very assumption that human nature is essentially constituted by an immaterial but substantial "soul"—the biblical language that had given rise to it in the first place came to be heard either as indefensibly "dogmatic" (precritical and therefore implausible) or else as simply unrelated to modern language and thought forms ("irrelevant").

The challenge facing the contemporary interpreter of the doctrine is therefore to bridge the interpretive gap between biblical and contemporary idiom, both linguistic and philosophical. I am proposing to bridge it by reading the *imago Dei* texts as a Christian doctrine of the formation, deformity, and reformation of the religious imagination. This theological locus thereby becomes a key to the meaning of revelation, that most embattled of doctrines in recent Christian theology.[27] H. Richard Niebuhr defines revelation as "that special occasion which provides us with an *image* by means of which all the occasions of personal and common life become intelligible."[28] Christ, embodying in his own "form" the inaccessible image of God, reveals God by offering himself as paradigm. But "where," in what "medium," can we conceive such a transaction to occur? If the argument of the preceding chapters is correct, that locus— the *Anknüpfungspunkt* of revelation—is the paradigmatic imagination. The theological task is to identify the "image of the invisible God"—to describe the "shape," the characteristic pattern that the New Testament calls the image of God in Christ. What sort of pattern is it, and what are the consequences of imagining it?

A number of recent theologians, most notably Hans Frei, have shed important light on the identity of Jesus Christ by treating it as a narrative issue. In contrast to the traditional distinction between the person and work of Christ, this approach sees personal agency as the key to personal identity: Christ *is* the one who *does* what the narrative about him reports. Frei uses the suggestive notion of a "narrative shape," a metaphor that is both verbal and visual, combining discursive with formal description.[29] What happens if we translate the theology of the *imago Dei* out of the thought forms of substantialist metaphysics into narrative terms? We will then look for the image of God in Christ by attending to the narrative shape of his life. He embodies the image of God in the living interaction of "character and circumstance" as depicted by the Gospel writers. Although they use certain apparently static images, such as suffering servant, Messiah, and Son of man, closer examination reveals all of these to be shorthand references to the story itself—ways of placing this story within the context of the older story of God's dealings with Israel. Jesus is identified (in the Apostles' Creed, for example) as the one who *did* certain things: he "was conceived by the Holy Ghost, born of the Virgin Mary, suffered under Pontius Pilate, was crucified, died, and was buried; he descended into hell; the third day he rose again from the dead; he ascended into heaven . . ." This "doing," of course, includes passive as well as active moments: he acts, but he also undergoes experience. It contains future acts as well, indicated by the further course of the creed. To know this man is to know him as the one who does these things—in other words, to know his story.

Expressed in terms of a functional theory of the imagination, the restoration of the image of God in Christ takes on new clarity. For it now becomes possible to state in anthropological terms *how* the image is renewed. The claim of Colossians that "He is the image of the invisible God" echoes what the Fourth Gospel puts in the mouth of Jesus: "He who has seen me has seen the Father" (John 14:9). Here the link between imagination and *revelation* is most direct and explicit. Unable to imagine what God is like or what it would mean to live in conformity to his will, we are helpless without model or analogy. Much as a scientist, lacking a theoretical model, is unable to penetrate the appearances of the natural world, we grope aimlessly, even when the "answers" are before our eyes. The frequently observed parallels in reports of scientific and religious discovery are rooted in this essential similarity. Creative advances in science have often been enabled in the first place by the imaginative insight of a single individual. ("What if we were to imagine the atom as a tiny solar system? . . .") The key is located in that inconspicuous copula of imagination, "as." An analogy has been proposed, a likeness between something with which we are already familiar and the unknown that we are trying to comprehend. The scientist then proceeds to articulate this hunch in a theoretical model, and the model gives rise to a new round of experiment and research. But the difference between scientific and religious discovery also becomes apparent here, for where in the world are we to find a model for *God*? The ways part here for two kinds of theology. The ancestor of one is St. Thomas, though his followers today include (in this regard, at least) many a Protestant as well. His is the way of "natural" theology, a search through the world for a likeness to God. The other way, the path of Paul, Augustine, and the Reformers, knows of no such "natural" path. For these thinkers, too, the knowledge of God depends on having some likeness to him. But the image of God cannot be conjured up by human creativity or insight; it can only be revealed by God himself. The claim that he has done so, concretely and specifically, is the cornerstone of Christian teaching.

Imitation and Imagination

Our interpretation of the *imago Dei* has so far been "chronological," following the "plot" of the Bible read as a single great story. A persuasive case can be made on systematic grounds, however, that the Christian doctrine of the divine image and the human imagination ought to begin not with creation but Christology. Consider, for example, this statement by the German Reformed orthodox theologian Ursin: the *imago Dei*, he argues, "will have to be estimated not by the state in which men began to be after the entry of sin, but by the reparation made through Christ, i.e., from the nature of man born again."[30] The grammar of Christian doctrine, in other words, mirrors the grammar of Christian experience, according to which the origin of our salvation and therefore of our knowledge of God is Jesus Christ alone.

What the previous section described—the reformation of the imagination according to the paradigm embodied in Jesus Christ—corresponds to the classical doctrine of justification. But justification is not a self-contained event (however dramatically the conversion of the imagination to Christ may sometimes occur); it is, rather, the beginning of a process. Just as the doctrine of justification has traditionally dealt with the discontinuity in the life of the sinner saved by Christ, so the doctrine of sanctification traces the consequences of that reorientation through the ongoing life of faith. This doctrine, too, has sometimes been expressed in terms of the *imago Dei*. Another theologian of Protestant Orthodoxy defines sanctification as a change in the human being, the *"terminus a quo* of which is the corruption of the image of God" and the *terminus ad quem* the "restoration of that image."[31]

Being conformed to this image means shaping one's life after Christ's life, patterning one's own living according to the pattern of his story, following the example of Jesus. The *imago Dei* is thus restored not as some kind of spiritual substance ("soul") but in the "narrative shape" of the Christlike life. This way of treating the doctrine of the *imago Dei* brings out its integral connection with the doctrine of *imitatio Christi.*

In the Pauline writings there is a particularly close relationship between images and forms on the one hand and imitation on the other. In Phil. 3:17, for example, Paul exhorts his readers to be "imitators of me," assuring them that they have "an example in us." His term is *typos*, that is, a "type," figure, or model. The impression of moral arrogance that may strike the modern reader of this phrase misses the thoroughly christological context of the passage. In verse 10 he climaxes a passionate account of his devotion to Christ with the hope that he "may share in his sufferings, becoming like him in his death." He uses the verb *symmorphizo* (which appears only in Christian writers), meaning literally "to be invested with the same form as," "to be conformed to," or "to take on the same shape as." For Paul, to be "in" Christ, means to be transformed by him: "if anyone is in Christ, he is a new creation" (2 Cor. 5:17). Just as the original creation of a human being, according to the Yahwist's account in Genesis 2, involved the molding of shapeless clay into the human form, so the re-creation of the human person "in Christ" involves a reshaping, a re-formation. The double relation of imitation and formation is most pithily captured in the injunction "Be imitators of me, as I am of Christ" (1 Cor. 11:1).

If the *imago Dei* is the model or paradigm for the renewal of human life, the imagination is the means by which it takes place. According to Col. 3:10 (the same imagery is found in Eph. 4:24), the "new nature" that we have "put on" "is being renewed in knowledge after the image of its creator." The Pauline theology of shaping or "form-ation" also emerges in Rom. 9:19 and following verses, where God is portrayed as potter (*ho kerameus*) or molder (*ho plasanti*) who shapes us like clay (*to plasma*). He borrows the image from the Hebrew prophets (cf. Isa. 29:16; 45:9; 64:8; and Jer. 18:6, where it also relates back to the Genesis 2 creation of Adam). A consistent set of images unites these passages and the ones mentioned earlier, enabling Paul to place creation and reconciliation in a common context. The "new creation" motif in Paul's theology (also echoing the prophets) is best understood in terms of this plastic imagery—a "new shape"—Paul's preferred "image of the image."

Other New Testament passages focus specifically on the transforming process itself, the metamorphosis of grace. "And we all, with unveiled face," writes Paul in 2 Cor. 3:18, "beholding [*or* reflecting] the glory of the Lord, are being changed into his likeness [*ten auten eikone metamorphoumetha*] from one degree of glory to another." The verb is the same one used in Matt. 17:2 for the *transfiguration* of Jesus and in Rom. 12:2, which exhorts Christians to "be *transformed* by the renewal of your mind." Some of these passages attribute the metamorphosis explicitly to the work of the Holy Spirit, which has (in terms of later doctrine) an external and an internal aspect. The process described in the New Testament can be paraphrased using the terminology of paradigmatic imagination. Externally, God takes shape in Christ, in whose image the imagination of the apostles is transformed, and who in turn give shape to the scriptures. Internally, the imagination of the reader or hearer of the Word is transformed by being conformed to the image of Christ. The chain of imaginative transformation extends still further: the transformed (sanctified) Christians (who are the "body," the physical shape, "of Christ") go on to impress the *imago* further through the pattern of their activity in the world.

This theology of the transforming image has had adherents in every age of the church, but it finds a particularly succinct expression in Origen. His own explanation of the transforming process is colored by Platonism, but it is not difficult to make the translation into the conceptuality of imagination. Drawing on New Testament passages such as the ones we have cited, Origen exhorts his second-century readers, "Let us therefore always fix our gaze on this image of God so that we might be able to be reformed in its likeness." His vivid sense of the devil makes for a dramatic version of the contrast between old and new images:

For if the human who has been made in the image of God, by contemplating against his nature the image of the devil, becomes like him through sin, so much more will he, by contemplating the divine image in whose likeness God has made him, receive through the WORD and his power that form which had been given him by nature.[32]

The bond uniting the Christian with Christ the Image, which Origen calls by the Platonic term *participation* and we are describing as imagination, is preeminently one of love: as the "image of the invisible God," Origen writes, "he himself grants participation in himself to all rational creatures in such a way that the participation each of them receives from him is commensurate with the passionate love with which they cling to him."[33] One of the advantages of reconceiving Christian revelation, justification, and sanctification in terms of the imagination is the automatic involvement of the whole person in the process of transformation. The tendency for modern theologians to become preoccupied by the epistemological consequences of sin and salvation is thereby avoided. The transformation of the imagination involves knowledge, conscience, and affections without the need to "relate" them conceptually.

The *imago Dei* is not only the original pattern of the human creation and the constitutive pattern of the new creation in Christ, but also the goal of creation. The "iconic" Christology of the New Testament, according to which the sinner is justified by imaginative appropriation of Christ as "image of the invisible God" and sanctified by being re-formed in the narrative shape of that image, has an eschatological dimension as well. Being "conformed to Christ" (Rom. 12:2) means allowing our paradigmatic imagination to become "Christomorphic" (a corrective to the usual moralistic reading of this injunction). A danger in the traditional threefold doctrinal scheme of creation–fall–redemption is that salvation in Christ, the restoration of the divine image, is made to appear simply as a return to the *status quo ante*. Paul's meditation on the "image of the man of dust" and the "image of the man of heaven," however, seems to lack the middle step. Its context is eschatological, his famous discourse on the resurrection: "Just as we have borne the image of the man of dust," he says—recalling the creation of Adam out of the "dust of the ground"—"we shall also bear the image of the man of heaven" (1 Cor. 15:49). This is the transformation to which he refers when he goes on to predict that "we shall be changed . . . at the last trumpet" (15:51–52). Though we share even now in the "new shape" of creation, we do so by anticipation of our *terminus ad quem*, the ultimate goal of our present faith. Origen ties this distinction to the "image-likeness" duality of Gen. 1:26: "while the human being did indeed receive the dignity of God's image in the first creation, the dignity of his likeness is reserved for the consummation."[34]

This chapter has argued that the long doctrinal tradition of interpretation of the *imago Dei* can be reformulated, without doing violence to its meaning for earlier generations of Christians, as a theology of the human imagination. The point of contact for divine revelation is, materially, the paradigmatic image of God embodied in Jesus Christ; formally, it is the human imagination—that ability of human beings to take elements of their "middle-sized" world as paradigmatic images of realities to which they would otherwise have no access. The argument is not a "natural theology," since the imagination is utterly dependent for its content on the image that it receives. It has no ability and no desire to create or construct it for itself (the true idolatry). On the other hand, Christian revelation so conceived remains an utterly human phenomenon, comparable with other use of imagination. The built-in ambiguity of imagination (its potential for truth and illusion) precludes turning the argument into a case for the superiority of Christian truth. As I will argue in the concluding chapter, this situation is just as it should be: not an embarrassment for Christian theology but the sign of its utter dependence on the grace of God.

Because we have access to the embodied image of God only by way of the imagination of the original witnesses, there is one further step to be taken before turning to the nature of Christian theology as the critical articulation of the grammar of the Christian imagination. The Reformer Melanchthon put it succinctly when he commented that it is in the scriptures that the "Godhead has portrayed its most complete image."[35] To that decisive portrayal of the image of God we must now direct our attention.

CHAPTER 6

The Normative Vision: The Function of Scripture

The Letter to the Hebrews opens with the announcement that God has now "spoken to us by a Son," who "reflects the glory of God and bears the very stamp [*charakter*] of his nature" (Heb. 1:2–3). This terse description of Christian revelation combines metaphors of hearing ("spoken to us") and seeing ("reflects the glory") with a third image—that of imprinting or impressing a form onto a plastic substance. This metaphor occurs in another well-known New Testament passage not usually linked by interpreters with the *imago Dei*: the story of Jesus' answer to the loaded question about paying Roman taxes, reported in all three synoptic Gospels (Mark 12:13–17 par.). Taking a coin, Jesus asks (the words are identical in all three versions): "Whose likeness [*eikon*] and inscription is this?" Often overlooked in the rush to discover political or economic lessons in the story is the analogical implication of the coin. Jesus, by assuming the coin to be one of the "things of Caesar" because it bears Caesar's image, implies an analogy to "God's things," which are likewise to be rendered to him. Where has God impressed *his* image as the sign of his claim? The question need only be made explicit for the answer to become obvious: in the human being, whom he has "stamped" with his image.

This imagery of impressing or imprinting provides another metaphor for describing the imagination as the divine-human *Anknüpfungspunkt*. The human likeness to God, worn away by sin, has been newly "minted" in the humanity of Christ. Through faith in him, according to the New Testament, the *imago Dei*, the *eikon* of God in Christ, is impressed upon the imagination of believers, conforming them to God (cf. Rom. 12:2). The faithful imagination thereby becomes "Christomorphic," *gottförmig*,[1] constituting a newly created analogy between God and humanity. The same metaphor is present, though usually dormant, in common speech—for example, in the notion of "making an impression on someone." If the previous chapter can be summarized in this imagery by saying that revelation is the impression that God makes on us, the task of the present chapter is to explain how that impression comes to be made. The main thesis of the book, expressed in another everyday idiom, is that God does it by appealing to our imagination. The sequence of the final three chapters can be explained briefly in metaphorical terms as follows: God has im-pressed his image, embodied in Jesus Christ, on the original witnesses, who have in turn ex-pressed that image in certain texts; these writings, which we therefore call sacred, once more im-press their form on us, the modern hearers, reshaping us in the image of God. This metaphor of successive molding or casting better conveys the process of transmitting the divine image than either of the more usual "images of the image": the picture or the statue.

The logic of the final three chapters can also be stated in more conceptual terms as a movement from revelation, through scripture, to theology. *Revelation* is the technical term for describing the inspiration of the original witnesses' imaginations. The doctrine of *scripture* goes on to describe the inspiration of the texts in which those witnesses recorded what had been revealed to them. *Theology*, finally, is the technical term for the critical interpretation of revelation by means of the interpretation of scripture. For all three, imagination plays a crucial role. Revelation is an act of imagination; scripture is a work of imagination; and theology is an interpretation of imagination.

The present chapter focuses on the middle term of this movement, the fulcrum between God's act of revealing and the response of Christian theology to that act. The doctrine of scripture must take account of three closely interrelated qualities of the Bible: its inspiration, its unity, and its authority. But "qualities" is an inadequate term, since each of them, like the concept of scripture itself, is best defined functionally according to its relation to paradigmatic imagination. Scripture is the concrete paradigm of the Christian imagination in the life of the believing community, the means by which we are enabled to imagine God.

Calvin's Spectacles: The Inspiration of Scripture

No theologian has expressed more forcefully than John Calvin the predicament in which human beings find themselves in trying to know God. In the opening pages of the *Institutes* he argues, first, that God's glory is manifest both outwardly in nature and inwardly in the human soul, and second, that this evidence is of no avail to us in the present life. "Although the Lord represents both himself and his everlasting Kingdom in the mirror of his works with very great clarity," he writes, "such is our stupidity that we grow increasingly dull toward so manifest testimonies, and they flow away without profiting us."[2] The consequences of original sin, he is claiming, are not only moral and religious but epistemological and theological as well: we are unable to attain a right knowledge of God even though the objective evidence confronts us at every turn. This impotent "natural theology" nevertheless plays a crucial role in Calvin's thought by underscoring the objectivity of the evidence for God and thus the culpability of the human beings who have made themselves blind to it.

God, of course, has not simply abandoned his creatures to their self-inflicted blindness but has provided a remedy in the scriptures. Calvin introduces the whole topic of scripture in a suggestive metaphor:

Just as old or bleary-eyed men and those with weak vision, if you thrust before them a most beautiful volume, even if they recognize it to be some sort of writing, yet can scarcely construe two words, but with the aid of spectacles will begin to read distinctly; so Scripture, gathering up the otherwise confused knowledge of God in our minds, having dispersed our dullness, clearly shows us the true God.[3]

Revelation, Calvin's metaphor implies, does not introduce new "content" into the world but rather corrects the astigmatism of the sinful imagination, thereby freeing us to see clearly what has been there all along. The scriptures are not something we look *at* but rather look *through*, lenses that refocus what we see into an intelligible pattern.[4]

Interpreting the role of scripture in this way allows us to bring the Christian use of the Bible into comparison with other imaginative acts, especially ones in which the imagination functions realistically. Michael Polanyi uses the very same metaphor in claiming that scientific theory is "like a pair of spectacles; you examine things by it, and your knowledge of it lies in this very use of it."[5] He particularly likes the analogy of a stereoscopic viewer, in which we use two-dimensional pictures "tacitly" but not focally in order to see a three-dimensional image.[6] For Christians the Bible functions analogously: its images permit us to see a dimension of depth in the world that is not otherwise apparent.

Thomas Kuhn likewise speaks on occasion of scientists viewing natural phenomena "through" a paradigm.[7] He also reports on some fascinating experiments concerning the effects of actual (nonmetaphorical) lenses on perception. A subject given goggles with inverting lenses actually learns in time to see the world right side up; the usual inversion of the retinal image is reversed. Experiments such as this lead Kuhn to conclude that "something like a paradigm is prerequisite to perception itself."[8] Paradigms, in other words, function like lenses; we depend upon them to give a meaningful gestalt to our experience of the world.

The Christian claim that the Bible is inspired by God[9] means that it is the instrument of revelation, the means by which God makes himself known in the present life of believers. This claim can be stated more precisely by saying that scripture embodies the paradigm through which Christians view the world in its essential relation to God, the images by which God in-forms the imagination of believers. The advantage of putting the claim this way is not that it becomes any more believable (as always, the imagination may deceive as well as reveal) but rather that it makes the claim intelligible to modern people. The chief indication of this intelligibility is that it allows us to compare the Christian use of the Bible with other uses of the imagination by people whose intent is realistic rather than fantastic or deceitful—people like natural scientists, historians, and at least some novelists and poets.

The ramifications of understanding scripture in this way can be brought out by exploring the eyeglass analogy a bit further. Suppose that an ophthalmologist is considering whether a particular pair of glasses will correct a patient's visual handicap. The doctor examines the glasses from every possible angle, measures the thickness and curvature of the lenses, tests the quality of the glass, and compares the data with standards listed in authoritative medical textbooks. Next the doctor examines the patient's eyes in great detail, recording every observable feature, and compares this data, too, with the scientific literature. But the doctor is unable to determine for certain whether the prescription is right. The problem, of course, is that the one test by which the lenses might be reliably evaluated has been omitted: having the patient put them on and look.[10]

Some philosophical questions are suggested by this parable. Does it imply that choosing eyeglass prescriptions is "subjective"? Surely not, if that is taken to mean that the doctor, or other outside observer, has no grounds for evaluating the patient's choice "objectively." (The patient might, for example, stumble over the furniture, complain of headaches, or get the big letters on the eye chart wrong. In that case the observer would be justified in doubting the patient's report that the glasses are right and suspecting other motives behind his or her insistence.) The choice of scripture, like the choice of eyeglasses, is personal but not therefore simply private or arbitrary: some scriptures, like some glasses, enable people to see better. Such choices can be tested only by their actual use;[11] but they have public consequences that enable them to be evaluated—though only indirectly—by outsiders. The limits of the eyeglass analogy for scripture spring from the vast differences between their functions. The consequences of bad physical vision are more easily identified (and remedied) than those of bad religious vision. The "grammar" of the two cases is nonetheless similar enough to justify Calvin's image and to suggest some implications about Christian use of the Bible.

The inspiration of scripture is thus a matter of right imagination. To call the Bible scripture is to claim that it enables its users rightly to imagine God and the world. In that case one might expect to find considerable attention to imagination in the Bible itself. A study of the occurrence of the word *imagination*, however, turns up very paltry results. In the first place, it is uncommon: there are only two occurrences in the Revised Standard Version of the New Testament, and they do not translate the same Greek term.[12] But in the second place, even those few references use the term in a pejorative sense. In the Magnificat of Luke's Gospel, God is praised as the one who "has scattered the proud in the imagination of their hearts" (1:51). The Greek word is *dianoia*, which is the organ of *noein*—in other words, the mind or understanding. Elsewhere in the New Testament, the same word is usually rendered as "mind." Plainly this term has only a tangential relationship to the paradigmatic imagination. The other occurrence of "imagination" yields no more encouraging results. In Paul's speech on the Areopagus in Acts 17, he exhorts his listeners "not to think that the Deity is like gold, or silver, or stone, a representation by the art and imagination of man" (v. 29). Here the term is *enthymesis*, typically translated as "thought," "reflection," or "idea." Twice in Matthew's Gospel (9:4; 12:25) it is used of Jesus "knowing the thoughts" of his interlocutors; similarly in Hebrews, the Word of God is described as "discerning the thoughts and intentions of the heart" (4:12).

These and similar passages, while indicating that no biblical term corresponds precisely to the concept of paradigmatic imagination, also contain hints of a different kind of connection, metaphorical rather than conceptual. Frequently, as in the Magnificat and the passage cited from Hebrews, the locus of these "thoughts" or "imaginations" is the *heart*. There are a number of indications that the biblical heart functions very much like the paradigmatic imagination. Two of these parallels are especially important. First, both heart and imagination are at once the seat of intellectual and emotional functions: the atheistic thoughts of the psalmist's fool are located in his heart (Ps. 14:1; 53:1), while the prophet can lament that his "heart is poured out in grief" (Lam. 2:11). Second, the biblical heart like the paradigmatic imagination is capable of lies as well as truth: "The heart is deceitful above all things" (Jer. 17:9), yet the "wise man's heart inclines him toward the right" (Eccles. 10:2).[13]

The negative parallel between heart and imagination is evident in the primeval history: when the "Lord saw that the wickedness of man was great in the earth, and that every imagination of the thoughts of his heart was only evil continually, . . . it grieved him to his heart" (Gen. 6:5-6). Here the human heart is both the seat of "thoughts" and the root of sin, and it is probably not just coincidental that the sinful human heart grieves God "to his heart." The corresponding positive parallel is expressed in Jesus' beatitude, "Blessed are the pure in heart, for they shall see God" (Matt. 5:8). On the one hand, this saying is eschatological, implying that the vision of God will be the reward of the blessed; in this sense it is parallel to Paul's expectation of seeing God "face to face." But it might also be read as saying that the pure in heart shall "see" God, that is, be able to imagine him rightly, in this life; in that case it is parallel to Paul's vision "through a glass darkly" (1 Cor. 13:12, KJV)—which brings us back to scripture as the spectacles of the imagination.

The most compelling argument of all for taking the heart to be the biblical correlate of the paradigmatic imagination is its role as the *Anknüpfungspunkt*, the point at which human and divine come most immediately and concretely into contact.[14] The heart is the place where the Word of God dwells (Deut. 30:14), the organ of faith (Rom. 10:10). Even the imagery parallels that of the imagination. There is no more precise summary of Christian revelation in the New Testament than Paul's statement that God "has shone in our hearts to give the light of the knowledge of the glory of God in the face of Christ" (2 Cor. 4:6). The metaphor of imprinting is suggested by Jeremiah's vision of God's new law written "upon their hearts" (Jer. 31:33). In summary we could say that according to these biblical writers the place where the image of God is newly impressed on the human being is the heart. The concept of paradigmatic imagination provides a contemporary conceptual apparatus by which Christian theology can interpret this biblical imagery, articulating it in terms that clarify the claims of Christian revelation vis-à-vis other human activity. In particular, it allows us to state with precision the way in which scripture functions as the medium of revelation.

Whether we call it the heart or the imagination, this human function is the anthropological locus, though not the substance, of revelation. It determines the way in which we think about revelation but not its contents. Not the imagination per se, in other words, is the theologically important point, but rather the images by which it imagines. Theologians at various periods of Christian history have acknowledged this distinction, but I will mention briefly just two of them.

The role of images and imagination is most important in general to those theologians who stress the indirect nature of revelation. The Aristotelian empiricism adapted for theology by Thomas Aquinas leads him to distinguish more sharply between the knowledge of God (revealed as well as natural) possible in this life and in the life to come than is the case, for example, in the more Platonic and mystical theology of his contemporary, St. Bonaventure. In addition to the role that Thomas attributes to images in natural reason, he speaks of revelation through images. "Prophetic visions," he says, "provide us with God-given images which are better suited to express divine things than those we receive naturally from the sensible world." Even these divinely ordained *phantasmata* do not enable us to know "what God is" but join "us to him as to an unknown." Revelation gives us a mode of access to God superior to that granted by natural reason but inferior to the direct vision that is our ultimate goal. Faith—the name for that intermediate kind of knowledge—thus has an indirect relation to its object; it "is not due to what is seen by the believer but to what is seen by him who is believed."[15]

A similar notion of indirect revelation through inspired images finds more recent expression in lectures by Austin Farrer, whose title, *The Glass of Vision*, recalls Paul's seeing "through a glass darkly" as well as Calvin's scriptural spectacles.[16] Farrer leaves no doubt that the Bible is where the inspired images are to be found: "Divine truth is supernaturally communicated to men in an act of inspired thinking which falls into the shape of certain images" (57). Despite his appeal to the supernatural, Farrer rejects the "old doctrine of inerrant supernatural dictation" of scripture as a "burden which our backs will no longer bear" (52). And though he speaks like Thomas of "God-given images," he disavows the Scholastic "hunt for theological propositions" along with the typically modern quest for a reliable historical record (43–44). Neither propositions nor history, but images are the bearers of revelation in the Bible. "The images, of themselves," Farrer maintains, "signify and reveal" (44). His own discussion of images is more metaphorical than conceptual, dominated by plastic imagery:

Through the secret act of God by which the Apostles were inspired there came upon us in imaged presentation the shape of the mystery of our redemption. It possessed and moulded their minds, it possesses and moulds ours: we are taken up into the movement of the life above all creatures, of the Son towards the Father in the Holy Ghost (56).

This eloquent statement of the revelatory interaction of divine image and human imagination suggests more than its author develops. I want to follow up on hints by theologians like Farrer and St. Thomas that scripture reveals through God-given images by interpreting the rich biblical imagery of the reshaped heart in terms of the more philosophical conceptuality of the paradigmatic imagination. In particular I want to say precisely what it means for the Christian understanding of scripture and its relation to other imaginative activity.

One other recent theologian has made a proposal about how scriptural images reveal that it will be instructive for us to examine: Paul Tillich's suggestive concept of an *analogia imaginis.* Rejecting any quest for the "historical Jesus" as not only pointless but impossible, he focuses instead on the "New Testament picture of Jesus." The transforming power of this picture "implies that there is an *analogia imaginis,* namely, an analogy between the picture and the actual personal life from which it has arisen." Tillich's application of the concept, however, is flawed by his apologetic claim that faith can "guarantee" the biblical picture "as an adequate expression of the transforming power of the New Being in Jesus as the Christ."[17] An ecstatic faith experience thus usurps the role of guarantee attributed by the New Testament itself to the Holy Spirit (2 Cor. 1:22; 5:5; Eph. 1:14). Rather than faith guaranteeing scripture, the New Testament claims that the Holy Spirit guarantees both faith and scripture. Protestant orthodox teaching, following Calvin, addressed this issue in the doctrine of the *testimonium spiritus sancti internum* as complement to the external testimony of Holy Scripture.[18] Employing the concept of paradigmatic imagination, we can paraphrase the point of the doctrine in contemporary terms: the external likeness of the scriptural images to the Word of God—the *analogia imaginis*—corresponds to the internal congruity of the faithful imagination to the scriptural images— what might be called the *analogia imaginationis.*

This correspondence between image and imagination—the revelatory *Anknüpfungspunkt*—therefore depends wholly on the initiative of divine grace and nevertheless appears in the wholly human form of imagination. Only in faith does the imagination correspond to God, so that the analogy of imagination is the analogy of faith.[19] The divine-human point of contact can therefore be described as the faithful imagination, the human power to imagine, conformed to the image of God. The inspiration of scripture, I have argued, is most adequately understood as its imaginative force—its power to re-form and trans-form the human imagination, grounded in that "secret act of God" that the New Testament calls the work of the Holy Spirit. Before turning to the implications of this view for the authority of scripture, we need to examine the imaginative shape of scripture as a whole—what has traditionally been called its unity.

The "Shape of the Mystery": The Unity of Scripture

After a long eclipse the canon has reemerged as a topic of serious attention by biblical scholars and theologians. The venerable dogma of the authoritative canon of scriptural books was an early casualty in the modern assault on all forms of heteronomy. To Enlightened proponents of reason and toleration in the seventeenth and eighteenth centuries, belief in a specific list of religious texts immune from criticism epitomized the authoritarianism and narrow dogmatism of "positive" religion. Still more devastating to belief in the scriptural canon was the historicism that followed in the nineteenth century. The presumed unity of doctrine in the various biblical books dissolved along with the literary unity of the texts themselves in the acids of historical-critical investigation. Attempts to salvage the lost unity of the Bible through such projects as "biblical theology" have often seemed little more than sophisticated attempts to do what fundamentalist "harmonies" do in a crudely precritical manner—to impose an artificial unity on scripture that cannot pass the test of disinterested critical scrutiny.

The modern protest against the unity of the canon is legitimate insofar as is has been directed against theological claims on behalf of the wrong kinds of unity. Charles Wood argues that the "canon is an unruly lot of material, which resists systematizing, reduction to essentials, or even harmonization." He describes it as a "whole rambling collection of diverse utterances spanning several centuries, cultures, and conceptualities, embracing many literary genres and techniques" and claims that "it functions less as a limitation than as a goad to our own thought."[20] This characterization of the Bible is surely accurate, and it serves as a protest and a warning against theological misuse of the doctrine of scriptural unity. It is especially pertinent to a theology accustomed to taking its cues mainly from philosophy. It does not, however, preclude other kinds of unity, especially ones modeled more on literature and the arts than on philosophical or mathematical systems.

There can be no question that the modern critical challenge to the canon—to the thesis that scripture is a unity—has made both positive and negative contributions to Christian theology; and attempting to undo this chapter of theological history, even if that were possible, would be folly. By freeing the study of the Bible from theological presuppositions, such as the dogma that every part of the Bible teaches the same doctrines, the empirical spirit of modernity has yielded a rich harvest of detail and fostered a new appreciation of the concrete particularity of the biblical writings. By bringing out the special character of innumerable strands of biblical tradition, modern scholarship has improved our grasp of the true biblical theolog(ies) while guarding against oversimplified harmonizing. At the same time, and for the same reason, it has left behind a bewildering picture of diversity that is at best unsettling to Christian believers and at worst inimical to Christian confidence that the Bible speaks the Word of God.[21]

Not all aspects of the modern assault on scriptural unity, however, stand up under critical scrutiny. The same positivist spirit, reaching its zenith in the late nineteenth and early twentieth centuries, that spawned the untenable dichotomies between fact and imagination, and between science and religion,[22] also infected prevailing views of the Bible. The assumption that empirical "induction" from discrete bits of data ("facts") is the only "scientific" method made the thesis of scriptural unity appear arbitrary. Like the associationist psychology of the day, biblical scholarship sometimes fell prey to the atomistic fallacy, assuming that scriptural unity could be maintained only on the basis of additive agreement among its component parts. The inadequacies of this view of the relations between wholes and parts have been shown in such diverse fields as gestalt psychology, Wittgensteinian philosophy, and recent philosophy of science.[23] Reconsideration of the canon in light of these developments leads to a quite different understanding of scriptural unity.

The position that I want to develop here could be called a gestalt view of the canon. To view the Bible as a unity, as Christians in all ages have done, is to see it according to a pattern in which all of its parts cohere, hang together as a whole. This unity is something quite different from maintaining that all the biblical books contain a common theology, treat the same themes, or otherwise share some common "essence." It is to hold that the multifaceted strands of biblical tradition manifest a family resemblance, that they "belong together," that the pattern they present to the imagination in concert is different from, and greater than, their individual patterns.

The sort of unity that Christians attribute to scripture can be clarified by considering the kinds of arguments that might legitimately be brought against it. For example, a dispute about the unity of the Bible might resemble a disagreement about the unity of a novel. A critic might argue that a certain episode is "out of character" for the protagonist.[24]

Arguments about harmonizing the justice and mercy of the biblical God can be understood on this analogy as disagreement about whether all of the actions attributed to God are "in character"—drowning all the inhabitants of the earth yet repeatedly forgiving the sins of Israel, for example. A novel, especially an epic novel like *War and Peace* or *Light in August*, can be exceedingly diverse, complex, and rambling and still be seen as a unity. Such a whole is quite different—has a different "grammar"—from a deductive system of thought or a hierarchical schema. Literary critics can and do argue about the meaning and coherence of novels, that is, about the patterns they embody. Much of the evidence they adduce has to do with the pattern of images in the work: the way its metaphors and symbolism give structure to the work as a whole. Theologians reason in a similar manner when, for example, Karl Barth interprets the "plot" of the Bible as God's covenant promised to Israel and fulfilled in Jesus Christ,[25] or when Calvin sees the world through scriptural spectacles as the "theater of the glory of God." Arguments about such theses are real arguments: evidence can be presented and opinions swayed, indicating that something is truly at stake in the question of unity, the issue of whether and how scripture can be construed as a coherent whole.

Though literary analogies are for obvious reasons especially appropriate to the consideration of scriptural unity, they are not the only suggestive comparisons. The function of imagination in music is an apt analogy of Christian revelation because it, too, is based on hearing rather than seeing. Mary Warnock, expounding Kant's view of the aesthetic imagination, invokes the example of a melody. "We had to hear the pattern *in* the sound," she writes. "Without imagination, there would have been just sound; imagination makes the sound, as it were, 'presentable,' and in so doing experiences the feeling of satisfaction in the discovery of order in chaos."[26] A better example even than a melody is polyphonic music: the unity of scripture is like the unity of a symphony. Here diversity, even dissonance, is quite compatible with a judgment that the work nevertheless functions as an aesthetic whole. David Kelsey uses the musical metaphor when he says that "calling a set of writings 'canon' means construing it as an ensemble . . . [but] does not entail any particular orchestration, any one mode of 'wholeness.' " The theologian who describes scripture as canon "takes on a responsibility to suggest what its singular 'wholeness' is *like*," something that "requires a metaphorical judgment, . . . an act of the imagination."[27]

The issue of the canon as we have considered it so far—how the individual components of scripture can be taken together as a whole—represents only part of the question of unity, what could be called its internal aspect. Acknowledgment of a canon also makes implicit reference to those texts that it excludes, and this selectivity can be called the external aspect of scriptural unity. Why have precisely these texts, and only these texts, been singled out for inclusion in the canon? Functional systems theory teaches us to conceive of a whole (a system in the technical sense of the theory) not so much with reference to what it includes but rather as a strategy for excluding everything else. "A system," according to the definition of Niklas Luhmann, "is its difference from the environment, an order for defining and maintaining a boundary."[28] Without necessarily endorsing the specifics of Luhmann's theory of religion as a social system, we can use his concept of system to clarify further the nature of the scriptural canon. The notion of scripture as a functional system conforms especially well with some recent attempts by biblical scholars to recover the importance of the canon. Brevard Childs emphasizes in particular that canon is a *process:* not a "late, ecclesiastical activity, external to the biblical literature itself, which was subsequently imposed on the writings" but rather a dynamic dialectical development extending "from the earliest stages of the New Testament to the final canonical stabilization of its scope."[29] The grammar of this process conforms closely with Luhmann's theory of the formation of systems, whose root function he identifies as the "stabilizing of a difference between inner and outer."[30] The fact that Luhmann is describing social systems rather than texts serves simply to underscore the interdependence of sociological and hermeneutical processes. As the early Christian church deepened and sharpened its religious vision through vigorous debates between rival parties within, and against competing groups without, it was both establishing its own identity (by distinguishing orthodoxy from heresy) and testing the revelatory claims of various documents (by distinguishing scripture from other writings). These were not two different processes but rather the sociological and hermeneutical aspects of a single dialectical development. The patient, struggling to achieve orientation in a bewildering world, tried out a number of lenses before settling finally on the right prescription.[31]

The judgment that scripture is canon is thus a judgment of paradigmatic imagination in which the various "parts" of the Bible are grasped in a single gestalt. Its unity is not a uniformity but a "wholeness," that is, a holistic pattern. The disagreements as well as the agreements about the canon in the history of the church can be made intelligible on this model.

Kelsey raises a possible objection to this view of the canon when he argues that ascribing *wholeness* does not necessarily entail *unity*. The latter "would consist of a coherence or even consistency among its contents. It could only be demonstrated by exegetical study. . . . But it is not logically necessary that the canon actually exhibit such 'unity' in order for it to be construed as some kind of 'whole.' "[32] The distinction is difficult to maintain, however; for coherence of some sort is surely implied in construing something as a whole. Kelsey suggests that "wholeness" could be grounded entirely in the use to which the scriptures are put by the church: "Taken together . . . [they] function *ensemble* when used in the common life of the church." But if the primary use to which the church puts its scriptures (the function that accounts for their being called scripture in the first place) is to render God to the paradigmatic imagination, their "wholeness" entails a kind of "unity" as well. What I am suggesting is that this unity has more in common with a visual gestalt or a functional system than with a class of like objects or a logical hierarchy.

A gestalt view of the canon thus allows us to conceive of scripture as a unity without attributing to it a uniformity that it manifestly does not possess. Historically, it allows us to see how the church fathers could have been guided by considerations beyond political expediency and apostolic authorship in the process of reaching a consensus about the canonical boundary. Apostolicity as the chief canonical principle, on this account, has to do less with the authorship of particular writings than with the integrity of a shared vision. There is, in fact, evidence that the church fathers viewed the issue of orthodoxy and heresy in gestalt terms. Irenaeus, in the example cited earlier, compares the Gnostic gospels to an art forgery, in which the stones of a royal portrait are rearranged into the form of an animal, which is then declared to be the likeness of the king.[33] Heresy, according to this analogy, is a "grammatical" error; it arises from a failure to grasp the proper "aspect," the characteristic way in which the pieces cohere to produce the revelatory vision. The heretic suffers from bad spiritual vision, an inability or unwillingness to use scripture Christianly, that is, according to the pattern shared by believers from the beginning.

Such a conception of scriptural unity also implies that the canon remains formally open. Karl Barth argues persuasively that the canon, as a witness of faith, must in principle remain subject to revision, even in the absence of specific objections to its traditional boundaries. His argument can be stated in terms of a gestalt view of the canon, which is in fact implied by the very language he uses. It is impossible to deny, he claims, that "the concrete shape [*Gestalt!*] of the canon can never be closed absolutely but only in a highly *relative* way, even with regard to the future."[34] The reason for his insistence is that the church does not create or authorize the canon but rather discovers and acknowledges it as already given.[35] Scripture is not under the control of the church; rather, the church is subject to the canon of scripture. But such a claim makes sense only if "canon" does not refer in the first instance to a particular collection of documents but rather to the criterion by which they are selected. For the church, that criterion is always Jesus Christ, the Word of God: Barth cites Luther's well-known principle that the test of scriptures is "whether they set forth Christ or not" ("*Christum treyben odder nit*"). Barth points out that this standard, appealed to throughout the ages by church and heretics alike, depends upon how the user understands "Christ."[36] The argument, stated in terms of the theory presented here, is about which texts truly render Christ to the imagination. The unity of the texts is a function solely of the unified vision they bring forth. The question of canon, to use an analogy from the visual arts, is like the question of whether a portrait is a "good likeness." Elements may be added to or removed from a picture or pattern without necessarily altering its identity. Whether a given change brings the subject into clearer focus or distorts it into something altogether different or incoherent is a judgment that can only be made ad hoc in each instance. The canonical boundary, therefore, can never be drawn so definitively as to preclude consideration of future proposals for change.

The Classic Rendition: The Authority of Scripture

By now it should be clear that scriptural unity is implicated in the even thornier problem of scriptural authority. For the religious issue at stake in the question of the Bible's unity is not just the totality or completeness of revelation but its *reliability:* "Are you he who is to come, or shall we look for another?" (Matt. 11:2; Luke 7:19). The Christian user of scripture seeks assurance that the God rendered imaginable through its words is really God and not merely a mask for some "God beyond God."[37] The doctrine of the unity of scripture speaks to this concern by insisting on the essential integrity of the biblical witness. Scripture proclaims the "full gospel": without dissolving the divine mystery, it nevertheless renders an imaginative vision of the true God that omits nothing essential to our salvation.

If the authority of scripture presupposes its unity, it even more obviously assumes its inspiration. But the question of authority goes beyond both these issues to ask *how* the Bible is normative. *In what way* is scripture authoritative for belief? The most direct answer is to say that biblical authority is *imaginative*. Scripture, rightly employed, enables its hearers to imagine God.

Proposing to link the concepts of imagination and authority will no doubt strike some people as contradictory. Is not the essence of imagination its freedom, its spontaneity, its independence of authority? The question reflects the pervasive influence of Romanticism on contemporary assumptions about imagination; it also ignores the systematic ambiguity at the heart of the concept, what I have called the *realistic* and *illusory* uses of imagination.[38] Whatever may be the case for creative fantasy, the use of imagination in truthtelling, in the service of reality, implies a normative aspect. The point becomes obvious in the light of other realistic uses of imagination—for example, in the natural sciences. The indispensable role of imaginative paradigms and models in science depends on their reliability; appropriate models enable scientific progress, whereas flawed ones distort the evidence and confuse the scientists who use them. Recent philosophy of science has done much to clarify the ways in which such imaginative structures function as scientific norms. If the claim that scriptural authority is essentially imaginative is to be useful, it will be necessary to show how scriptural images function normatively in Christian faith and practice.

Recent theological proposals for understanding scripture in terms of the concept of the *classic* provide a useful point of departure. David Tracy offers a "theory of the religious classic" in *The Analogical Imagination*, which he advances as the "heart of the argument of the entire book."[39] He defines classics as "certain expressions of the human spirit [that] so disclose a compelling truth about our lives that we cannot deny them some kind of normative status." As such, classics represent "a *normative* element in our cultural experience."[40] Tracy's most notable departure from traditional theories of the classic is his broadening of the concept to include more than just texts. His list (which appears in varying forms in the book) includes images, rituals, symbols, persons, and sometimes events, as well as various kinds of texts. Especially intriguing about this "nonclassicist notion of the classic" is its claim to "restore a nonauthoritarian notion of authority and norm."[41]

Tracy's proposal to understand the normativeness of scripture on the model of the classic as cultural norm is especially promising because it holds out the possibility of reconceiving theological authority in contemporary terms, at the same time rendering that authority comparable with other, generally acknowledged forms of textual authority. The way in which he works out his "theory of the classic," however, undermines its usefulness by presupposing an unsatisfactory "encounter" theory of meaning and a correspondingly inadequate concept of religion. The weakness of Tracy's position can best be articulated by employing a critical distinction introduced by George Lindbeck.

In *The Nature of Doctrine* Lindbeck offers a threefold typology for classifying theories of religion and doctrine.[42] The first is the *propositional* view, represented by traditional orthodoxy and contemporary fundamentalism, which takes cognitive propositions to be the primary substance of religion and therefore of doctrine. Second is the *experiential-expressive* approach to religion, represented primarily by liberal Protestants since Schleiermacher and by "ecumenically inclined Roman Catholics." This approach "interprets doctrines as noninformative and nondiscursive symbols of inner feelings, attitudes, or existential orientations" (16). Lindbeck advocates an alternative theory of religion, which he calls *cultural-linguistic.* It is the newest of the approaches and one increasingly influential in religious studies but largely neglected by theologians. On this view a religion is a "comprehensive interpretive scheme," a "cultural and/or linguistic framework or medium that shapes the entirety of life and thought" for its adherents (32–33). This approach quite deliberately "reverses the relation of the inner and the outer" assumed by the experiential-expressivism that dominates contemporary theology. "Instead of deriving external features of a religion from inner experience," Lindbeck writes, "it is the inner experiences which are viewed as derivative" (34). Borrowing insights of cultural anthropologists like Clifford Geertz, Lindbeck argues that "to become religious involves becoming skilled in the language, the symbol system of a given religion," and an adequate account of religion thus requires "thick description" (34, 115).

Tracy's view of religion, and especially of the religious classic, epitomizes Lindbeck's experiential-expressive type and demonstrates its inadequacy. The classic, according to Tracy, claims our attention "on the ground that an event of understanding . . . has here found expression."[43] Understanding, especially religious understanding, is always a "hermeneutical event," a "disclosure," in one of Tracy's favorite terms. Classics are the external correlates of these inner experiences—"*expressions of the human spirit*" whose normative status is grounded in the compelling quality of the experiences themselves.[44] The dangerous naïveté of grounding normative truth claims in subjective experience ought to be obvious in a century that has produced such religious expressions as the "German Christians" and Jonestown. Tracy and other theologians of normative "disclosures" fail to take seriously the profound ambiguity of religious experience, its potential for demonic and destructive "expressions" as well as sacred ones. In traditional doctrinal terms, we can say that Tracy's theory of the classic is incapable of distinguishing orthodoxy from heresy, since both share in the same dynamics of religious experience. As a description of socioreligious reality, Tracy's disclosure model is plausible; as the basis for the authority of scripture, it is flawed, precisely because it cannot tell us why some compelling disclosures ought to be rejected and others made normative for faith.

Another theologian who uses the concept of the classic as a means of redescribing in contemporary terms the normative function of the Bible is Sallie McFague. But her account, like Tracy's, is largely vitiated by the unargued assumption that theology is the articulation of prior religious experience. "The Bible," she writes, "is absolute or authoritative in . . . the way that a 'classic' text is authoritative: it continues to speak to us."[45] Though she cites Tracy's notion of classic approvingly, McFague prefers the language of James Barr, who describes the Bible as the "classic model" for Christians.[46] For Barr, in fact, the description amounts to a formal definition of Christianity itself: "Christian faith is faith which relates itself to this classic model."[47] Barr remains vague about just how the Bible functions as model, saying only that it models the "understanding of God." McFague, too, leaves the notion of classic undeveloped, but links it to the concept of models in explicit dependence on recent philosophy of science. She describes the "classic model" metaphorically as an "interpretive grid or screen," an image belonging to the same family as spectacles and lenses. But for McFague the direction of interpretation is the reverse of that proposed by Calvin, Kuhn, and Lindbeck, for she understands the interpretive grid as the means by which "many dimensions of *Christian experience* of God are given shape."[48] The movement from inner religious experience to outer theological expression is especially pronounced in McFague's "quest of a feminine model for expressing the divine-human relationship."[49] The entire discussion assumes that this relationship is something experienced by human beings *before* it finds expression in language. Having presupposed that "experience is central to religion" because it provides the models for understanding God, McFague is unable to adduce criteria for determining whose experience should be normative.

Against the prevalent view that religion "expresses" something originating within human experience, Lindbeck wants to reverse the direction of interpretation. "A religion," he maintains, "is above all an external word, a *verbum externum*, that molds and shapes the self and its world, rather than an expression or thematization of a preexisting self or of preconceptual experience" (34). His preferred metaphors (e.g., "molds and shapes") reveal that Lindbeck conceives of religion and its relation to culture in terms of what I have called the paradigmatic imagination. Although his own favored analogy for religion is language- —hence cultural-*linguistic*[50]—the account of religion that he offers might more appropriately be called "imaginative." Indeed, at one point he suggests that "language" might be replaced by "some conceptual and/or symbolic interpretive scheme" as a "condition for religious experience" (37). This scheme or paradigm, he argues, "gains power and meaning insofar as it is embodied in the total gestalt of community life and action" (36).

Applying the reversal of the relationship between inner and outer proposed by Lindbeck to the theory of scripture as classic produces a quite different picture of the cultural role of normative texts from the one suggested by Tracy and McFague. The texts that become a culture's classics (for whatever reasons: the motives are immaterial to the theory) are the ones that give shape and substance to the experience of the individuals and groups constituting the culture. Classics do not express experience so much as they produce it by embodying the community's paradigms, thus serving as models and exemplars of experience. This account of the classic is strictly functional: any text that people in fact commonly employ as a favored imaginative model is by definition a classic. Such a theory is "nonclassicist" in Tracy's term; that is, it remains neutral about the question of which texts *ought* to be classics. The more culturally radical elements in a community will tend to attack its classics, proposing to replace them by other, more appropriate candidates for classic status; conservatives ("classicists") will invoke and defend the authority of the prevailing classics. The evidence that certain texts do in fact function in this classical way is overwhelming. One of Kuhn's many ways of using the word *paradigm* in *The Structure of Scientific Revolutions* is to designate scientific textbooks that have come to embody the definitive exemplars for doing science—works such as Newton's *Principia* and Darwin's *Origin of Species*. We can improve on Kuhn's often loose terminology by saying that such works are classics because they exemplify the paradigm, the pattern or grammar that the community in question (physicists or biologists, in these examples) accepts as normative for its common enterprise. By using the term too broadly, Tracy obscures the specific function of the classic. He includes not only texts but also certain "events, images, rituals, symbols and persons."[51] What all of these items really have in common is pattern, and when Tracy describes them as classics he is indicating that each of them may function paradigmatically. But events and persons ordinarily achieve paradigmatic status in a community through their embodiment in texts, and it would be clearer to limit the term *classic* to such specifically textual paradigms. A classic, in other words, ought to be defined as a literary paradigm, a paradigm embodied in textual form.

The Bible carries authority for the Christian community by embodying the classic paradigm of the Christian imagination. Scripture is the concrete exemplar in the life of the believing community, by which it is enabled to imagine God, and hence to imagine the world in its essential relation to God. As such, scripture is the means by which individual and group identity is formed and reformed, and it is the means by which the community of believers seeks to transform the world around it by converting the world's imagination to conformity with the Word of God. Of course the Bible in its diversity contains many paradigms, a host of models for imagining Christianly. But the singular is nevertheless justified—scripture embodies *the* Christian paradigm—by the unity of the vision it renders. Under the aspect of the canon, the diverse parts of scripture are constellated as a whole, and this gestalt becomes in turn the lens through which the fragmentary elements of human experience come together in a coherent unity.[52] The focal point of that unity is the final topic to be addressed in this account of scripture and the religious imagination.

Focusing the Christian Imagination

Karl Barth's initial answer to the question "What is it that makes precisely the Bible of the Old and New Testaments the *canon?"* seems to invite the charge of *Offenbarungspositivismus:* "The Bible makes itself the canon!" He explicates this bald assertion, in terms that recall the metaphor with which this chapter began, by saying that the Bible is canon because "it *impresses* itself as such." But he does not attempt to ground this scriptural "self-impressing" (*dieses Sich-Imponieren*) on the experience itself, on the impression that is made on us, but rather on the specific content that produces the impression. "By the power of its content the scripture makes its impression." And that content, according to Barth, is summarized in the name Jesus Christ.[53]

The question we have been pursuing—how scripture is authoritative—can be formulated more precisely by asking what aspect of scripture is normative. The term *aspect* is employed here in Wittgenstein's sense: it designates a particular gestalt, the whole according to which something is being construed, the pattern by which it is organized and constituted. As we have seen, this act is the definitive function of the paradigmatic imagination: seeing "as," that is, under one aspect rather than another. David Kelsey has argued persuasively that "it is the *patterns* in scripture, not its 'content,' that makes it 'normative' for theology."[54] But this formulation appears directly to contradict Barth's claim that the Bible's content is the basis of its authority. The contradiction can be resolved by redescribing the relations in terms of the paradigmatic imagination. Kelsey's formulation is unfortunate insofar as it pits pattern against content. Jesus Christ is the definitive *content* of scripture because he is the focal point for construing the canon Christianly. But to construe something is to imagine it according to a paradigm, to recognize its definitive *pattern*. The point can be illustrated by biblical examples. The story of the coming of the Holy Spirit at Pentecost is the point in the New Testament at which the light dawns for the original Christian community. Peter's speech (Acts 2:14–36), often cited as an early example of the *kerygma*, the essential gospel message in compact narrative form, provokes in its hearers the "dawning of an aspect," according to which the story of Jesus becomes the focus for a re-imagining of the history of salvation. For those who in hearing it were converted (cf. Acts 2:37–42)—the usual religious term for the dawning of an aspect—the various parts of the story were reconstituted in a new and meaningful whole. The old parts were still there—the Jewish scriptures remained essential to the new story—but they were no longer "parts" in the same sense, because their meaning had been redefined in terms of a new and different constitutive pattern: the Jewish scriptures had become the Old Testament.

This example raises a more general issue, one that has generated the greatest controversy concerning the construal of the Christian canon: the relation of Old Testament to New. Hartmut Gese, echoing a persistent minority report heard in the church from Marcion to Harnack, has recently argued for the "dispensability of the Old Testament" on the grounds that its typological interpretation in the New Testament itself renders it superfluous: "What good is this anticipation when the fulfilled truth stands in full view?"[55] But the type, or figure, is not rendered dispensable by its fulfillment, any more than (for example) John the Baptist can be omitted from the gospel story.[56] To say that a particular part finds its significance in relation to a larger whole, having its focus elsewhere, does not make it dispensable. It remains a part, perhaps an essential one. A good statement of the majority view on the Christian

canon is offered by Dietrich Bonhoeffer at the end of his brief introduction to *Creation and Fall*: "When Genesis says 'Yahweh,' historically or
psychologically it means nothing but Yahweh. Theologically, however,
i.e. from the Church's point of view, it is speaking of God." The church,
Bonhoeffer says, "sees the creation *sub specie Christi*."[57] Because Christ is
the paradigm for the Christian theological imagination, the entire scripture is viewed differently. The focus on Christ alters none of the Old
Testament elements, but it defines a new gestalt, a vision of how everything hangs together in a meaningful pattern (cf. Col. 1:17).

Christians acknowledge the authority of the scriptures of Old and
New Testaments because only they render Christ, the image of God, fully and coherently to the imagination. Attending to scripture is therefore
the touchstone of the Christian life, because it is the revelatory point of
contact between God and the people of God. Christians, like all others
who orient themselves beyond the middle-sized world of immediate experience, use their imagination in certain concrete ways. Those ways
may be as different from others as a duck from a rabbit, but the very act
of imagining makes Christians comparable with all other human ima-
giners. As Bonhoeffer recognized, seeing the world *sub specie Christi* is
the paramount theological activity for Christians. Our final task is to examine that definitive Christian enterprise.

CHAPTER 7

The Faithful Imagination: The Task of Theology

Paul Ricoeur once expressed his hermeneutical goal in the aphorism "The symbol gives rise to thought." His aim, he said, was to discover a "criticism that is no longer reductive but restorative," a method in which interpreting the symbol does not render it dispensable. Such a hermeneutic would restore the immediacy of myth and symbol without returning to the "primitive naïveté" of a precritical age. "But if we can no longer live the great symbolisms of the sacred in accordance with the original belief in them," Ricoeur continued, "we can . . . aim at a second naïveté in and through criticism. In short, it is by *interpreting* that we can *hear* again."[1] I believe that the account of the paradigmatic imagination developed in the preceding chapters is especially well suited to explain how and why "the symbol gives rise to thought," and to show in the Christian case how the imaginative world of the Bible can be theologically appropriated in such a way as to enable a second naïveté.

The present chapter aims to bring the philosophical analysis of paradigmatic imagination in chapters 3 and 4 into explicit relations with the theological discussion in chapters 5 and 6 in order to clarify the specific function of theology. I want first to return to the topic of metaphor, touched upon briefly in the discussion of paradigmatic imagination in chapter 4,[2] in order to consider recent proposals that theology be defined as metaphoric. I will argue that theology is better conceived as the means by which the Christian community carries out the hermeneutical task implicit in a view of the Christian life as faithful imagination. The remainder of the chapter will elaborate several consequences entailed by this account of theology. The first concerns the problem of theological truth claims, raised most acutely by the fictional status of many biblical narratives. A second issue, posed by the charge of fideism that this account of theology may appear to invite, concerns the nature of faith understood as the submission of the religious imagination to the paradigmatic vision of scripture. The issues of faith and fideism lead to a consideration of the specific nature of the God imagined by Christian faith, including some implications for theological hermeneutics. Finally, I want to demonstrate how the specifically practical consequences of a theology conceived in terms of imagination imply a reformulation of the relation between religious theory and practice.

Metaphor, Imagination, and Theology

A broad consensus rejecting the classical view of metaphor as mere ornament has emerged from the work of philosophers of language, literary critics, and theologians in recent years. According to the classical tradition, represented by few theorists today but still generally taken for granted by nonspecialists, metaphor departs from the real or authentic use of language for aesthetic and rhetorical reasons by substituting figurative language for its literal equivalent. The new consensus, on the other hand, understands metaphor as an authentic and central use of language, not reducible to other, more literal terms. The classical view of metaphor is substitutionary; the new consensus could be called substantive, since it takes metaphorical speech to be a legitimate and central function of language, capable of communicating in ways that cannot be duplicated in nonmetaphorical terms. Especially influential have been the views of I. A. Richards, Max Black, and Paul Ricoeur,[3] though many others have participated in the process as well. The case against the substitution view of metaphor has been made extensively and persuasively by other writers and can safely be taken as a point of departure for further consideration of metaphor as a subject of hermeneutical importance for theology.[4]

The more difficult question of how and why metaphorical speech is uniquely communicative has led to a greater variety of viewpoints. I want therefore to describe with some care how I understand the functioning of metaphorical discourse and in so doing to determine precisely how metaphor can be defined in relation to imagination. The theological significance of imagination will become apparent only against this background.

One of the more interesting attempts to make theological sense out of metaphor has been undertaken by Eberhard Jüngel.[5] He argues persuasively against the long tradition of viewing metaphor as "inauthentic" speech by going back to its ancient roots. Aristotle treats the *metaphora* as one kind of *onoma* (name or noun) that we use (together with the *rhema*, or verb) to make true or false assertions about things. But the metaphor is different from the true noun, the *onoma kyrion* or "governing name," which it replaces for rhetorical purposes. Jüngel calls attention to the fact that this view of metaphor presupposes that the entire world of things can be expressed without metaphors. The use of metaphors is justified by Aristotle because they make learning pleasurable and encourage the hearer to new knowledge. Jüngel finds the Achilles heel of this view in the phenomenon recognized by the post-Aristotelian tradition as *catachresis* or *abusio*—necessary metaphors, for which there are no "governing nouns." This apparent exception to the rule leads Jüngel to develop his "suspicion" that many of the words taken to be governing nouns were originally metaphors. The result is a picture of language as a dynamic history of metaphoric expression and conceptual definition, in which the "metaphoric structure" of language is the hallmark.

Jüngel draws two important conclusions from the history of metaphor theory. First, he finds significance in the fact that even the classical theory was forced to admit exceptions to the general rule that metaphors have only rhetorical justification. The existence of a special term for these "necessary metaphors" is testimony to their frequency and "suffices to call the entire traditional theory of metaphor into question."[6] More interesting, he shows how these anomalies in the classical theory become the clue to a new paradigm for metaphor: his picture of language as a historical dialectic in which ongoing metaphorical creativity is the driving force.

Jüngel's other main conclusion from the history of metaphor theory is more questionable. He is convinced that Aristotle's attention to the rhetorical force of metaphor is correct, even though he rejects the implication that it therefore has no direct function in the articulation of truth. According to Aristotle, metaphoric language finds its justification in the responsibility of the speaker not only to utter the truth but also to communicate it to the hearer. By employing an unusual word, even though not literally true, the speaker breaks the hearers out of their normal linguistic rut and allows them to hear the truth. Metaphor employs unusual words in order to jar us awake when the familiarity of usual words has dulled our attentiveness. Jüngel calls this trait of metaphor its "vocative character" (*Anredecharakter*) and treats it as an essential feature of metaphor and thus of language itself. He believes that he can have it both ways: metaphor is essentially related to the character of language as address, yet it can also communicate the truth. He wants to transform Nietzsche's cynical thesis that truth is nothing but a "moving army of metaphors, metonymies, and anthropomorphisms" into a positive acknowledgment of metaphor "*as the event of truth*," the paradigmatic case of the "translation of being into language."[7] At the root of theology is an *experience* (Jüngel calls it an "experience of experience"),[8] a linguistic event that can only be *expressed* metaphorically. "The language of faith is constituted by *metaphora*," he claims, and "metaphors are expressed discoveries."[9] The job of theology is to "articulate" this prior experience of faith. The difficulties entailed by Jüngel's argument are similar to those of another contemporary theologian whose views I want also to consider.

For Sallie McFague the key to theology is also metaphor, the "heart" of which she describes succinctly as a "basic movement by indirection from the known to the unknown."[10] Adapting a view of metaphor indebted especially to I. A. Richards and Max Black, she argues for the necessity of "unsubstitutable" metaphors in speaking of God. But her theological appropriation of metaphor ultimately fails because she, like Jüngel, gets the relationship between language and experience backward. She assumes throughout (apparently without recognizing it and thus without offering any evidence) that human beings have experiences, including experiences of their relationship with God, which they subsequently *express* in language, metaphorical language being the most appropriate kind. She speaks, for instance, of the "imagery emerging from experiencing the relationship with God," arguing that feminine as well as traditional masculine imagery properly expresses that experience.[11] The assumption that the authority for theological language lies in prelinguistic religious experience leads her to a method in which the "divine-human relationship" serves as the experiential criterion for judging the adequacy of various theological models, defined as extended metaphors. The criterion is vague at best and hopelessly subjective at worst, admitting of no publicly identifiable controls. The root problem is that McFague misses the fact that "experience" is already a function of paradigmatic imagination, from which it cannot be extracted in a nonimaginative form in order to serve as foundation and criterion for religious language. Her method is the theological kin to philosophies of science that want to employ a language of pure description in order to evaluate the adequacy of models and theories. It is ironic that she appeals for support to the very philosophers of science (including Thomas Kuhn) who have done most to discredit such methods. The principle that all data are theory-laden applies to the data of religious experience just as it does to the data of scientific observation. Trying to use prelinguistic experience as a theological criterion involves an implicit contradiction: it is like wanting to remove one's glasses in order to check their reliability against a "direct" view of the world. Neither theologians nor natural scientists can make an end run around the imagination.

Both Jüngel and McFague depend ultimately on foundational arguments, apparently believing them to be the only alternative to relativism. Janet Soskice, referring to the same essay by Nietzsche that raises the specter of relativism for Jüngel, exposes the underlying assumption. "The point that speakers use language according to precedents and established belief," she writes, "is not a new one (it was Vico's point and Thomas Kuhn's, too), but commonly it has been taken to imply a relativism like that of Nietzsche."[12] Such relativism, it should be pointed out, can take the form either of an antireligious skepticism or of fideism.

A satisfactory account of the relation between metaphor and theology first requires a clearer understanding of the logical grammar of metaphoric utterance than that provided by either Jüngel or McFague. To this end I propose to employ Soskice's theory of metaphor,[13] though not without some adjustments that are necessary, first, to clear up points of confusion in her account, and second, to bring metaphor into more explicit relation with paradigmatic imagination. Only then will it be possible to account adequately for the theological significance of metaphor.

Though there is widespread agreement today (against the classical tradition) that a metaphor cannot simply be replaced by a corresponding literal expression, there is disagreement about how metaphor works and why its meaning is irreducible to literal terms. Max Black dismisses the "comparison view" of metaphor as simply a special case of the unsatisfactory "substitution view." The comparison view, taking metaphor to be a "condensed or elliptical *simile*," according to Black, wrongly supposes that the "metaphorical statement might be replaced by an equivalent literal *comparison*."[14] Black is not alone in insisting on an important difference between metaphor and simile, but Soskice argues persuasively that these two tropes, "while textually different, are functionally the same" (59). But she gets into difficulty herself when she tries to explicate this functional identity. She rightly criticizes Black for failing "to mark the fact that the good metaphor does not merely compare two antecedently similar entities, but enables one to see similarities in what previously had been regarded as dissimilars" (26). It is therefore surprising that she nevertheless follows Black in denying that metaphors involve comparisons.

At the root of Soskice's difficulty (it is the only serious quarrel I have with her theory) is her inadequate attempt to distinguish analogy—

which necessarily involves comparison—from metaphor. Devoting less than three pages to a discussion of analogy, she defines it as a "linguistic device [that] deals with language that has been stretched to fit new applications, yet fits the new situation without generating for the native speaker any imaginative strain" (64). The notion of "imaginative strain" is an intriguing one, but surely not the definitive mark of analogy. It is simply wrong to claim that we can distinguish analogical from metaphorical usage "by the fact that from its inception it seems appropriate" (65). Some of the most fruitful analogies—in the sciences, philosophy, theology, and the arts—produce enormous imaginative strain, and ones that do not are typically not very informative. The whole point of an analogy is to illumine one term by showing a pattern of significant similarities with another. (To speak, as McFague and others do repeatedly, of a pattern of similarity-in-difference is redundant, for that is precisely what distinguishes *similarity* from *identity* . Whether in everyday speech or in philosophical discourse, to say that one thing is *like* another necessarily implies a degree of unlikeness as well; otherwise one would say "the same as.") Some analogies, like some metaphors, occasion more imaginative strain than others.

Soskice is on stronger ground in her critique of Black's "interactive view" of metaphor, especially of his insistence that a metaphor has two subjects, a primary and a secondary one. She prefers I. A. Richards's distinction between the *tenor,* or "underlying subject," of a metaphor and the *vehicle* by which it is presented (45). Because these two thoughts are active together in metaphoric utterance, she calls this theory an "interanimative" view of metaphor. "It is only by seeing that a metaphor has one true subject which tenor and vehicle conjointly depict and illumine," she writes, "that a full, interactive, or interanimative, theory is possible" (47). This theory is especially effective in accounting for metaphors expressed not only by nouns (e.g., "Man is a wolf") but also by adjectives ("giddy brink," "writhing script") and other parts of speech. She also rightly emphasizes that a metaphor may be implicit, not identifiable with any of the specific *words* in the utterance.[15] This account of metaphor is unquestionably superior to Black's, yet both Soskice and Black overlook an essential element of the logical grammar of metaphor: its use of analogy.

The familiar distinction between literal and figurative speech, employed by most theorists of metaphor (including Black and Soskice), contains a clue to the underlying analogical grammar of metaphor. The key issue in the distinction concerns the mode of reference: in the literal case, a word is used to name an object directly; but in the case of metaphor, reference is made indirectly by invoking an analogy. We might put the matter more formally by calling the first ("literal") case *ostensive* reference and the second ("figurative") case *heuristic* reference. A person refers ostensively by pointing directly to the subject; in speech this is done by the use of its *name*, defined as its conventional linguistic label. Understood in this way, names can be defined in contradistinction to metaphors. A name in the strict sense has no meaning except its referent: it is a linguistic sign for referring to something. (The fact that many, perhaps most, names are metaphorical or figurative in origin is no argument against this definition. Whatever their history, names *now* no longer function heuristically but ostensively.)[16] A speaker refers to something heuristically by directing attention to something else—to a model or paradigm with which it is analogous. Understanding, in such a case, depends on the hearers' grasping an explicit or implicit analogy: for understanding to take place, they must "get the point," or "see the light." Black's "interactive" view is right in emphasizing the dynamic quality of metaphor in contrast to ostensive speech. He is also right in noting that two terms are essentially involved. But he errs in calling them both the "subjects" of the metaphor and in denying that a comparison is involved in their interaction. As Soskice points out, only one of the two terms is the metaphor's *subject* (what it is "about").

Soskice offers a more compelling account of the logical grammar of metaphor—but without recognizing the full implications of what she has discovered. As a result, she remains vague about the central metaphoric interaction between "vehicle" and "tenor." The source of the problem is her inexplicable refusal to acknowledge the analogical heart of metaphor. She defines metaphor as *"speaking about one thing in terms which are seen to be suggestive of another"* (49). The vague and cumbersome phrase "in terms which are seen to be suggestive of"[17] is the crux of the matter. She argues that metaphor "characteristically [involves] the consideration of a model or models" (49) but overlooks the fact that models give rise to "suggestive" terms precisely because they posit analogies. "Metaphorical construal," she writes, "is characterized by its reliance on an underlying model," which need not be explicit (50). She qualifies this definition by saying that it describes a "secondary level" of metaphorical meaning. But there is nothing secondary about it: the invocation of a model (the "vehicle") that serves as an analogical basis of comparison with the subject under discussion (the "tenor") is the very essence of metaphor. What is puzzling about Soskice's argument is her refusal to call this relation analogy.[18]

Metaphoric speech, in other words, requires the ability that I have called paradigmatic imagination. A metaphor is an explicit or implicit linguistic model employed by a speaker for the purpose of depicting a subject analogically. Like other uses of paradigmatic imagination, metaphor makes accessible something that would otherwise lie beyond our linguistic grasp; metaphors, for this reason, cannot be replaced by literal equivalents. Once the pivotal importance of the underlying analogical model has been acknowledged, Soskice's account of metaphor can be sharpened. First, both the labels "interactive" and "interanimative" are misleading insofar as they deflect attention from the single focus and unidirectional grammar of metaphoric speech. The "vehicle" is in fact the *metaphor* itself, in the concrete sense of the word,[19] and the "tenor" is its *subject*—what the metaphor is about. Soskice and Black are correct in emphasizing that metaphoric speech involves interaction among ideas, but the focal idea is the metaphor itself. Of course, the metaphor "interacts with" or "animates" its subject; we can recognize a metaphor only by its function within a sentence. But what initiates and enables that interaction in the first place is a quite specific linguistic "artifact"—the metaphor—a concrete image taken from the familiar "middle-sized" world and employed "paradigmatically" by the speaker for the purpose of depicting an otherwise inaccessible subject.[20] The speaker thereby appeals to the hearers' paradigmatic imagination through the use of metaphor.

The problem with attempts like those of Jüngel and McFague to define theology in terms of metaphor is not that they are wrong about the centrality of metaphor in religious language but rather that they mistake its function. Religious language is not the expression of prelinguistic religious experience but rather speech arising out of commitment to specific religious paradigms. People with different paradigmatic commitments characteristically have different experiences. What is *given* to the believer, and therefore to the theologian, is not a foundational experience but a religious paradigm: a normative model of "what the world is like," embodied in a canon of scripture and expressed in the life of a religious community. The way to recognize Christians—and, I am convinced, other religious people as well—is not by looking for experiences lying "behind" their language but rather by observing how they imagine themselves in the world. Experience, in other words, is not the ground of religious imagination so much as its product. Metaphor has always been understood to be "imaginative" language, and rightly so, because it stems from the underlying paradigmatic commitments of speakers. It is therefore an important clue to the religion of the speakers—a point of methodological significance for both religious studies and theology.

Analyzing metaphor in terms of the paradigmatic imagination shows that the confusion about "metaphorical theology" involves a misunderstanding of the nature and function of metaphor generally and of the relation of religious language and experience in particular. The conclusion can be briefly stated as follows: because *religion* is imaginative, religious language is metaphorical, and *theology* is hermeneutical. The religious vision of "what the world is like" embodied in the scriptures of the Old and New Testaments is for Christians the paradigmatic norm for human life and thought. Christian faith can be characterized accordingly as *faithful imagination*—living in conformity to the vision rendered by the Word of God in the Bible. Theology is one function of that faithful life, performing the task of critical interpretation. Biblical literalists, on the one hand, confuse this function by denying the imaginative character of scripture, thus in effect identifying revelation with theology. Liberal theology, on the other hand, confuses the function of theology by reversing the priority of imagination and experience, thus in effect making experience the criterion for revelation rather than the other way around. A truly critical theology performs the task of interpreting the imaginative language of scripture on behalf of the community seeking to live in conformity to its vision. Like all interpretive activity, theology will therefore be historically and culturally grounded, not speaking from some neutral vantage point but in and for its human context. One corollary is that the theological task will never be completed this side of the Eschaton, since human beings are by nature historical and changing. Interpretation, like love and bodily nourishment, is required for the sustenance of human life. Theology provides that sustenance for the religious community, which becomes malnourished when it neglects the vital function of interpretation.

Fact, Fiction, and Scriptural Truth

Theology, according to the foregoing account, is better described as hermeneutical than metaphorical. Its job is to *interpret* the metaphorical language of religious life and faith, which in the Christian case is grounded in the Bible, its classic or paradigmatic text. Since so much of Christian scripture consists of realistic narrative (a point that has recently drawn considerable theological attention), hermeneutical concern with the meaning of scriptural texts inevitably becomes implicated in questions of their truth.

The work of Hans Frei has given us a clearer understanding of how the realistic narratives of the Bible have come to be read since the dawn of modern criticism.[21] Especially illuminating is the distinction that Frei draws between literal meaning and historical reference. Precritical Christian thinkers did not really make the distinction; they generally read the stories literally and simply assumed that the events took place as described. Modern thinkers, on the other hand, have learned to question the historicity of the narratives, but in so doing, Frei argues, they have confused the literal sense of the texts with their historical reference. From one end of the theological spectrum to the other, nearly everyone has assumed that taking the stories literally means affirming their historical veracity. For the supernaturalists or fundamentalists the identification of literal and historical has meant defending the ostensive historical truth of the texts. Theological liberals, on the other hand, also assume the identity of literal meaning and historical reference, but they have sought to detach the meaning of the texts from their literal-historical sense. In other words, the liberal alternative has been to abandon the literal reading of the Bible in order to preserve its religious value. Especially noteworthy is the tacit agreement of both sides that reading the texts literally is the same thing as taking them to be historically accurate reports. Stated in Frei's terminology, nearly everyone has assumed that acknowledging the "history-like" quality of biblical narratives means affirming their "historical likelihood."[22] By common consent a "biblical *literalist*" has come to mean one who affirms the *historical* reliability of narrative texts in scripture.

Frei's work has contributed to a growing interest in the concept of narrative among theologians and philosophers of religion. One of the advantages of the concept is that it enables interpreters to attend to the meaning of texts while bracketing the question of truth: accurate historical reports and the purest fictions are both narratives. Attention to narrative gives theologians some breathing room by allowing the literal sense of the text to come into focus without its becoming immediately confused with historical questions. At the same time, of course, narrative interpretation offers theologians a chance to duck awkward questions about the *truth* of the stories. If narrative is used for this purpose, it will simply become the latest in a long line of devices by which modern theology has tried to evade the challenges posed to religious belief by the critical spirit of modernity. The undertone of embarrassed defensiveness that can frequently be heard in liberal theology has done as much to weaken its case as the explicit arguments of its critics.

If the rediscovery of biblical narrative is not to be co-opted as a protective strategy to immunize faith against secular criticism,[23] the question of narrative truth must be faced squarely. The first step is to examine the problem, the apparently fictional status of many scriptural narratives, in the light of recent developments in philosophy and hermeneutics, with special attention to the distinction between historical reference and textual meaning. It will then be possible to show how the question of fiction and scriptural truth is transformed when it is understood in terms of the interaction between the paradigmatic text of scripture and the faithful imagination of the religious community.

The problem can be stated simply. The usual modern term for a narrative text having no claim to truth is *fiction*. Modern biblical interpretation, by combining historical-critical method with the identification of literal sense and historical reference, has seemed to consign large portions of the Bible to fiction. The dominant thrust of apologetics since the European Enlightenment has thus been directed toward rescuing the Bible from fictional status. Conservative attempts to effect the rescue by demonstrating the historical accuracy of the narratives have done little to convince any but the already committed and have probably contributed to the erosion of the Bible's plausibility for other modern readers. Liberal apologists, likewise accepting the identification of meaning and reference, have sought to show that biblical narratives "really" have a nonhistorical (e.g., ideal, mythical, or existential) meaning.[24] But in that case the literal sense of the texts (since it is not factual) can only be assumed to be fictional, and therefore untrue. If conservatives have wanted to return to a precritical "first naïveté," liberals have embraced historical criticism while trying to save the faith by abandoning the truth claims of the literal text. The task at hand is to see whether there is another option, a "second naïveté" that would allow scriptural narrative to be read literally without sacrificing either the truth claims of the text or the critical integrity of the interpreter.

By calling the identification of literal meaning and historical reference into question, Frei has placed the whole matter of what it means to call a text fictional in a new light. The same philosophical developments that have undermined claims that science is true because it directly describes the "facts," or that metaphors are merely ornamental, also calls into question the claim that "fiction" can be simply opposed to "fact" and automatically dismissed as untrue. As the preceding chapters have shown, all imaginative forms—including models, metaphors, and myths—share in the inherent ambiguity of the paradigmatic imagination. Whether or not they are true is a judgment that can be made only on a case-by-case basis, and only by respecting the holistic grammar of paradigms. In the case of narrative texts, their truth depends not on their ostensive historical reference but rather on their claim to exemplify an aspect of the real world.

In discussions of fiction in religion, one often encounters the name of Hans Vaihinger, who may be regarded as the first thinker to formulate an explicit theory of fiction and apply it to religion. Vaihinger, who called his work *The Philosophy of "As If,"* was part of the late nineteenth-century movement to reappropriate Kantian philosophy after the demise of Idealism. His subtitle indicates the program he sought to carry out over several decades: *A System of the Theoretical, Practical, and Religious Fictions of Mankind.* He tells us that he chose his title because he was convinced "that 'As if,' i.e. appearance, the consciously-false, plays an enormous part in science, in world-philosophies and in life."[25] Especially in the fields of ethics, aesthetics, and religion, he argues, "we operate intentionally with consciously false ideas, or rather judgments," whose "secret life" he sought to lay bare. Vaihinger was convinced that the fullest articulation of the "as if" philosophy had been undertaken by Kant, though he had sometimes expressed himself with unfortunate ambiguity. An example of Vaihinger's reading of Kant is his paraphrase of Kant's interpretation of the virgin birth of Jesus: "The 'Idea' of the virgin conception is another expedient religious fiction, a beautiful, suggestive and useful myth!"[26] It would make Kant's real intention plainer, he argues, to replace the concept of the "objectively, practically real idea" with what Vaihinger calls the "equivalent but clearer expression, *expedient fiction.*"[27]

Whether or not Vaihinger's reading of Kant's philosophy of religion is correct is not the issue at hand. For whatever Kant may have intended, his way of dividing up consciousness into a "theoretical" realm of empirically based science and a "practical," nonscientific realm of ethics, aesthetics, and religion has been enormously influential in the religious thought of the past two centuries. And Vaihinger is surely not alone in drawing the conclusion that religion, for better or for worse, is a wholly practical matter inhabiting an "as if" world of symbol, myth, and fiction. It is important to note that this group comprises not only skeptics and unbelievers but also a number of thinkers who, like Vaihinger, value religion and see in fictionalism a viable apologetic strategy in the modern world.

But the fictionalist case is doubly flawed. On the one hand, its philosophical underpinnings have been eroded by the pragmatic and anti-foundationalist critiques of recent philosophy, especially the philosophy of science. The naively realistic view of scientific theories as direct descriptions of reality ("fact") has given way to positions that frankly acknowledge the symbolic and relative nature of basic scientific concepts. In an instructive parallel to debates about fiction in religion, philosophers of science now argue whether theoretical models and paradigms should be considered "useful fictions" or whether they are representations of reality.[28] At least one philosopher, Richard Braithwaite, has argued explicitly for fictionalism in both science and religion.[29] From the religious side as well, there are good grounds for rejecting the fictionalist case. To claim that Christian believers, for example, act *as if* they lived in a world created by God and redeemed by Jesus Christ is precisely to beg the crucial question. Surely most Christians, both pre- and postcritical, have understood themselves to be making assertions about reality, about the way things are, whether or not they can supply a second-order theory to justify that intent. They may be right or wrong in what they assert about reality, but it misrepresents their intent to describe them as producing fictions, "useful" or otherwise.

The issue of fiction, especially when raised in Vaihinger's terms as the question of "as if," recalls the more recent philosophical debates about "seeing and seeing as." The analysis of those issues in chapter 4 led to the conclusion that a speaker's use of the connective *as* signals an awareness of multiple "aspects" (in Wittgenstein's sense), alternative paradigms according to which something can be seen—"as this" or "as that" kind of object.[30] Wittgenstein himself acknowledges that "seeing as" involves the question of fiction. Speaking of an arbitrary written figure, he comments, "I can see it in various aspects according to the fiction [*Erfindung*] I surround it with."[31] But in that case a fiction may become the means—perhaps the only available means—of seeing what is really there. It is just this kind of consideration that has undermined fictionalism in science, the view that paradigms or models, however useful they may be heuristically or psychologically, are not "literally true." Scientists do not view natural phenomena *as if* the model were true but *according to* the pattern exemplified by the model. The question of truth is misplaced when it is directed to the imaginative paradigm itself in abstraction from its application. Truth is not a property of the model or the narrative text per se but rather a function of the use to which it is put. For the physical scientist, for example, the question of truth is not whether light is "really" composed of tiny particles but whether describing light as particles most adequately interprets the natural phenomena under observation. Similarly, the truth question for the theologian is not whether the parting of the Red Sea "really" happened but whether this narrative, in the context of the scriptural canon, adequately renders to the imagination God's act in saving the people of Israel. Whether scientifically or religiously, the issue of fiction is a red herring, a survival from an earlier time when philosophers thought that scientists were in the business of collecting uninterpreted facts and theologians looked for the meaning of texts in the events they described.

The legitimate question obscured by confused discussion of fact and fiction concerns the reliability of imagination as an organ of truth. In place of the flawed fictionalism of "as if," I am proposing a subtle but important shift of connective: not "as if" but "as" is the key to the logic of religious belief. What characterizes religion is not understanding the world *as if* . . . but rather understanding it *as* . . . The fact-fiction duality tries to distinguish between "is" and "is not": whatever *is* the case merits the designation "fact"; what *is not* so is called "fiction." The move to "as if" may soften the negative implications of "is not," suggesting that fictions have useful functions to fulfill, but the underlying dichotomy remains unchanged: to live in the world *as if* it were the creation of a beneficent God entails that in fact it *is not*, however useful it may be to maintain the fiction. Such is not the case, however, if we substitute "as" for "as if." When Calvin, for example, admonishes us to see the world *as* the theater of God's glory, he means that it really *is*. Why not, then, say "is" instead of "as"?

One of the more inconspicuous but intriguing signs of the emerging pluralism of the modern age has been the growing prominence of the word *as*, especially in the titles of serious works of nonfiction.[32] The writer who looks at something *as* something else is signaling awareness of other, different ways of viewing the same object. Such a writer is ordinarily commending his or her own way of seeing, though not always (e.g., the intent may be playful, fantastic, or satirical). The grammar of *as*, one could say, is not ontological but analogical. The point of using *as* is heuristic: not to affirm that something is or is not the case but rather to draw attention to one possibility among others by proposing an analogy. If a viewer of Wittgenstein's well-known example reports that he sees the figure as a rabbit, he communicates two things to us simultaneously: (1) the pattern or gestalt currently governing his perception of the figure and (2) his awareness of alternative possibilities. He is implicitly appealing to a comparison by using the word *rabbit*, which proposes that this figure is *like* an already familiar model. (A viewer unaware of alternatives would report that it *is* a rabbit, not that it can be seen *as* one.) The ontological indeterminacy of *as* can be made apparent by everyday examples. Critic A might reasonably write, for example, "This novel can be read as a parable of moral choice, but such a reading distorts the book's deeper meaning." This judgment acknowledges the possibility of a particular way of construing the whole, while at the same time denying its validity. One can imagine two kinds of rebuttals. Critic B could agree that the book can be read as a parable while maintaining that this is the correct reading; critic C, on the other hand, might disagree with both on the grounds that the book cannot plausibly be read as a parable of moral choice.

Seeing something as something else is an ability, a "faculty" in the classical sense of the word. That ability is what I have called the paradigmatic imagination, defined as the analogical faculty, the ability to see one thing as another. Living in the modern world makes demands on imagination in a way that traditional worlds did not, because it forces us to be continually aware of multiple options, of a myriad of sometimes competing, sometimes compatible ways of seeing. The little word *as*, the "copula of imagination," is thus a sign of the modern age. The paradigmatic imagination—the "as" faculty—can bring conceptual precision to Ricoeur's suggestive distinction between a "first" and a "second naïveté."[33] The first inhabits the world of "is," blissfully unaware of other possibilities. The second lives in a world of "as," construing reality according to a particular vision in full awareness of other options. Imagination is integral to both, for the only way to have a world is to imagine it. But the first imagines implicitly ("knows") while the second imagines explicitly—not as if, but as. This account of modern pluralism avoids fictional reductionism not by returning to an epistemological absolute but by a more consistent relativism. Whether it can help us with the question of the truth of religious narratives remains to be considered.

Modern writers about the Bible have been especially prolific in the production of "as" titles. An earlier generation of educators tried to read the "Bible as literature," while most biblical scholars were preoccupied with the "Bible as history." More recently, in a particularly significant trend, treatments of canon and biblical authority have begun to appear in this form. Krister Stendahl, for example, has written "The Bible as a Classic and the Bible as Holy Scripture," and Brevard Childs has followed his *Introduction to the Old Testament as Scripture* with *The New Testa-*

ment as Canon.[34] This development is significant theologically, because it signals a move beyond the typically modern terms of argument about the Bible, which has taken place according to the logic of "is" and "is not," of "fact" versus "fiction." The defenders of orthodoxy have argued that the Bible is divinely inspired scripture; their opponents have responded that it is not, because it is a historically conditioned human document. The newer approach proposes that the Bible be read *as* scripture—which acknowledges the possibility, and perhaps the legitimacy, of other ways of construing the same texts. Since the beginnings of modernity, theologians have made the circuit from the implicit assumption that the Bible *is* scripture to the explicit reading of the Bible *as* scripture.

Fideism and the Faithful Imagination

Theological programs that attempt to insulate the truths of scripture or doctrine from the icy winds of historical criticism are frequently attacked as fideistic. The foregoing account of religious truth claims, employing concepts from the likes of Wittgenstein, Kuhn, and Frei, will no doubt appear to some as an example of what has been dubbed Wittgensteinian fideism.[35] The charge is a serious one, and I therefore want to show why the present argument is not vulnerable to it. The hallmark of "Wittgensteinian fideism" is the attempt to immunize theological assertions against hostile criticism by treating the assertions as aspects of particular, self-referential "language games," worldviews, or paradigms. Its operative assumption is that, since there are no viable epistemological absolutes, all languages must be treated in their own terms, and it makes no sense to call one "truer" than another. The error of the position is not its relativism but its unwarranted assumption that choices among language games are arbitrary. But all paradigms are not created equal, as even a cursory look at the natural sciences ought to make clear. The view that they are is often justified by a careless appeal to Kuhn.[36] But his point about the role of paradigms in the sciences, as I have argued, is not that paradigm switches are arbitrary and therefore irrational but rather that they are logically holistic; they cannot be made piecemeal, since they involve changes in the basic ordering pattern itself. People are in fact influenced by arguments—in religion as well as science—to move from one paradigm commitment to another. And retrospectively they are often able to adduce compelling reasons for having done so. That such a position involves a fiduciary element—a commitment to one way of seeing among others—does not entail that it is fideistic. Religious faith commitments, like scientific paradigms, are not exempt from criticism, but their holistic grammar requires that for such criticism to be effective it must be addressed to the position as a whole. A paradigm is refuted only by appeal to a more persuasive paradigm. The Bible, read literally and used scripturally, makes that kind of appeal.

The issue of fideism is closely related to another controversial issue, the relationship of religious studies and theology. Here, too, the role of paradigmatic imagination is clarifying. If religions, as I have argued, are in the business of construing the world in terms of imaginative paradigms, the critical study of religion will involve the identification, examination, and comparison of those paradigmatic structures without prejudice to their truth claims. Theology, by its very nature, is paradigm-specific; its job is the articulation of the vision entailed by a given religious commitment. But for Christian theologians today (and for any other tradition inhabiting a religiously pluralistic world) attention to religious studies is no longer optional. Theological concern with religion represents the methodological difference between a first and a second naïveté. As long as religion is understood as an enterprise governed by the paradigmatic imagination, Christian theologians can engage in the task of religious studies without falling prey to the danger, against which Karl Barth warned so vehemently, of making religion the criterion for theology. By the same token, scholars of religion not only can but must attend to theology, since it represents important religious data—a major aspect of the phenomena under study.[37]

If this way of distinguishing between religious studies and theology is correct, we have reached the point at which further delineation of the task of theology must itself be theological. So far, virtually everything that has been said about Christian theology could be said *mutatis mutandis* about any other paradigm-specific theology. What remains to be said takes the particular paradigmatic commitment of Christians as its criterion. A comment that Frei makes about the resurrection narratives in the New Testament in fact characterizes Christian theology generally: "Commitment in faith and assent by the mind constrained by the imagination are one and the same."[38] What makes the Bible scripture for the believer is precisely that "constraint," the inescapable conviction that, in hearing the story *as* the Word of God, it truly *is* the Word of God. The appearance of fideism is rooted in this surprising move from "as" to "is." Seen from outside the world of the narrative itself (in methodological terms, from the standpoint of religious studies) the "as" governs: Christians (virtually by definition) are those who hear the Bible *as* the Word of God and who accordingly see the world *as* the "theater of God's glory." Imagining the world according to the biblical story, they find themselves persuaded that the story is true; others, no doubt, will hear it differently—as a piece of "hyperfiction,"[39] perhaps. Seen from within that imagined world, on the other hand (in methodological terms, from the standpoint of theology) the "is" governs: the Bible *is* the Word of God, because it speaks with the authority of the Holy Spirit, who is, of course, a central actor in that very story.

Modern, critically trained Christians can, then, in good conscience be literalists of the second naïveté. Fully aware that there other ways of construing both the Bible and the world, they are nevertheless persuaded that the most realistic way to view the world is through the spectacles of scripture. They strive to see the world as it is depicted in the Bible and to act in accordance with that vision. Unlike those living in a precritical "first" naïveté, these believers can acknowledge with Soskice that the "way in which we divide up the world is not the only way this might adequately be done."[40] As critical thinkers they recognize that their own truth claims, like those of others, depend on right imagination; but unlike so many modern critics, both religious and antireligious, they recognize, too, that there can be no "direct" or "neutral"—that is, no nonimaginative—access to reality. The philosopher Santayana, writing on imagination, comments that "whatever picture of things we may carry about in our heads we are bound to regard as a map of reality."[41] Religions are maps of reality,[42] and Christians are convinced that their map, in Soskice's preferred term, is reality-depicting.[43]

This kind of literal reading is compatible with the recognition that scripture contains fictional elements—at least, if fiction is understood to mean "not referring to actual historical occurrences"—since neither the meaning nor the truth of the texts is identical with their historical reference. There are at least two ways in which Christian theology can affirm the fictional status of certain scriptural texts. One is commonplace (though often overlooked) and true of all uses of imagination; the other has to do with the peculiar nature of the God who is depicted in Christian scripture.

In the first case, Christian use of scripture is comparable to other uses of imagination involving what may be called fictional elements. To imagine is to put elements together into a meaningful whole, to conceive according to a particular gestalt. But this activity frequently involves "fictional" as well as "factual" elements. Everyday visual experience can serve as a model: when I look at a physical object—the lamp across the room, for example—I do not remain "agnostic" about the side of it that I cannot see directly; rather, I see it *as* a whole, including its hidden aspects. A similar logic leads us to trust the judgment of experts in areas extending beyond their immediate, "factual" knowledge. Those who know someone well enough, for example, can be trusted to imagine rightly how that person would behave in other, unknown circumstances. Frei, in discussing the depiction of Jesus in the Gospels, claims that "we are actually in a fortunate position that so much of what we know about Jesus . . . is more nearly fictional than historical in narration." Especially in the passion-resurrection sequence, Frei writes, "it is precisely the fiction-like quality of the whole narrative . . . that serves to bring the identity of Jesus sharply before us and to make him accessible to us."[44] The issue at stake for believers, in that case, is not whether the text is fact or fiction but whether the author is to be trusted. If the evangelists are what believers take them to be—namely, the ones in the best position to tell us who Jesus is (though not necessarily the "facts" about him)—we are right to trust them. But this faith is at bottom a trusting in the authors' imagination, which may include "fictional" as well as "factual" aspects. The faithful imagination of the believer allows itself to be formed by the imagination of the scriptural texts.

Focusing on the concept of faith runs a particular risk of misunderstanding unless the "topical" nature of Christian theology is taken seriously. Karl Barth rightly criticizes the modern tendency to "pursue theology as *pisteology*, the science and doctrine of Christian faith."[45] The emphasis on faith in the present argument does not imply that it constitutes the anthropological foundation or systematic center of theology; it follows rather from its relation to our immediate concern with the human ability to imagine. "Faith" is the nearest analogue in Christian doctrine to the philosophical concept "paradigmatic imagination." Both terms designate a point of contact between a human knower and the reality apprehended. Viewed from the standpoint of this concrete concern with human imagining, Christian faith appears in the form of faithful imagination.

As a form of imagination, faith is not an immediate knowledge. To apprehend the image of God in faith is not to have the unmediated vision of God; to be able to imagine God rightly is not to see God face to face. We do not need to imagine what we have directly at hand. Imagination belongs, therefore, in the language of traditional Christian dogmatics, to the *regnum gratiae*, to the present age between the times, in which believers look forward in expectation because they can look back to the decisive event of salvation. Imagination is thus the organ of faith: neither its ground, nor its goal or perfection, but rather a penultimate means of grace in a world whose final redemption remains the object of hope.

An epistemological limit, implied by the thesis that God encounters us in imagination, is confirmed by scripture. The New Testament writers affirm in various ways that "we walk by faith, not by sight" (2 Cor. 5:7). The conviction that Jesus Christ is the image of God includes not only the recollection of his life, death, and resurrection among us but also the expectation of his future return in glory. Faith—"the assurance of things hoped for, the conviction of things not seen" (Heb. 11:1)—therefore includes a not-knowing, a mystery whose ultimate unfolding cannot be part of our present experience.[46] The assurance that we are already "God's children" includes the acknowledgment that "it does not yet appear what we shall be" even though "we know that when he appears we shall be like him" (1 John 3:2). The *Anknüpfungspunkt* of revelation is therefore the *faithful* imagination, trust in the images of scripture in the absence of direct vision.

The penultimate character of faith is a key to overcoming the impasse of "natural theology" or "positivism of revelation."[47] Just as theology based on the human faculty of imagination would fall into the first error, so a theology that confused imagination with sight would succumb to the second. Whenever biblical revelation is taken as a given quantity, a supernatural deposit of truth at the disposal of the theologian, the theology of grace is corrupted into a theology of glory and the positivity of the gospel is distorted into a theological positivism. The positivity of the images of faith is a mark of their penultimate status. The faithful imagination is the mirror in which the image of God is reflected "dimly" (*en ainigmati*, "enigmatically"), never to be confused with the promised vision of God "face to face" (1 Cor. 13:12). Christians, especially those who follow the Protestant Reformers, know God solely on the basis of his Word, heard in the words and reflected in the images of the Bible, which for this reason is called Holy Scripture. Whatever knowledge of God they may claim to have from other sources can be recognized as such only through the lens of scripture and thus cannot be used to verify scriptural truth. Because this knowledge is mediated by the interaction of scriptural image and faithful imagination, no formal or material attribute of the biblical text itself could possibly certify it as an expression of realistic rather than illusory imagination. The fact-fiction decision takes place entirely on the ground of faith. The attempt to derive the truth of faith from the faculty of imagination leads to the Scylla of "natural theology," but an appeal to the written text of the Bible itself as sufficient grounds for the truth of its contents amounts to the Charybdis of "revelation positivism."

The Hermeneutics of the Cross

There is another, quite different reason why Christian "literalists of the second naïveté" can affirm the fictional status of scriptural texts. This reason is theological in the strongest sense of the word, because it is based on the character of the God who is the protagonist of Christian scripture. This approach to the question of fiction has nothing to do with the nature of human imagination in general and everything to do with the God whom Christians imagine. The point is strikingly expressed in a passage from Kierkegaard, which, because it is not widely known, I want to cite in full:

The absolutely greatest thing that can be done for a being, greater than anything one could make it into, is to make it free. It is exactly here that omnipotence is required. This seems odd, as it is precisely omnipotence which has the capacity of making dependent. But if one thinks about omnipotence, one will see that it is precisely in this concept that there must also lie the capacity to retreat into oneself again in an expression of omnipotence, in such a way as to allow that which owes its existence to omnipotence to be independent. Therefore it is the case that one *person* cannot make another completely free, because he who has power is himself entrapped by it, and therefore always comes into an incorrect relation to the person whom he wants to liberate. In addition to this is the fact that all *finite* power (talentedness, etc.) contains a finite self-love. Only *omnipotence* can take itself back while it gives away, and this relationship means, of course, exactly the independence of the recipient. God's omnipotence is therefore His goodness. For it is goodness to give away entirely, but in such a way that, by omnipotently taking oneself back again, one makes the recipient independent. . . . The art of power consists precisely in the capacity to set free. But this never admits of achievement between man and man. Even though it always needs to be emphasized again and again that this [setting free] is the highest thing, only omnipotence is truly capable of it.[48]

Kierkegaard's insight focuses on the relation between love and freedom, as that relation is reflected in the relation between God and his creatures. The chief anthropological consequence of God's love for his creatures, Kierkegaard is saying, is their freedom. God loves human beings so much that he allows them to be free. What is remarkable in the passage, however, is that Kierkegaard conceives this endowment of creaturely independence—including especially independence from *God*—precisely as the expression of divine *power*. The truly omnipotent God, in other words, is one who is able to create a being who is not dependent on God.[49] But it is equally important to grasp that this freedom is an integral aspect of the divine love for the creature and not an extrinsic principle that must first be related to it.

The theological relationship between divine love and human freedom is the key to the theme, addressed repeatedly by twentieth-century theologians, of the weakness of God. Among the most striking expressions of this motif are passages in the late prison letters of Dietrich Bonhoeffer. "God lets himself be pushed out of the world on to the cross," Bonhoeffer writes from Tegel prison in July 1944. "He is weak and powerless in the world, and this is precisely the way, the only way, in which he is with us and helps us."[50] In spite of the emphasis on divine weakness in these passages, there are indications that Bonhoeffer, like Kierkegaard, understands God's worldly weakness as the manifestation of his real power. He contrasts the "religious" emphasis on divine power in the world, which makes of God a *deus ex machina*, with the "God of the Bible, who wins power and space in the world by his weakness."[51] The point, which superficial interpretations of Bonhoeffer miss, is not that God is weak (or dead) but rather that worldly weakness (including death) is the means by which God exercises his power. Those who view the world biblically will recognize in God's refusal to play *deus ex machina*, his unwillingness to save us from our freedom, the expression of his love for us. *Out of love* God "lets us live in the world without the working hypothesis of God."[52]

From this perspective—Luther called it theology of the cross—the deepest theological significance of narrative, and precisely of fictional narrative, becomes apparent in what might be called a "hermeneutics of the cross." What, after all, could be more fitting for the God who does not force himself on the world, who even allows himself to be forced "out of the world and on to a cross," than to present himself to the world in a story—even one that can be read as a "fiction"? The true Christian, says Luther, knows "God as hidden in sufferings."[53] Expressed in the terminology of the paradigmatic imagination, the point can be put this way: God offers himself to the imagination of his creatures by means of a "fictional" narrative—that is, one whose truth cannot be independently ascertained. In this way God "captures the imagination" of the faithful, the only kind of conquest that leaves them free. In theology, as distinguished from all other "sciences," the difference between fact and fiction ultimately depends on God the Spirit.[54] Theologians can only focus all their powers of imagination on their subject, the Word of God revealed in scripture. Theological work, humanly regarded, may well remain indistinguishable from works of the "fictive imagination." Of course, Christians will find provisional confirmation of the story's truth in its continuing ability to illumine their own lives and the world around them. Seeing the world through scriptural spectacles, theologians will continue to affirm the intelligibility of the vision it renders, and preachers will continue to appeal to the Bible's power to illuminate reality. But such confirmation can only be provisional for a Christian community living under the sign of the cross, since God's power remains hidden under weakness until Christ's return in glory. The theologian, therefore, trusting the imagination of the prophets and apostles, works in *faith* that the Spirit (the guarantee) vouches for the ultimate truth of the story, which in the meantime can only be dimly grasped from afar.

If this story is true, however, it will affect our interpretation of the world as well. The story of the world, in that case, is not "a tale told by an idiot" but rather one told by the Holy Spirit. In this way, the Bible can once again interpret the world, as it did in a precritical age of primitive naïveté. Such a state of affairs ought to free theologians and preachers to follow the story of salvation with critical intelligence and unfettered imagination, not concerning themselves with its validity or factuality, since that is precisely the one question not subject to their control.

The Theory and Practice of Imagination

The hermeneutical function of Christian theology implies that its proper form is not "systematic" in the philosophical or foundational sense; that is, theological propositions are not deduced from axioms or derived from first principles. Rather, theology as an interpretive discipline ought to be "local" or topical, the elaboration of specific *loci*, whose relationships to one another are ad hoc rather than a priori, and whose character and content are relative to the questions being asked at a particular time and in a particular situation. This view of theology, which has found advocates from the Protestant orthodox theologians of the seventeenth century to Karl Barth in the twentieth,[55] is also implied by the arguments presented here. The unity of Christian truth is to be sought not in theology or doctrine but in revelation, in the scriptural canon read as a whole. Theology, like other hermeneutical enterprises, endeavors to interpret the manifold aspects of that imaginative unity in order that its logic, the coherence of its elements, may be intellectually apprehended. Doing theology in this way is more like doing literary criticism than elaborating a philosophical system. Christian theology is systematic in the way that the grammar of a natural language is systematic rather than in the sense assumed by foundational philosophies.[56]

Modern theologians have been prolific in producing progammatic proposals, most of which are never implemented. One of the chief advantages of defining the theological task in relation to the problematics of imagination is its fruitfulness for reconceiving a broad range of specific theological issues, both systematic and practical. Our earlier discussions of revelation (chapter 5) and scripture (chapter 6) demonstrate how a number of particular Christian doctrines can be reformulated systematically in terms of imagination: for example, the doctrines of God, human nature, sin, justification, and scripture. An equally important advantage of interpreting the divine-human *Anknüpfungspunkt* as imagination, however, is its implications for practical theology. All too often the practical tasks of the church have either been ignored by systematic theology or artificially tacked onto it as an afterthought. Perhaps for this reason, the field of practical theology has fallen under the influence of nontheological disciplines (for example, economics, sociology, clinical psychology) or has degenerated into the mere inculcation of technique (church administration, social action, sermon preparation, pastoral counseling, and the like). The issue of the contact point for revelation is an inherently practical one, for it involves the question of how the Word of God becomes effective in human experience and action.

Protestant theology has always seen the focus of divine-human encounter in the proclamation of the gospel, which takes place usually and typically in preaching. Proclamation, formulated in terms of the present argument, can be described as an appeal to the imagination of the hearers through the images of scripture. The preacher's task is to mediate and facilitate that encounter by engaging his or her own imagination, which becomes the link between scripture and congregation. The preacher must therefore pay particular attention to the imagery of the biblical text, seeking to present it with such clarity and force that it will be seen and heard by the congregation. To save sinners, God seizes them by the imagination: the preacher places himself at the service of this saving act by the obedient and lucid engagement of his own imagination. All of the preacher's technical preparation—biblical languages, exegetical method, sermon organization, skillful use of language, oral delivery—will be in vain unless subordinated to this central purpose.

The Bible itself offers some images of imaginative proclamation. One of the most vivid examples is the sermon delivered by the prophet Nathan to King David, who had misused the powers of his office to commit murder and adultery (2 Sam. 12:1 ff.). Nathan appeals to the imagination of the king by telling him a story. From David's standpoint the narrative has every appearance of a fictional tale (the scene is set in "a certain city," verse 1; the action involves a stylized rich man and poor man; etc.). David might well have taken the story to be fantasy, directed to the illusory imagination. His reaction in verses 5–6, however, indicates that he

assumes the story to be realistic but never imagines any relationship between himself and the protagonists except that of the sovereign whose
duty it is to ensure justice among his subjects. Nathan's climactic "You
are the man" instantly transforms David's perception of the relationship
between image and reality. Nathan has used David's own powers of
imagination to provoke an insight into his true status before God.
David's contrite response (verse 13) makes clear that he has got the
point. Had Nathan confronted him instead with a discourse on the sixth
and seventh commandments or a moral harangue on the virtues of
statesmanship and marital fidelity, he might have provoked only defensive denial and angry counterattack. The success of the appeal to the
imagination, however, was not finally in the hands of the preacher, for
Nathan could have no way of ensuring David's contrition; all he could
do is to proclaim the word of Yahweh in the most vividly imaginative
way possible. A similar logic pervades the parables of Jesus in the New
Testament. We, as hearers, are asked to imagine ourselves as a Samaritan
encountering a robbed and beaten stranger on the road, a merchant who
has found an exquisite pearl, or a blind man who has received his sight.
Our response, like David's, reveals whether we have got the point—a
truth underscored in many passages by the injunction, "He who has ears
to hear, let him hear."[57] The preacher can try to communicate the images
so as to bring them to bear on our present situation, while leaving our
response to the inspiration of the Holy Spirit.

The ambiguity of reality and illusion inherent in imaginative discourse takes on practical significance in proclamation, for the preacher
must use imagination in order to call our usual assumptions about reality into question by means of imaginative forms that may initially appear
illusory to the hearers—as did Nathan's to David. Understanding that
the field of action is the imagination may help to clarify the preacher's
task, especially in contemporary culture, where "images" are created
and manipulated by advertisers and politicians, and illusion is marketed
as reality.[58] Paul's observations about the divine "foolishness" and
"weakness" (1 Cor. 1:25) might reasonably be extended to the proposition that the illusions of God are more real than the realities of men.

But the practical theological consequences of the imaginative shape
of revelation are not limited to the discursive level of homiletics. The
importance and function of the other elements of worship are also implied, and they in turn serve to underscore the fact that imagination is
not limited to the intellectual or moral level of human perception. Liturgical action, especially the sacraments, need not be justified indirectly
as "expressions" of theological truth, for they appeal directly to the

imagination in their own right. The Lord's Supper is no mere illustration of the gospel but rather its embodied proclamation: "For as often as you eat this bread and drink the cup, you *proclaim* the Lord's death until he comes" (1 Cor. 11:26). The function of music in Christian worship is no mere adornment but rather an imaginative "language" of proclamation and faith. The musical imagination is a particularly apt analogy of revelation itself. Mary Warnock's paraphrase of Kant on the aesthetic imagination, cited earlier as a metaphor of scriptural unity, is also applicable in the practical context of worship:

We had to hear the pattern *in* the sound. Without imagination, there would have been just sound; imagination makes the sound, as it were, "presentable," and in so doing experiences the feeling of satisfaction in the discovery of order in chaos.[59]

The faithful imagination learns to hear the melody of revelation in the polyphony of scripture. Proclamation can be thought of as singing the scriptural melody so that others may also learn to hear and enjoy it and to join in the singing. The Psalms, both in their content and by their very presence in the canon, offer an expression and scriptural attestation for this view.

These practical consequences of theological imagination show how the Word of God encounters and transforms the whole person. God does not appear, on this interpretation, to address the intellect, the feelings, or the conscience separately; and it does not require a subsequent theory to relate the various human faculties to each other and to revelation. Imagination is not so much a particular faculty as the integration in human experience of the various human abilities and potentialities. The integrative function of imagination in apprehending patterns of meaning externally also allows an integral response on the part of the imagining subject. To imagine myself, for example, as the random product of the forces of physical nature, or as a member of the master race, or as destined to fail at everything I attempt, or as a sinner redeemed from death and hell by the sacrifice of Christ—each of these images calls forth a total response, having intellectual, emotional, and volitional aspects.

Untold numbers of people in our century, including leading theologians, have been challenged by Marx's eleventh "Thesis on Feuerbach": "The philosophers," Marx wrote in 1845, "have only *interpreted* the world, in various ways—the point, however, is to *change* it." The diverse mix of theological proposals, political programs, and moral convictions known today as liberation theology represents only the most recent attempt by Christians to respond to Marx's challenge. But such theological responses have all too often accepted uncritically a doctrine of theory and its relation to practice that cannot survive the scrutiny of either a careful philosophical analysis of historical experience or a theological analysis of its conformity to scripture. According to the Marxist account, religious doctrine is simply a form of ideology that serves the economic and political interests of the ruling classes, and religious practice masks the real relations obtaining in the social world and diverts the energy of the oppressed that might otherwise be used to change reality. The deepest irony of Marxism is that its greatest power to influence events in the modern world has resulted not so much from its revolutionary political activity as from its vision—that it, the way in which Marxist thinkers have *interpreted* history and human affairs.

Our analysis of the paradigmatic imagination and its implications for religion suggests a fundamentally different relationship between the activity of the human spirit and the processes of historical change than the one propounded by Marxist philosophers and their theological admirers—one that eschews altogether the misleading dichotomy of "theory and practice." The examples both of modern science and the history of religion point to the same conclusion: that the most powerful way to change the world is precisely by interpreting it.

Notes

Introduction

1. Gotthold Ephraim Lessing, "On the Proof of the Spirit and of Power," in *Lessing's Theological Writings*, trans. and ed. Henry Chadwick (Stanford, CA: Stanford Univ. Press, 1957), 51–56.
2. This analysis, though applicable primarily to the North American situation, also has implications for the historical European base of Christian theology. If I am not mistaken, the prevailing winds of theological influence (often cursed but never changed) are at long last shifting from an easterly to a westerly direction (with strong gusts from the south). To mix metaphors still further, even leading German theologians are being drawn into the orbit of the American discussion, as evidenced in their footnotes and by their increasing participation in American conferences and scholarly meetings.

Chapter 1. Religion as Imagination in Modern Thought

1. David Tracy, *The Analogical Imagination: Christian Theology and the Culture of Pluralism* (New York: Crossroad, 1981); Gordon D. Kaufman, *The Theological Imagination: Constructing the Concept of God* (Philadelphia: Westminster Press, 1981). See my reviews of Kaufman's book in *Religious Studies Review* 9 (1983): 219–22, and of Tracy's in *Zygon* 17 (1982): 419–21.
2. The privileged position of epistemology in modern philosophy has been illuminatingly described and criticized by Richard Rorty in *Philosophy and the Mirror of Nature* (Princeton, NJ: Princeton Univ. Press, 1979).
3. Hans W. Frei, building on a suggestion by Alasdair MacIntyre, develops a useful distinction between two types of modern atheism in "Feuerbach and Theology," *Journal of the American Academy of Religion* 35 (1967): 250–56. I refer here to Frei's first kind of atheist, who, in the tradition of Hume, holds that religious statements are either meaningless or false. The second type of atheism, epitomized by that of Feuerbach, is not so easily distinguished from theism and is far more important for modern theology, as will become apparent later in this chapter.
4. The terms, and especially the metaphors, used by the various mediating theologians themselves to identify their project would be an interesting subject for study. Among the commonest are the "kernel-husk" image (in which the theological task is pictured as a kind of winnowing) and the notion of the tradition as a mere "vehicle," in which the real essence is presumably just along for the ride.
5. For a survey of the development of the modern idea of imagination, see James Engell, *The Creative Imagination: Enlightenment to Romanticism* (Cambridge: Harvard Univ. Press, 1981).
6. Herman-J. de Vleeschauwer, *The Development of Kantian Thought* (New York: Thomas Nelson & Sons, 1962), 82–88; Engell, *Creative Imagination*, chap. 10.

7. Engell, *Creative Imagination*, 137.

8. Cf. Immanuel Kant, *Religion Within the Limits of Reason Alone*, trans. Theodore M. Greene and Hoyt H. Hudson (New York: Harper & Brothers, 1960), 142; and Matthew Tindal, *Christianity as Old as the Creation* (1730; reprint, Stuttgart–Bad Cannstatt: Friedrich Frommann Verlag [Günther Holzboog], 1967), 298.

9. For a critical discussion of the problem of religious "positivity" in German philosophy from Kant to Hegel, see Garrett Green, "Positive Religion in the Early Philosophy of the German Idealists" (Ph.D. diss., Yale University, 1971). Chaps. 1 and 2 deal with Kant's *Religion*.

10. Allen W. Wood lists a number of examples from the *Religion* in *Kant's Moral Religion* (Ithaca, NY: Cornell Univ. Press, 1970), 193–94 and notes.

11. Immanuel Kant, *Die Religion innerhalb der Grenzen der blossen Vernunft*, ed. Karl Vorländer, Philosophische Bibliothek vol. 45 (Hamburg: Verlag von Felix Meiner, 1956), 62 (*Religion Within the Limits of Reason Alone*, 52).

12. Ibid., 62 n. (trans., 53 n.).

13. Ibid., 188–90 (trans., 156–58).

14. "Selbst der Wahnsinn hat daher diesen Namen, weil er eine bloße Vorstellung (der Einbildungskraft) für die Gegenwart der Sache selbst zu nehmen und ebenso zu würdigen gewohnt ist" (ibid., 188 n.; cf. trans., 156 n.).

15. See *Immanuel Kant's Critique of Pure Reason*, trans. Norman Kemp Smith (New York: St. Martin's Press, 1965), A118, A124, B151–52, et passim.

16. Johann Gottlieb Fichte, *Grundlage der gesammten Wissenschaftslehre*, cited by Engell, *Creative Imagination*, 226.

17. Emil Fackenheim, in a useful appendix on the meaning and translation of *Vorstellung*, argues in favor of the "conventional but obscure and artificial 'representation' because all more natural terms have false connotations" (*The Religious Dimension in Hegel's Thought* [Bloomington, IN: Indiana Univ. Press, 1967], 154–55). Though he may be right about such candidates as *notion, idea*, and *picture-thinking*, it is odd that he does not even consider *imagination*.

18. Frederick Copleston's summary offers (as is so often the case) a particularly lucid overview. See *A History of Philosophy* (Westminster, MD: Newman Press, 1963), 7:226–30. Another useful discussion is J. Glenn Gray's "Introduction: Hegel's Understanding of Absolute Spirit," in G. W. F. Hegel, *On Art, Religion, Philosophy* (New York: Harper & Row, Harper Torchbooks, 1970), 1–21. Gray's elucidation of the term *Aufhebung* in Hegel is the best that I know; unfortunately he does not include a discussion of *Vorstellung*.

19. Gray, "Hegel's Understanding of Absolute Spirit," 17.

20. Michael Rosen, *Hegel's Dialectic and Its Criticism* (New York: Cambridge Univ. Press, 1982), 108–9.

21. Copleston, *History of Philosophy* 7: 235.

22. Georg Wilhelm Friedrich Hegel, *Enzyklopädie der philosophischen Wissenschaften im Grundrisse (1830)*, ed. Friedhelm Nicolin and Otto Pöggeler, Philosophische Bibliothek 33 (Hamburg: Verlag von Felix Meiner, 1959), §3; cf. Rosen, *Hegel's Dialectic*, 59.

23. An excellent brief account (which deserves to be more widely known) of Hegel's interpretation of Christianity and its *Aufhebung* into philosophy is Stephen D. Crites, "The Gospel According to Hegel," *Journal of Religion* 46 (1966): 246–63.

24. Rosen, *Hegel's Dialectic*, 92 (Rosen's emphasis).

25. Crites, "Gospel According to Hegel," 260.

26. Samuel Taylor Coleridge, *Biographia Literaria; or, Biographical Sketches of My Literary Life and Opinions*, ed. James Engell and W. Jackson Bate, vol. 7, pts. 1–2, of *The Collected Works of Samuel Taylor Coleridge*, Bollingen Series 75 (Princeton, NJ: Princeton Univ. Press, 1983), 1:304.

27. The phrase is quoted from Copleston, *History of Philosophy* 8:155, who gives Coleridge less than five pages; similar comments by other writers abound.

28. See Claude Welch, *Protestant Thought in the Nineteenth Century* (New Haven: Yale Univ. Press, 1972–85), 1:110–13. Welch takes William Paley's *Natural Theology* (1802) as the epitome of the "supernaturalist rationalism of the post-Lockean theology of 'evi-

dences' " that dominated British theology in the early nineteenth century. Jeremy Bentham, Welch maintains, "emerges as the real alternative to Coleridge, the great symbol of what the eighteenth century stood for and therefore of what had to be combated."

29. See Engell, *Creative Imagination*, esp. chap. 13, for a review of this tradition. The quoted phrase is from Basil Willey, "Coleridge on Imagination and Fancy," *Proceedings of the British Academy* 32 (1946): 174. Willey's lecture offers a particularly clear and persuasive analysis of Coleridge's famous distinction. It reappears in slightly altered form in Basil Willey, *Nineteenth Century Studies: Coleridge to Matthew Arnold* (New York: Columbia Univ. Press, 1949), 10–31.

30. Coleridge, cited by Willey, "Coleridge on Imagination and Fancy," 177 (*Nineteenth Century Studies*, 16).

31. Willey, "Coleridge on Imagination and Fancy," 177–80 (*Nineteenth Century Studies*, 16–19).

32. Coleridge, *Biographia Literaria* 1:168–70.

33. Engell, *Creative Imagination*, 149.

34. Willey, "Coleridge on Imagination and Fancy," 183 (*Nineteenth Century Studies*, 30).

35. Engell, *Creative Imagination*, 362.

36. J. Robert Barth, *Coleridge and Christian Doctrine* (Cambridge: Harvard Univ. Press, 1969), 23.

37. Willey, "Coleridge on Imagination and Fancy," 182 (*Nineteenth Century Studies*, 28).

38. Willey, "Coleridge on Imagination and Fancy," 182 (*Nineteenth Century Studies*, 29).

39. James C. Livingston, *Modern Christian Thought: From the Enlightenment to Vatican II* (New York: Macmillan, 1971), 90.

40. Coleridge, *Biographia Literaria* 1:156.

41. Coleridge, *The Statesman's Manual*, in *Collected Works* 6:29. Cf. Barth, *Coleridge on Christian Doctrine*, 22.

42. Hans Frei comments on Strauss's adaptation of the Hegelian distinction between *Vorstellung* and *Begriff* as follows: "The difference between representation and concept, which distinguished between them as forms while affirming the identity of their content, was—in the early view of Strauss and his friends—Hegel's most important contribution to theology (though it may be doubted that Hegel himself would have accorded this relation the same high significance or, for that matter, have distinguished them quite as sharply as Strauss did)" ("David Friedrich Strauss," in *Nineteenth Century Religious Thought in the West*, ed. Ninian Smart et al. [New York: Cambridge Univ. Press, 1985], 1:230).

43. Emanuel Hirsch, *Geschichte der neuern evangelischen Theologie* (Gütersloh: Verlagshaus Gerd Mohn, 1949–51), 5:492.

44. David Friedrich Strauss, cited by Peter C. Hodgson, "Strauss's Theological Development from 1825 to 1840," Editor's Introduction to *The Life of Jesus Critically Examined*, ed. Peter C. Hodgson, trans. from 4th German ed. by George Eliot, Lives of Jesus Series (Philadelphia: Fortress Press, 1972), p. xxiii. The bracketed interpolations are Hodgson's.

45. Acknowledging that Strauss's own "quest was theological rather than historical," Frei nevertheless concludes that the "book's form or strategy outstripped his own intention," bringing about a lasting reorientation of theological discussion: "he assured the priority of the historical over the conceptual argument in the attack on traditional christology" ("David Friedrich Strauss," 228, 223, 224).

46. Hodgson, "Strauss's Theological Development," p. xxvi.

47. David Friedrich Strauss, *Das Leben Jesu, kritisch bearbeitet*, 4th ed. (Tübingen: Verlag von C. F. Osiander, 1840), 1:54–55 (*Life of Jesus*, 65; see n. 44).

48. See Hodgson's account of how the work came to be translated by Eliot and his discussion of the translation of *Vorstellung* and *Begriff* ("Strauss's Theological Development," pp. xlvii–l).

49. Ludwig Feuerbach, *Das Wesen des Christentums* (Stuttgart: Philipp Reclam Jun., 1969), 26; *The Essence of Christianity*, trans. George Eliot (New York: Harper & Row, 1957), p. xxxix. Hereafter the reference to the English edition will follow the German citation, though I have departed from Eliot's translation where it seems appropriate.

50. Hirsch, *Geschichte der neuern evangelischen Theologie* 5:578.
51. Feuerbach, *Wesen des Christentums*, 53–54; *Essence of Christianity*, 13.
52. Ibid., 76 (trans., 29–30).
53. Ibid., 53 (trans., 13).
54. From the opening sentence of Marx's "Contribution to the Critique of Hegel's Philos-
    ophy of Right," in *Karl Marx and Friedrich Engels on Religion* (New York: Schocken
    Books, 1964), 41 (ital. omitted).
55. Ibid., 41–42. Cf. original German in Karl Marx, *Die Frühschriften*, ed. Siegfried Landshut
    (Stuttgart: Alfred Kröner Verlag, 1971), 207. The emphasis in all these citations is
    Marx's own.
56. Ibid., 42.
57. The eleventh and last of Marx's "Theses on Feuerbach," ibid., 72.
58. See n. 3.
59. Cf. Frei, "Feuerbach and Theology," 253–55.
60. Friedrich Engels, extracts from *Anti-Dühring*, in *Karl Marx and Friedrich Engels on Reli-
    gion*, 147.
61. E.g., ibid., 136 (Marx), 149 (Engels).

Chapter 2. A Theological Dilemma

1. Freud's views are most evident in his 1927 essay *The Future of an Illusion*, trans. W. D.
   Robson-Scott, rev. and ed. James Strachey (Garden City, NY: Doubleday, Anchor
   Books, 1964), especially the concluding section 10; for Durkheim's views, see the conclusion of *The Elementary Forms of the Religious Life*, trans. Joseph Ward Swain (New
   York: The Free Press, 1965), 462–96. Needless to say, the naive positivism of these
   thinkers' views of science in no way lessens their important contributions to the study
   of religion.
2. See H. Martin Rumscheidt, *Revelation and Theology: An Analysis of the Barth-Harnack Correspondence of 1923* (Cambridge: Cambridge Univ. Press, 1972).
3. Emil Brunner, "Theologie und Kirche," *Zwischen den Zeiten* 8 (1930): 398 n.
4. Brunner is assuming that the chief danger posed by theological concern with a "point
   of contact" for revelation is that it may concede too great a role to human free will,
   thereby compromising the grace of God as the sole source of revelation—thus repeat-
   ing the error of Pelagius, so vehemently opposed by Augustine and officially con-
   demned as a heresy by the church in the early fifth century ("Die andere Aufgabe der
   Theologie," *Zwischen den Zeiten* 7 [1929]: 262).
5. Ibid.
6. Karl Barth, *Die kirchliche Dogmatik* (Zurich: Theologisher Verlag Zürich, 1932–67), 1/1:
   25–30 (hereafter *KD*); *Church Dogmatics*, ed. G. W. Bromiley and T. F. Torrance, trans.
   G. W. Bromily et al. (Edinburgh: T. & T. Clark, 1956–69), 1/1: 26–31 (hereafter *CD*).
   Translations from Barth are mine; for the convenience of the reader references are provided to the published English translation. All references to *CD* 1/1 refer to the 2d ed.
   (1975).
7. *KD* 1/1: 249 (*CD* 1/1: 236).
8. *KD* 1/1: 249 (*CD* 1/1: 237).
9. Both Brunner's *Natur und Gnade* and Barth's *Nein!* are included in Walther Fürst, ed.,
   "Dialektische Theologie" in Scheidung und Bewährung 1933–1936 (Munich: Chr. Kaiser Verlag, 1966), 169–258. An English translation by Peter Fraenkel, published as *Natural Theology* (London: Geoffrey Bles, 1946), has been reissued in a facsimile edition (Ann
   Arbor, MI: University Microfilms International, 1979). Page references are to the original editions of Brunner's and Barth's works, whose pagination is provided in the Fürst
   anthology; translations are mine, though references are given to the published English
   translation.
10. Brunner, *Natur und Gnade*, 19–20 (*Natural Theology*, 32); partially cited by Barth, *Nein!* 26
    (*Natural Theology*, 89).

11. The term *Offenbarungspositivismus* to describe Barth's theology was first used by Dietrich Bonhoeffer in his letter of 30 April 1944 from Tegel Prison to Eberhard Bethge (trans. in Dietrich Bonhoeffer, *Letters and Papers from Prison*, enl. ed., ed. Eberhard Bethge [New York: Macmillan, 1971], 280), in a sense that is clearly pejorative but not elaborated. More illuminating is a passage in the letter of 5 May 1944 (p. 286), where Bonhoeffer accuses Barth of replacing "religion" with "a positivist doctrine of revelation [*eine positivistische Offenbarungslehre*]," which refuses to distinguish levels of significance in dogma, setting up a "law of faith" that says in effect, "Like it or lump it! [*friß, Vogel, oder stirb*]." Whether or not Barth can finally be exonerated of the charge, no serious student of his theology can fail to feel its force. It remains *the* challenge to theologians who would appropriate Barth's thought in their own work. See also Bonhoeffer's letter of 8 June 1944 (pp. 328-29).

12. *KD* 1/1: 35-36 (*CD* 1/1: 36).

13. *KD* 1/1: 128-36 (*CD* 1/1: 125-31).

14. See Richard Rorty, *Philosophy and the Mirror of Nature* (Princeton, NJ: Princeton Univ. Press, 1979), and the works cited there. Ronald F. Thiemann provides a lucid account of the philosophical critique of epistemological foundationalism and its consequences for theological method in *Revelation and Theology: The Gospel as Narrated Promise* (Notre Dame, IN: Univ. of Notre Dame Press, 1985), chaps. 1-4. See esp. pp. 43-46 and his brief definition of foundationalism, pp. 158-59 n. 20.

15. Here I am suggesting that the two kinds of foundationalism described in the Introduction are related: that the theological foundationalism explicitly rejected by Barth is in fact an outgrowth of the prevailing philosophical foundationalism identified and criticized by Rorty and others.

16. Thiemann, *Revelation and Theology*, 43.

17. Brunner, "Die andere Aufgabe der Theologie," 262.

18. *KD* 1/1: 251-53 (*CD* 1/1: 238-40).

19. *KD* 1/1: 251 (*CD* 1/1: 239).

20. *KD* 1/1: 253 (*CD* 1/1: 240).

21. *KD* 2/1: 134 (*CD* 2/1: 121); Barth's emphasis.

22. The phrase is from Antony Flew's contribution to the "Theology and Falsification" debate, in *New Essays in Philosophical Theology*, ed. Antony Flew and Alasdair MacIntyre (London: SCM Press, 1955), 97. Flew is pointing out the fallacy— rampant, he believes, among modern theologians—of making an assertion and then qualifying it to the point where nothing significant is any longer being asserted.

23. There remain dangers, of course, in the use of such tools. Since speaking English involves using analogies drawn from all kinds of experience, the theologian may inadvertently import inappropriate assumptions into his or her theology through the uncritical use of language. Even an apparently nontheological tool like mathematics could get a theologian into trouble if used carelessly, for example, in a discussion of the Trinity. But such dangers are not unique to theology and cannot at any rate be avoided by refusing to use the tools.

Chapter 3. The Priority of Paradigms

1. See Introduction, pp. 3-4.

2. *KD* 1/2: 304-97 (*CD* 1/2: 280-361). See chap. 2, n. 6.

3. The unfortunate mistranslation of the title of §17 of the *Church Dogmatics* has occasioned serious misunderstanding of Barth's theology of religion. By rendering *Aufhebung* as "Abolition," the translators have left the impression that for Barth revelation is the simple opposite of religion. In fact, Barth uses the term in the deliberately double sense of Hegel to indicate *both* the "abolition" of religion *and* its preservation at a higher level. Otherwise, he could hardly have spoken of "True Religion" in the third subsection.

4. The dichotomy is prevalent among spokesmen for both "science" and "religion." Bronislaw Malinowski's division of human communities into "two distinguishable do-

mains, . . . the domain of Magic and Religion and that of Science" (*Magic, Science and Religion and Other Essays*, ed. Robert Redfield [Boston: Beacon Press; Glencoe, IL, Free Press, 1948], 1) is typical of scientific attitudes until very recent times. Likewise Paul Tillich speaks for many modern theologians when he claims that "scientific truth and the truth of faith do not belong to the same dimension of meaning" and therefore cannot come into legitimate conflict (*Dynamics of Faith* [New York: Harper & Brothers, 1957], 81).

5. See discussion chap. 1.

6. Max Black makes the point explicitly in the concluding sentence of his essay "Models and Archetypes": "Science, like the humanities, like literature, is an affair of the imagination" (in *Models and Metaphors: Studies in Language and Philosophy* [Ithaca, NY: Cornell Univ. Press, 1962], 243).

7. Thomas S. Kuhn, *The Structure of Scientific Revolutions*, 2d ed., enl. (Chicago: Univ. of Chicago Press, 1970). Page references to this edition will be given parenthetically in the text.

8. Several of the early responses to Kuhn's theory are collected in Imre Lakatos and Alan Musgrave, eds., *Criticism and the Growth of Knowledge* (New York: Cambridge Univ. Press, 1970); a more recent anthology is Gary Gutting, ed., *Paradigms and Revolutions: Appraisals and Applications of Thomas Kuhn's Philosophy of Science* (Notre Dame, IN: Univ. of Notre Dame Press, 1980). The huge volume edited by Frederick Suppe, *The Structure of Scientific Theories*, 2d ed. (Urbana, IL: Univ. of Illinois Press, 1977), surveys the broader movement in recent philosophy of science as well as the debate surrounding Kuhn.

9. Margaret Masterman, "The Nature of a Paradigm," in Lakatos and Musgrave, *Criticism and the Growth of Knowledge*, 59-89.

10. Kuhn acknowledges that he would have liked to retain the term *paradigm* for "these problem-solutions" since "they are what led me to the choice of the term in the first place." Only because he believes that he has "lost control of the word" does he replace it with the term *exemplar*. (See his "Reflections on My Critics," in Lakatos and Musgrave, *Criticism and the Growth of Knowledge*, 272.) For reasons that I develop later in this chapter, I believe that the term *paradigm* is a better choice and therefore take steps to regain control over it.

11. Stephen Toulmin, *Human Understanding* (Princeton, NJ: Princeton Univ. Press, 1972), 1:114.

12. Henry George Liddell and Robert Scott, comps., *A Greek-English Lexicon*, 9th ed. (Oxford: Clarendon Press, 1940), 1307-8.

13. Though the noun *paradeigma* does not appear in the New Testament writings, related verbal forms occur twice in the sense of "to hold (someone) up to contempt," or as we might say, "to make an example of someone." Cf. Matt. 1:19 and Heb. 6:6. (William F. Arndt and F. Wilbur Gingrich, *A Greek-English Lexicon of the New Testament and Other Early Christian Literature*, 4th rev. ed. [Chicago: Univ. of Chicago Press, 1957], 619.)

14. Ludwig Wittgenstein, *Philosophical Investigations*, trans. G. E. M. Anscombe, 2d ed. (New York: Macmillan, 1958), pt. 2, p. 194. Wittgenstein adapted the figure from Joseph Jastrow, *Fact and Fable in Psychology* (Boston: Houghton Mifflin, 1900), 295. Wittgenstein's simpler and clearer version is more effective in demonstrating the gestalt shift.

15. Norwood Russell Hanson, *Patterns of Discovery: An Inquiry into the Conceptual Foundations of Science* (Cambridge: Cambridge Univ. Press, 1958), 17 (Hanson's emphasis).

16. Wittgenstein, *Philosophical Investigations*, pt. 2, p. 193 (Wittgenstein's emphasis).

17. Wolfgang Köhler, *The Task of Gestalt Psychology* (Princeton, NJ: Princeton Univ. Press, 1969), 163-64.

18. Andras Angyal, "The Structure of Wholes," *Philosophy of Science* 6 (1939): 25-37.

19. Kuhn, *Structure of Scientific Revolutions*, 11.

20. Albert Einstein, *The Method of Theoretical Physics* (Oxford, 1933), cited by Hanson, *Patterns of Discovery*, 119.

21. Hanson, *Patterns of Discovery*, 120.

22. Ibid., 87.

23. Kuhn, *Structure of Scientific Revolutions*, 6. See chap. 10 for his explication of these transformations.

24. Imre Lakatos, for example, claims that for Kuhn paradigm change in science "is a mystical conversion which is not and cannot be governed by rules of reason. . . . Scientific change is a kind of religious change" ("Falsification and the Methodology of Scientific Research Programmes," in Lakatos and Musgrave, *Criticism and the Growth of Knowledge*, 93). As though the charge of religion were not enough, Lakatos goes on to claim that "in Kuhn's view scientific revolution is irrational, a matter for mob psychology" (178; ital. omitted). John Watkins, in less strident tones, points to passages in which Kuhn mentions theology as a parallel to science and concludes that "Kuhn sees the scientific community on the analogy of a religious community and sees science as the scientist's religion" ("Against 'Normal Science,'" in Lakatos and Musgrave, *Criticism and the Growth of Knowledge*, 33). The assumption of such critics—that to suggest a parallel between science and theology is automatically to deprecate science—reveals more about their own prejudices than about Kuhn's theory. But they are also missing the main point: not that science is modeled on religion but rather that both manifest similar "grammatical" qualities. I am arguing that this unexpected similarity is an important clue to the role of imagination in both science and religion.

25. See discussion earlier in the chapter for examples and references.

26. Hanson, *Patterns of Discovery*, 11. He gives a number of other examples in the same chapter.

27. Basil Mitchell, *The Justification of Religious Belief* (New York: Oxford Univ. Press, 1981), 84. Mitchell's whole summary and evaluation of the debate between Kuhn and his critics (chaps. 4 and 5) is instructive.

28. The metaphor of the leap is used here in full awareness of its implications for theological notions of a "leap of faith." Despite a deeply held modern prejudice going back to Kierkegaard, such leaps are neither unique to religious experience nor irrational; rather, they are psychological symptoms of the "paradigmatic" grammar of religious experience. Here, as in so many theological confusions, we have a "case of the misplaced mystery"—an illegitimate mystification of religion (for apologetic purposes) that serves only to obscure the real mystery of faith.

29. Kuhn, "Reflections on My Critics," 266.

30. Kuhn, *Structure of Scientific Revolutions*, 150.

31. Kuhn, "Reflections on My Critics," 267.

32. Kuhn, *Structure of Scientific Revolutions*, 147.

33. Ibid., 115.

34. Alfred North Whitehead, *Process and Reality* (New York: Harper & Row, 1929), 25.

Chapter 4. Religion and the Paradigmatic Imagination

1. H. Richard Niebuhr, *The Meaning of Revelation* (New York: Macmillan, 1941), 93.

2. George Whalley, *Poetic Process* (London: Routledge & Kegan Paul, 1953), 85. Significantly, Whalley also refers to this crystallization as a "paradeigmatic event."

3. Immanuel Kant, *Critique of Pure Reason*, trans. Norman Kemp Smith (New York: St Martin's Press, 1968), B 151. Kant's views on the imagination were nevertheless anything but simple. See discussion in chap. 1, pp. 13–15.

4. See discussion of "picturability" later in this chapter.

5. I am indebted to Charles M. Wood for calling my attention to this kind of imagination.

6. Ludwig Wittgenstein, *Philosophical Investigations*, trans. G. E. M. Anscombe, 2d ed. (New York: Macmillan, 1958), pt. 2, pp. 193ff.

7. Calling this level "highest" does not imply a value judgment; it is higher in the logical or evolutionary sense that it presupposes and depends on the lower levels. The "higher animals" are not necessarily more valuable than the "lower" ones, just more recent and more complex. Similarly, the interpretive imagination is higher—more complex—than the transcendental and perceptual imagination.

8. Dilthey's attempt to distinguish natural scientific *Erklären* from humanistic *Verstehen*, which has been the source of considerable confusion in hermeneutics, is no longer tenable in the light of recent philosophy of science. For a summary and critique of Dilth-

ey's position, see Wolfhart Pannenberg, *Theology and the Philosophy of Science*, trans. Francis McDonagh (Philadelphia: Westminster Press, 1976), chap. 2. A shortcoming of Wayne Proudfoot's important recent book *Religious Experience* (Berkeley and Los Angeles: Univ. of California Press, 1985) is its confusing attempt to resurrect Dilthey's dualism (without attending to the critical discussion of it summarized by Pannenberg). Proudfoot's version culminates in an unconvincing attempt to distinguish "descriptive reduction" from "explanatory reduction" (196–98). This false duality causes him to overlook the fact that religious people as well as scholars of religion are involved in both understanding and explanation. In Pannenberg's terms, "Where we understand, no explanations are needed. It is only where we do not understand that explanations are required" (153).

9. Cf. 1 John 1:1.

10. Cf. Ray L. Hart's phenomenological treatment of paradigmatic events in *Unfinished Man and the Imagination: Toward an Ontology and a Rhetoric of Revelation* (New York: Herder & Herder, 1968), 285–90. "The paradigmatic event," according to Hart's definition, "is . . . an event of extraordinary 'importance' in that it manifests the pattern by which other events are co-ordinated" (286). Especially important is his comment that the "imaginative language [of the New Testament] is the underived language of faith, language in closest proximity to the paradigmatic events themselves" (290). The theological implications of the paradigmatic imagination for the authority of scripture is my topic in chapter 6.

11. Margaret Masterman, "The Nature of a Paradigm," in Imre Lakatos and Alan Musgrave, eds., *Criticism and the Growth of Knowledge* (New York: Cambridge Univ. Press, 1970), 67. She calls this feature the "paradigm's basic property."

12. Edward Casey makes the seemingly incredible claim that "although I can misperceive, I cannot misimagine" (*Imagining: A Phenomenological Study* [Bloomington, IN: Indiana Univ. Press, 1976], 167; Casey's emphasis). The claim is justified only within the narrow limits of his sharp (and problematic) distinction between phenomenological and epistemological questions and his treatment of imagination solely in terms of the former. As I have tried to demonstrate, the most striking feature of imagination is precisely its "epistemological" ambiguity. Casey's entire treatment of imagination falls under the category that I have called fantasy—the free, "idle" use of the imagination with no realistic intent (cf. Casey's own examples, pp. 26–33). Because in some cases we can know *only* by imagining, it follows that we are also susceptible to *mis*imagining. Again, ordinary language bears clear testimony: if it is impossible to misimagine, what could be meant by a "failure of imagination"? (An example: "I can't imagine what it would be like to be poor and black.")

13. See above, chap. 1, n. 3, and pp. 22–26.

14. Niebuhr, *Meaning of Revelation*, 108.

15. The most ambitious articulation of functional systems theory (including its application to religion) has been undertaken by the German sociologist Niklas Luhmann, who is indebted both to the Husserlian phenomenological tradition and to the ideas of Talcott Parsons. Expressed in Luhmann's terminology, I am proposing a "relationizing" (*Relationierung*) of religion by taking the paradigmatic imagination as the "reference problem" (*Bezugsproblem*). The result is to replace two-term direct comparisons with functional three-term relations, in which religion is not only examined with reference to its use of imagination but also compared with other, nonreligious uses of imagination (cf. Luhmann, *Funktion der Religion* [Frankfurt am Main: Suhrkamp Verlag, 1977], 9–10). In this way one can illumine religion by viewing it as comparable to science and literature in respect to the use of imagination without "grounding" religion in a foundational theory of imagination. For a summary of Luhmann's theory of religion and a critical discussion of its application to theology, see Garrett Green, "The Sociology of Dogmatics: Niklas Luhmann's Challenge to Theology," *Journal of the American Academy of Religion* 50 (1982): 19–34.

16. A useful summary and critical discussion of the analogical features of science and literature in relation to religion is presented by Ian G. Barbour in *Myths, Models, and Paradigms: A Comparative Study in Science and Religion* (New York: Harper & Row, 1974), esp.

chapters 2–6. Barbour's application of these features to religion (chap. 7) and to Christian theology (chap. 8) is less helpful because he takes for granted an "experiential-expressivist" definition of religion, which assumes that "religious experience" is the subject matter of theology (see George Lindbeck, *The Nature of Doctrine: Religion and Theology in a Postliberal Age* [Philadelphia: Westminster Press, 1984]). The issues of metaphor and analogy will be developed further in chapter 7.

17. Barbour, *Myths, Models, and Paradigms*, 14.

18. See discussion in chap. 1, pp. 16–17, 21–23.

19. Eberhard Jüngel, "Metaphorische Wahrheit: Erwägungen zur theologischen Relevanz der Metapher als Beitrag zur Hermeneutik einer narrativen Theologie," in *Metapher: Zur Hermeneutik religiöser Sprache*, by Paul Ricoeur and Eberhard Jüngel, special issue of *Evangelische Theologie* (Munich: Chr. Kaiser Verlag, 1974), 71–122. Jüngel cites Nietzsche's essay "Ueber Wahrheit und Lüge im aussermoralischen Sinne," in *Nachgelassene Schriften, 1870–1873*, vol. 3, pt. 2 of *Werke: Kritische Gesamtausgabe*, ed. Georgio Colli and Mazzino Montinari (Berlin and New York: Walter de Gruyter, 1973), 369–84. For a further discussion of Jüngel's theory of metaphor and its application to theology, see chapter 7, pp. 127–34.

20. The term *metaphor* is itself a good example of the metaphoric origin of abstract terms. It derives from the Greek for "bear across" or "carry over" (the etymological equivalent of the Latin-based term *transfer*). The original users of the term recognized an analogy between carrying something physically from one place to another and the way in which certain words are used to "carry over" or "transfer" meaning from something familiar to something in need of illumination. The fact that people can now use the abstract term *metaphor* successfully without being aware of the analogy embedded in its etymology is proof of its evolution from metaphor to concept. The metaphoric content has been "forgotten" or become "frozen." (Stephen Crites reports that the word retains a nonmetaphoric use in modern Greek, where it is the term for a moving van! ["The Spatial Dimensions of Narrative Truthtelling," in *Scriptural Authority and Narrative Interpretation*, ed. Garrett Green (Philadelphia: Fortress Press, 1987), 100].) Similarly, people who speak today of "incentives" intend no analogy to singing, any more than those who discuss the "derivation" of words expect their hearers to think of streams. Much of the verbal awkwardness perpetrated in the name of "inclusive language" could be avoided by attending to this linguistic principle: *chairman* long ago lost its original metaphoric reference to a male seated at the head of the table.

21. An example of this tendency is Ernesto Grassi, *Die Macht der Phantasie: Zur Geschichte abendländischen Denkens* (Königstein/Ts.: Athenäum, 1979), which nevertheless contains useful information about the history of metaphor and its interpretation.

22. The discussion is summarized in Barbour, *Myths, Models, and Paradigms*, 51–53.

23. Hanson, *Patterns of Discovery: An Inquiry into the Conceptual Foundations of Science* (Cambridge: Cambridge Univ. Press, 1958), 9–10.

24. Ibid., 6.

25. I have conducted this experiment several times with classes, using slides of shifting-gestalt figures projected on a screen. The conversation among the students invariably becomes a model of persuasion and conversion, complete with arguments about the "obvious" and gasps of recognition when someone suddenly "sees the light." Useful visual examples are reproduced in Hanson, *Perception and Discovery: An Introduction to Scientific Inquiry* (San Francisco: Freeman, Cooper, 1969), and E. H. Gombrich, *Art and Illusion: A Study in the Psychology of Pictorial Representation* (New York: Pantheon Books, 1960).

26. The logic of "as" will be developed further in chapter 7, pp. 137–45.

27. Hanson, *Patterns of Discovery*, 119 (Hanson's emphasis).

28. Ibid., 124.

29. Ibid., 125. The parallel between the neutrino and the Trinity is a strictly methodological one and should not be misunderstood as ontological. The kinds of unpicturability are obviously quite different in the two cases. Employing my earlier typology, the neutrino's unpicturability is spatial; in the case of the Trinity, it is logical. The parallel is a negative one: in both cases the observer is unable to make use of models taken directly

from the "picturable" world of ordinary experience and must therefore employ imaginative constructs.

30. Ibid., 126 (my emphasis).
31. Ibid., 122 (my emphasis).
32. For this reason, Kant's definition of imagination as representation (cited earlier, see n. 3) is finally inadequate. Representation is too likely to be understood as a kind of picturing, whereas imagination often involves other, "nonrepresentational" ways of making its objects accessible.
33. John Wisdom, *Paradox and Discovery* (New York: Philosophical Library, 1965), 54 (my emphasis). Cf. Barbour, *Myths, Models, and Paradigms*, 52.
34. See Stephen Sykes, *The Identity of Christianity: Theologians and the Essence of Christianity from Schleiermacher to Barth* (Philadelphia: Fortress Press, 1984).
35. See Garrett Green, "Positive Religion in the Early Philosophy of the German Idealists" (Ph.D. diss., Yale Univ., 1971).
36. Pannenberg, *Theology and the Philosophy of Science*, 276–96, 299. The translation sometimes erroneously has "positivism" instead of "positivity."
37. *Die Religion in Geschichte und Gegenwart*, 1st ed. (Tübingen: J. C. B. Mohr [Paul Siebeck], 1913), s.v. "Positiv."
38. Dietrich Bonhoeffer's late prison letters contain a devastating critique of this tendency in twentieth-century theology. See discussion in chap. 7, pp. 146–47.
39. The latter failing is exemplified by Ninian Smart's attempt to define religion so broadly that it finally dissolves into a hopelessly vague concept of "worldviews," thereby sacrificing the chief value of a definition in the first place; namely, to tell us what makes a religion a religion and not something else. See his *Worldviews: Crosscultural Explorations of Human Beliefs* (New York: Charles Scribner's Sons, 1983).
40. To cite just one example: Jonathan Z. Smith's provocative "redescription of canon from the perspective of an historian of religion" suggests unexpected and unexplored parallels between exegetical concern with canon by Christians and the other Western "Peoples of the Book," and the exegesis of lists and catalogs in nonliterate traditions ("Sacred Persistence: Toward a Redescription of Canon," in *Imagining Religion: From Babylon to Jonestown* [Chicago: Univ. of Chicago Press, 1982], 36–52). Especially fascinating is Smith's conclusion that "for nonliterate peoples, canon is most clearly to be perceived in divinatory situations" (52). If Smith is correct, my analysis of the Christian canon in chapter 6 might have interesting implications for understanding Ndembu or Yoruba divination—and vice versa. Likewise, my description of Christian theology in chapter 7 might be used comparatively to identify analogues to theological interpretation in religious traditions that have been assumed to be utterly nontheological.

Chapter 5. The Image of God

1. Emil Brunner, "Die andere Aufgabe der Theologie," *Zwischen den Zeiten* 7 (1929): 264 n. 3.
2. See discussion in chapter 2, pp. 32–33.
3. A useful brief survey of the history of the *imago Dei* doctrine, including references to key passages in ancient, medieval, and modern theologians, is found in Otto Weber, *Foundations of Dogmatics*, trans. Darrell L. Guder (Grand Rapids: Wm. B. Eerdmans, 1981), 1:558–79. Weber's analysis of the theological issues raised by the tradition is also helpful.
4. Augustine, *City of God*, bk. 12, chap. 23, trans. by M. Dods in *Basic Writings of Saint Augustine*, ed. Whitney J. Oates (New York: Random House, 1948), 2:205. He draws the same conclusion from the juxtaposition of the creation in the image of God and the charge of dominion over nature: "man was made to the image of God in that part of his nature wherein he surpasses the brute beasts. This is, of course, his reason or mind or intelligence, or whatever we wish to call it." St. Augustine, *The Literal Meaning of Gen-*

esis, vol. 1, *Books 1–6*, trans. John Hammond Taylor, Ancient Christian Writers 41 (New York: Newman Press, 1982), 96.

5. St. Thomas Aquinas, *Summa Theologiae* la.93, 6, in Blackfriars ed. (New York: McGraw-Hill, 1963), 13:67.

6. Martin Luther, *Lectures on Genesis, Chapters 1–5*, vol. 1 of *Luther's Works*, ed. Jaroslav Pelikan (St. Louis: Concordia Publishing House, 1958), 62.

7. Gerhard von Rad concludes that the "text speaks less of the nature of God's image than of its purpose," which he identifies closely with the charge of dominion over nature. "Just as powerful earthly kings, to indicate their claim to dominion, erect an image of themselves in the provinces of their empire where they do not personally appear," von Rad reasons, "so man is placed upon earth in God's image as God's sovereign emblem." He comes very close to identifying the nature of the image directly with its function: "The decisive thing about man's similarity to God, therefore, is his function in the non-human world" (*Genesis: A Commentary*, trans. John H. Marks [Philadelphia: Westminster Press, 1961], 57–58).

8. The earthy simplicity and dramatic power of the Yahwist's story is captured in the voice of the American black preacher in the conclusion of "The Creation" by James Weldon Johnson (in *God's Trombones: Seven Negro Sermons in Verse* [New York: Viking Press, 1959], 20):

> Up from the bed of the river
> God scooped the clay;
> And by the bank of the river
> He kneeled him down;
> And there the great God Almighty
> Who lit the sun and fixed it in the sky,
> Who flung the stars to the most far corner of the night,
> Who rounded the earth in the middle of his hand;
> This Great God,
> Like a mammy bending over her baby,
> Kneeled down in the dust
> Toiling over a lump of clay
> Till he shaped it in his own image;
> Then into it he blew the breath of life,
> And man became a living soul.
> Amen. Amen.

Johnson, like the ancient Hebrew storyteller, has no qualms about associating the image of God with Adam's physical shape. He also brings out effectively, especially in his striking maternal image, the drama of the divine condescension—not, as is usual, with reference to human redemption but here to the original creation.

9. See, for example, John Calvin, *Commentaries on the First Book of Moses Called Genesis*, trans. John King (Grand Rapids: Wm. B. Eerdmans, 1948), 1:93–94. A useful summary and compendium of quotations on the *imago Dei* from the Reformed dogmatic tradition is found in Heinrich Heppe, *Reformed Dogmatics: Set Out and Illustrated from the Sources*, rev. and ed. Ernst Bizer, trans. G. T. Thomson (1950; reprint, Grand Rapids: Baker Book House, 1978), 232–38.

10. Karl Barth's long excursus on the *imago Dei* contains a valuable historical and theological summary, reaching from the creation accounts of Genesis to the Pauline *eikon*-Christology of the New Testament (*KD* 3/1: 214–33 [*CD* 3/1: 191–206]; see chap. 2, n. 6). At one point, however, in his effort to overcome a one-sidedness in dogmatic tradition, Barth seems to reject totally the doctrine that the image of God identifies an original human ideal that was subsequently lost. The Old Testament, he claims, offers no support for the view that the divine likeness is something "that man has *lost* through the

fall, whether partially or wholly, formally or materially" (*KD* 244; cf. *CD* 220, which omits Barth's crucial emphasis). While excusing the Reformers because they operated out of the background of medieval theology, he denies any biblical basis for the doctrine of a *status integritatis* that was subsequently lost through sin, arguing that the "biblical saga speaks neither in Gen. 1 nor Gen. 2 nor elsewhere of such an original ideal man." But Barth himself has emphasized only a few pages previously that the *imago* of Genesis posits not an *analogia entis* but an *analogia relationis* (*KD* 219 [*CD* 195]). Surely the Genesis narrative does intend to portray, not an *Idealmenschen*, but rather an ideal divine-human *relationship* at creation. And a major point of the subsequent depiction of the primeval history is the tragic consequences flowing from the original couple's willful disturbance of that relation. Barth is right to underscore the fact that the saving relationship between God and Israel, far from being abrogated by sin, really begins in earnest with the fall; and he is likewise justified in stressing that the "free and gracious will of the Creator by which man is to be one with whom He can deal as with an equal" is by no means lost. But this emphasis ought not to obscure the equally important claim of the story that we have indeed lost something—namely, a free and natural access to God, which ought to pertain but does not. "Objectively," from God's side, the *imago* remains after the fall, but as far as human experience is concerned, it is as good as lost. Another way to state it: the image of God is still there, but human beings no longer have eyes to see it.

11. Irenaeus *Adv. haer.* 1, 8, 1, in *The Ante-Nicene Fathers*, ed. Alexander Roberts and James Donaldson (New York: Charles Scribner's Sons, 1899), 1:326. Cf. Robert M. Grant, *The Secret Sayings of Jesus* (Garden City, NY: Doubleday, 1960), 92.

12. H. McKeating, "Idolatry," in *The Westminster Dictionary of Christian Theology*, ed. Alan Richardson and John Bowden (Philadelphia: Westminster Press, 1983), 280–81.

13. Thomas F. Torrance, *Theological Science* (New York: Oxford Univ. Press, 1969), 22, summarizing a point made by John Macmurray. Torrance's whole discussion of seeing and hearing is instructive (pp. 19–25).

14. Ibid., 19.

15. See chap. 7, 139–42, for a discussion of "is" versus "as."

16. Cf. Wittgenstein, *Philosophical Investigations*, §301: "An image is not a picture, but a picture can correspond to it."

17. The etymology of *pattern* is in fact not visual but (presumably) mimetic: it derives from Latin *patronus*, "patron"—thus one to be emulated. This history reflects the close relationship between imagination and imitation discussed later in the chapter.

18. Two examples can be cited from recent Christian theology. One is the widely influential position of Paul Tillich, who dismisses all concrete images of God as idolatrous—or at least potentially so. Perhaps the extreme of his position emerges in his critique of the very idea of "God," which is at best an insufficient pointer to the "God beyond God." The other example is the current assault by proponents of "inclusive language" on the specificity of biblical, liturgical, and theological language about God. This campaign is already having unfortunate practical effects on worship in some Christian churches, as language about God becomes increasingly vague and impersonal. Especially distressing is the altering of the language of scripture, liturgy, and hymns on ideological grounds, without regard for the integrity of the texts, and without confronting the historical, aesthetic, and theological issues involved.

19. Patrick Henry, "The Formulators of Icon Doctrine," in *Schools of Thought in the Christian Tradition*, ed. Patrick Henry (Philadelphia: Fortress Press, 1984), 75.

20. St. John of Damascus, *On the Divine Images: Three Apologies Against Those Who Attack the Divine Images*, trans. David Anderson (Crestwood, NY: St. Vladimir's Seminary Press, 1980). Citations given in the text refer to this edition.

21. John Calvin, *Institutes of the Christian Religion*, book 1, chaps. 11–12. Citations in the text refer to the Library of Christian Classics 22, ed. John T. McNeill, trans. Ford Lewis Battles (Philadelphia: Westminster Press, 1960).

22. The contrast between these two Christian traditions is vividly represented where I live in southern New England in the juxtaposition of richly ornate Orthodox churches built by recent Greek immigrants and the whitewashed meetinghouses still used by the descendants of the earlier English Puritan settlers of the region.

23. See esp. 1.11.12 (p. 112), where Calvin refers explicitly to "sculpture and painting." An examination of his use of the term *image* shows that he always means it literally—that is, *picture*.

24. This distinction shows up in a fascinating context in the tradition of "the icon made by God" (*Theoteuchtos eikon*) or image "not made by the hand of man," celebrated in the Eastern Orthodox service of the Holy Face. This tradition derives from various legendary accounts about an image of Jesus sent to Abgar, king of Edessa. This God-given image is sharply distinguished from all humanly crafted images. See Leonide Ouspensky, *Theology of the Icon* (Crestwood, NY: St. Vladimir's Seminary Press, 1978), 59–68. The Abgar legend has recently surfaced in a bizarre context in the modern West: in the controversy about the authenticity of the Shroud of Turin.

25. Failure to distinguish adequately between idolatry and the legitimate uses of the religious imagination has created a dilemma for some contemporary heirs of the Reformed tradition—a kind of "idolophobia" leading to theological paralysis of the imagination. A recent case is Gordon Kaufman, for whom every "image/concept" of God presents a theological dilemma. On the one hand, theology, having no direct intuition of God, cannot do without the image; but on the other hand, every image of God, being finite, contradicts the nature of God and is to that extent idolatrous. For a fuller critique of Kaufman's concept of imagination in theology and the dilemma to which his view of idolatry leads, see my review article, "Reconstructing Christian Theology," *Religious Studies Review* 9 (1983): 219–22.

26. Both English *obey* and German *gehorchen* come from verbs meaning "to hear."

27. I agree with Ronald F. Thiemann, *Revelation and Theology: The Gospel as Narrated Promise* (Notre Dame, IN: Univ. of Notre Dame Press, 1985), that the doctrine of revelation can be defended and is "Worth the Trouble" (the title of his introduction). His account of the troubles besetting the doctrine is very helpful, and his own proposal to understand revelation as "narrated promise" is persuasively presented. As I will argue below, I hesitate to attribute so exclusive a role to *narrative*, which I believe can be more adequately understood theologically as one of the forms—a particularly important one in Christianity—of the Christian religious imagination.

28. H. Richard Niebuhr, *The Meaning of Revelation* (New York: Macmillan, 1941), 109. My italics are a deliberate attempt to shift the emphasis from the occasion to the image. Niebuhr's often brilliant insights into the role of imagination in revelation are obscured by his "somewhat Kantian" dichotomy between "pure" (he means "theoretical") and practical reason (p. viii). The effect of this dualism is to locate revelation in a communal "inner history," which Niebuhr never succeeds in uniting with "outer history" (see esp. chap. 2). The result is to tie revelation to a private and privileged "experience" rather than to the public images that give shape to Christian experience—a classic case of what George A. Lindbeck calls "experiential-expressivism" in theology. See *The Nature of Doctrine: Religion and Theology in a Postliberal Age* (Philadelphia: Westminster Press, 1984).

29. Hans W. Frei, *The Eclipse of Biblical Narrative* (New Haven: Yale Univ. Press, 1974).

30. Heppe, *Reformed Dogmatics*, 233.

31. Johannes Braunius, in ibid., 565.

32. *Origen: Spirit and Fire: A Thematic Anthology of His Writings*, ed. Hans Urs von Balthasar, trans. Robert J. Daly (Washington, DC: Catholic Univ. of America Press, 1984), 55. The passage is taken from Origen's homily on Genesis.

33. Ibid., 57. The passage is taken from Origen's teaching on the preexistent soul of Christ, so troublesome for his supporters in the light of later christological orthodoxy. For the context, see *On First Principles* 2.6.3.

34. Ibid., 56 (*On First Principles* 3.6.1). This way of distinguishing "image" and "likeness" has remained a characteristic of Eastern Christianity. "To be in the image of God is to have the possibility of acquiring the divine likeness" (Ouspensky, *Theology of the Icon*, 185).

35. *Cum in illis absolutissimam sui imaginem expresserit divinitas.* Philip Melanchthon, Dedicatory Letter to *Loci communes theologici* (1521), in *Melanchthon and Bucer,* ed. Wilhelm Pauck, Library of Christian Classics 19 (Philadelphia: Westminster Press, 1969), 19.

Chapter 6. The Normative Vision

1. Karl Barth's term: *KD* 1/1: 253 (cf. *CD* 1/1: 240); see chap. 2, p. 37. For the method used in citing the *Church Dogmatics,* see chap. 2, n. 6.
2. John Calvin, *Institutes of the Christian Religion* 1.5.11, cited from the translation by Ford Lewis Battles, ed. John T. McNeill, Library of Christian Classics 20 (Philadelphia: Westminster Press, 1960), 63.
3. Ibid., 1.6.1 (p. 70).
4. Cf. Jonathan Z. Smith's suggestive, but insufficiently developed, notion of a "focusing lens" ("The Bare Facts of Ritual," in *Imagining Religion: From Babylon to Jonestown* [Chicago: Univ. of Chicago Press, 1982], 53–65). He cites examples from ancient Greek and Jewish religion in which the "temple serves as a *focusing lens,* marking and revealing significance" (54). Later in the essay Smith applies the same metaphor in interpreting a ritual that enacts an idealized hunt: the ritual, he claims, "provides a focusing lens on the ordinary hunt which allows its full significance to be perceived" (65). If Smith is right about sacred space and ritual in these traditions, they apparently perform a function analogous to that of scripture for the Christian, embodying a normative pattern for the shaping of the religious imagination.
5. Cited by Ronald F. Thiemann, "Revelation and Imaginative Construction," *Journal of Religion* 61 (1981): 255–56.
6. Ibid., 254–55. A similar analogy, perhaps even better for scripture, is the red and blue glasses one has to wear while viewing the old 3-D movies. The same "objective" image on the screen looks blurred and distorted without the glasses but "real" when viewed through them.
7. E.g., Thomas S. Kuhn, *The Structure of Scientific Revolutions,* 2d ed. (Chicago: Univ. of Chicago Press, 1970), 128.
8. Ibid., 112–13. To some of their contemporaries, the early Christians seemed to be wearing inverting lenses: the Thessalonian Jews charged that they had "turned the world upside down" (Acts 17:6).
9. The locus classicus is the statement in 2 Tim. 3:16 usually translated "all scripture is inspired by God," in which the key Greek term is *theopneustos.* See David H. Kelsey, *The Uses of Scripture in Recent Theology* (Philadelphia: Fortress Press, 1975), 18–20. Hans W. Frei recounts the development of the concept of *Theopneustie* in German theology and exegesis of the eighteenth century in *The Eclipse of Biblical Narrative: A Study in Eighteenth and Nineteenth Century Hermeneutics* (New Haven: Yale Univ. Press, 1974), 164–78.
10. Cf. Wittgenstein's advice to *"look and see"* whether things share a common essence or manifest family resemblances: "Don't think, but look!" (*Philosophical Investigations,* trans. G. E. M. Anscombe, 2d ed. [New York: Macmillan, 1958], §66).
11. Cf. Luke 6:43–45.
12. There are also just three occurrences of the verb *imagine,* translating three unrelated Greek words. For references and Greek terms, see Clinton Morrison, *An Analytical Concordance to the Revised Standard Version of the New Testament* (Philadelphia: Westminster Press, 1979), 294.
13. A wealth of further examples is provided by R. C. Dentan, "Heart," in *The Interpreter's Dictionary of the Bible,* ed. George Arthur Buttrick (New York: Abingdon Press, 1962), 2:549–50. Dentan also comments that the "conception of heart in the NT is identical with that in the OT."
14. One of Dentan's four main definitions of the biblical concept of heart is the "point of contact with God." As the "central and unifying organ of personal life" (ibid., 549), the heart "is directly open to God and subject to his influence" (550). Dentan offers numerous examples.

15. Thomas Aquinas, *Summa Theologiae* 1a.12, 13, cited from the Blackfriars trans.
16. Austin Farrer, *The Glass of Vision* (London: Dacre Press, A. & C. Black, 1958), contains the Bampton Lectures of 1948. The title page bears the motto "Now we see through a glass darkly" from 1 Cor. 13:12. Page references will be given parenthetically in the text.
17. Paul Tillich, *Systematic Theology*, vol. 2, *Existence and the Christ* (Chicago: Univ. of Chicago Press, 1957), 114-15.
18. *Die Religion in Geschichte und Gegenwart: Handwörterbuch für Theologie und Religionswissenschaft*, ed. Kurt Galling (Tübingen: J. C. B. Mohr [Paul Siebeck], 1962), 6:702-3.
19. Cf. Rom. 12:6 and Barth's concept of the *analogia fidei*, especially KD 1/1: 257 (CD 1/1: 243-44).
20. Charles M. Wood, "The Aim of Christian Theology," *Perkins Journal* 31 (1978): 25.
21. For an account of the issues (as they relate to the New Testament), as well as a discussion of the consequent theological problems, see James D. G. Dunn, *Unity and Diversity in the New Testament: An Inquiry into the Character of Earliest Christianity* (Philadelphia: Westminster Press, 1977), esp. the summary and conclusions, pp. 369-88.
22. See discussion in chap. 1.
23. See the discussion of wholes and parts in chap. 3, pp. 50-59.
24. A recent interchange between a Jewish and a Christian theologian raises the issue of the canon in precisely these terms. Responding to Ronald F. Thiemann's interpretation of Matthew's Gospel (*Revelation and Theology: The Gospel as Narrated Promise* [Notre Dame, IN: Univ. of Notre Dame Press, 1985]), Michael Goldberg challenges Thiemann's claim that the God of Matthew's Jesus is identical with the God of Israel. "At many crucial junctures in Matthew's story line," Goldberg argues, "the character of the work and person of Jesus Christ appears to be strikingly *out of character* for the One, who by dint of certain characteristic redeeming acts attributed to him in the going out from Egypt, originally became acknowledged as Israel's God and Lord. . . . Indeed, in light of the story of the Exodus, God might well be *unrecognizable* in Jesus Christ" ("God, Action, and Narrative: *Which* Narrative? *Which* Action? *Which* God?" *Journal of Religion* 68 [1988]: 51; Goldberg's emphasis). Goldberg, however, fails to note the ways in which his own reading of the biblical narrative (particularly as focused on the Exodus) has also been shaped by a postbiblical history of interpretation—in his case, rabbinic Judaism. The nub of the issue concerns the governing paradigm: whether the whole narrative is to be read "in light of the story of the Exodus" or in light of the story of Jesus. For our purposes the striking point about this debate is the two theologians' *agreement* about how theological arguments appealing to a narrative should be conducted: by attention to such matters as "the continuities of the story line, theme, and characterization" (Goldberg, p. 40).
25. See Kelsey's illuminating interpretation of Barth's view of scripture "rendering an agent" by narrative depiction of Jesus (*Uses of Scripture*, 39-50).
26. Mary Warnock, *Imagination* (Berkeley and Los Angeles: Univ. of California Press, 1976), 50.
27. Kelsey, *Uses of Scripture*, 107 (Kelsey's emphasis). His whole discussion of scripture and canon is instructive (pp. 100-108).
28. Niklas Luhmann, *Soziologische Aufklärung: Aufsätze zur Theorie der Gesellschaft*, vol. 2 (Opladen: Westdeutscher Verlag, 1975), 211.
29. Brevard S. Childs, *The New Testament as Canon: An Introduction* (Philadelphia: Fortress Press, 1985), 21. The brief chapter entitled "The Canon as an Historical and Theological Problem" (pp. 16-33) offers a lucid summary of recent scholarly debate on the canon along with a statement of the author's own position.
30. Luhmann, *Soziologische Aufklärung: Aufsätze zur Theorie sozialer Systeme*, vol. 1, 4th ed. (Opladen: Westdeutscher Verlag, 1974), 116.
31. Luhmann's thesis that the primary function of system building is the reduction of complexity is also suggestive for interpreting the formation of the scriptural canon. The church fathers struggled to achieve a scriptural "system" sufficiently complex to render Christ truly to the religious imagination without blurring or distorting that vision or producing a self-contradictory "double vision." According to this reading, the can-

on reflects a consensus that four Gospels, despite elements of tension among them, give a truer rendering of Jesus Christ than any one alone; on the other hand, it rejects the Gnostic portrayals of Jesus as basically incompatible with this gestalt. Similarly, the church fathers embraced the unity of the biblical God of both covenants, despite his greater complexity, rather than accepting Marcion's simpler but distorted solution.

32. Kelsey, *Uses of Scripture*, 106.

33. Irenaeus *Adv. haer.* 1, 8, 1 (for full citation, see chap. 5, n. 11). Childs also appeals to this passage, commenting that the heretics "operated from the wrong context" and "had no true concept of the whole" (28).

34. *KD* 1/2: 527; Barth's emphasis (cf. *CD* 1/2: 476).

35. Barth denies that the church creates the canon, arguing that its responsibility comes "after the fact" (*nachträglich*)—namely, to ascertain (*feststellen*) the truth that God has already revealed (*KD* 1/2: 524 [*CD* 1/2: 473]).

36. *KD* 1/2: 529 (*CD* 1/2: 478). Luther's verb *treyben*, which he glosses with "teach" and "preach" in the sentences immediately following, has some suggestive possibilities for a gestalt view of the canon. *Treiben* can mean to cause something to come forth or bloom (such as blossoms in a greenhouse); it can also refer to that which causes something to rise (dough) or ferment (wine). I believe that the textual equivalent is to "render": scriptures are to be evaluated by "whether they render Christ or not."

37. The reliability of revelation is given theological expression in Barth's distinction between the primary and secondary objectivity of God. Ronald F. Thiemann offers the following summary: "Because his secondary objectivity (revelation) is his self-manifestation, revelation is a *reliable* manifestation of the primary objectivity which is its ground. We can be confident that when we encounter God in his revelation we have encountered him as he really is. There is no hidden essence of God different than that which is available in revelation." "Revelation and Imaginative Construction," *Journal of Religion* 61 (1981): 260.

38. See discussion in chap. 4, pp. 62–70.

39. David Tracy, *The Analogical Imagination: Christian Theology and the Culture of Pluralism* (New York: Crossroad, 1981), p. xii. His presentation of the theory of the classic in chap. 3 leads to a consideration of the specifically religious classic in chaps. 4 and 5.

40. Ibid., 108 (my emphasis).

41. Ibid., 100.

42. George A. Lindbeck, *The Nature of Doctrine: Religion and Theology in a Postliberal Age* (Philadelphia: Westminster Press, 1984). Specific references will be cited parenthetically in the text.

43. Tracy, *Analogical Imagination*, 102.

44. Ibid., 108 (my emphasis).

45. Sallie McFague, *Metaphorical Theology: Models of God in Religious Language* (Philadelphia: Fortress Press, 1982), 19.

46. Ibid., 61; cf. James Barr, *The Bible in the Modern World* (New York: Harper & Row, 1973), chap. 7.

47. Barr, *Bible in the Modern World*, 115 (cited by McFague, *Metaphorical Theology*, 61).

48. McFague, *Metaphorical Theology*, 61 (my emphasis).

49. Ibid., 177.

50. The metaphor of language as Lindbeck uses it can be traced to Wittgenstein, who has profoundly influenced many of the thinkers favored by Lindbeck. For reasons that should be clear from the present work, I believe that the paradigmatic imagination offers a more precise and articulate conceptuality for understanding religion than the linguistic analogy. At the heart of language is its patterned or gestalt quality ("grammar" in Wittgenstein's sense) and its status as an activity rather than an essence. Language is a skill, something we learn how to *do* by "internalizing" its grammar.

51. Tracy, *Analogical Imagination*, 108. The list is not always quite the same: cf. pp. 100, 102, for other versions.

52. George Herbert's poem "The H. Scriptures" contains some striking images of the unity and interconnection of scripture, and of scripture's connection with Christian experi-

ence.·The second of the two stanzas is held together by the imagery of stars and their constellations:

> Oh that I knew how all thy lights combine,
>> And the configurations of their glorie!
>> Seeing not onely how each verse doth shine,
> But all the constellations of the storie.
> This verse marks that, and both do make a motion
>> Unto a third, that ten leaves off doth lie:
>> Then as dispersed herbs do watch a potion,
> These three make up some Christians destinie:
> Such are thy secrets, which my life makes good,
>> And comments on thee: for in ev'ry thing
>> Thy words do finde me out, & parallels bring,
> And in another make me understood.
>> Starres are poore books, & oftentimes do misse:
>> This book of starres lights to eternall blisse.

The image of scriptural writings as a constellation expresses well the paradigmatic nature of the Bible's unity. Herbert also brings out the way in which the scripture interprets the reader, and how its patterns unify and illumine extrascriptural reality ("parallels bring"). (Cited from *The Works of George Herbert*, ed. F. E. Hutchinson [Oxford: Clarendon Press, 1941], 58.)

53. Barth, *KD* 1/1: 109–11 (cf. *CD* 1/1: 107–8). The translators' unfortunate use of "impose" for Barth's term *imponieren* introduces a suggestion of compulsion. Barth is saying that the Christian reader of scripture finds it to be "impressive," not an "imposition."
54. Kelsey, *Uses of Scripture*, 193 (Kelsey's emphasis).
55. Hartmut Gese, *Zur biblischen Theologie: Alttestamentliche Vorträge* (Munich: Chr. Kaiser Verlag, 1977), 10.
56. For the origins and significance of typological interpretation, see Erich Auerbach, "Figura," in *Scenes from the Drama of European Literature* (1959; reprint, Gloucester, MA: Peter Smith, 1973), 11–76; and Frei, *Eclipse of Biblical Narrative*.
57. Dietrich Bonhoeffer, *Creation and Fall: A Theological Interpretation of Genesis 1–3* (London: SCM Press, 1959), 7–8.

Chapter 7. The Faithful Imagination

1. Paul Ricoeur, *The Symbolism of Evil*, trans. Emerson Buchanan (New York: Harper & Row, 1967), 350–51 (Ricoeur's emphasis).
2. See chap. 4, pp. 69–70.
3. I. A. Richards, *The Philosophy of Rhetoric* (New York: Oxford Univ. Press, 1936); Max Black, *Models and Metaphors: Studies in Language and Philosophy* (Ithaca, NY: Cornell Univ. Press, 1962, esp. chaps. 3 and 13, and "More about Metaphor," in *Metaphor and Thought*, ed. Andrew Ortony (Cambridge: Cambridge Univ. Press, 1979); Paul Ricoeur, *The Rule of Metaphor: Multi-Disciplinary Studies of the Creation of Meaning in Language*, trans. Robert Czerny et al. (Toronto: Univ. of Toronto Press, 1977).
4. For extensive bibliographical references and the best critical discussion of metaphor with which I am acquainted, see Janet Martin Soskice, *Metaphor and Religious Language* (New York: Oxford Univ. Press, 1985). See also Ian G. Barbour, *Myths, Models, and Paradigms: A Comparative Study in Science and Religion* (New York: Harper & Row, 1974), esp. 12–16, 42–45.
5. Eberhard Jüngel, "Metaphorische Wahrheit: Erwägungen zur theologischen Relevanz der Metapher als Beitrag zur Hermeneutik einer narrativen Theologie," in *Metapher:*

Zur Hermeneutik religiöser Sprache, by Paul Ricouer and Eberhard Jüngel, special issue of *Evangelische Theologie* (Munich: Chr. Kaiser Verlag, 1974), 71-122.

6. Ibid., 100.

7. Ibid., 105-8 (Jüngel's emphasis). For the Nietzsche reference, see chap. 4, n. 19.

8. Jüngel, *Gott als Geheimnis der Welt: Zur Begründung der Theologie des Gekreuzigten im Streit zwischen Theismus und Atheismus* (Tübingen: J. C. B. Mohr [Paul Siebeck], 1977), 40-41.

9. Jüngel, "Metaphorische Wahrheit," 78, 104.

10. Sallie McFague, *Metaphorical Theology: Models of God in Religious Language* (Philadelphia: Fortress Press, 1982), 31.

11. Ibid., 167.

12. Soskice, *Metaphor and Religious Language*, 150.

13. Ibid., esp. the critique of Max Black's "interactive" theory (pp. 38-43) and the presentation of her own "interanimation" theory (pp. 43-51). Subsequent references to this book will be given parenthetically in the text.

14. Black, *Models and Metaphors*, 35-37. Soskice (*Metaphor and Religious Language*, 42-43) demonstrates inconsistencies in Black's views here and in "More About Metaphor." It should also be noted that Black is plainly wrong in speaking here of an "equivalent *literal* comparison." The case in point is Schopenhauer's calling a geometrical proof a mousetrap, a comparison that is surely not literal but figurative. As I shall argue below, the point missed by both Black and Soskice is that the comparison is *analogical*.

15. Her example is a passage quoted by Richards:

> A stubborn and unconquerable flame
> Creeps in his veins and drinks the streams of life.

She points out that the *"fever is never explicitly mentioned,"* thus proving that "it is thoughts and not words which are active together" in the metaphor (pp. 45-46).

16. The distinction between names and metaphors suggests a historical hypothesis that I find compelling but lack the expertise to investigate: that names always precede metaphors, which are analogical applications of names. If we suppose, for example, that "Tree" was originally the name I chose to refer to the thing shading the entrance to my cave, I might subsequently apply this proper name metaphorically to other things resembling Tree by calling them "trees." If the metaphor becomes widely accepted by others in my linguistic community, it will eventually lose its metaphoric force and become conventional (and its metaphoric origins will be forgotten). I see evidence for the hypothesis in the ongoing process of linguistic development (e.g., the evolution of *sputnik* and *gerrymander* from specific reference to generic application). At any rate, the philosophical point I am making does not depend on the historical thesis.

17. This connective phrase can in fact be reduced to the single word *as*: metaphor means "speaking of one thing *as* another." See discussion later in this chapter.

18. Black at one point locates the similarity between the use of models and metaphors in the fact that both require the "analogical transfer of a vocabulary" (*Models and Metaphors*, 238), without seeming to notice that he has found the key to metaphoric speech. He is speaking here only of what he calls "theoretical models," but his entire discussion of models (in chap. 13, "Models and Archetypes") in effect demonstrates that all models posit analogies. Even "scale models," the simplest and most "literal" kind, are analogical: the model is meant to be like its subject in every respect except size.

19. Note that the original meaning of *metaphor* was the same as *vehicle*, a sense it retains in modern Greek as well! See chap. 4, n. 20.

20. "In making scale models, our purpose is to reproduce, in a relatively manipulable or accessible embodiment, selected features of the 'original.' . . . We try to bring the remote and the unknown to our own level of middle-sized existence" (Black, *Models and Metaphors*, 221). Once again, Black seems to miss the wider application of his remarks. The logic described in this passage applies to all models, hence to metaphor as well.

21. Hans W. Frei, *The Eclipse of Biblical Narrative: A Study in Eighteenth and Nineteenth Century Hermeneutics* (New Haven: Yale Univ. Press, 1974).

22. Ibid., 11-12.

23. A critique of "protective strategies" in religion is developed by Wayne Proudfoot in *Religious Experience* (Berkeley and Los Angeles: Univ. of California Press, 1985), esp. 199-209. Characteristic of such strategies is the attempt "to restrict accounts of religious experience and belief to the perspective of the subject" (211). Under the guise of "taking the belief at face value," such apologists are in effect "construing it in such a way as to preclude its falsity" (205). Although Proudfoot's criticism of such strategies is persuasive, his related attempt to distinguish between "descriptive and explanatory reduction" is not. He advocates a scholarly "neutrality" (204), apparently uncommitted to theory. But a purely descriptive language is as much a chimera for religious studies as for the natural sciences. Religious paradigms are not invulnerable to criticism, but it cannot be launched from some "neutral" (and thus privileged) position. Even scholars of religion cannot evade the paradigmatic imagination.

24. Not all theological liberals have dismissed history with quite the alacrity that this claim might suggest, since they affirm a significant residue of historically accurate material that is religiously significant. This concession, however, is insufficient to salvage the traditional connection between the truth of the text and its literal sense.

25. H[ans] Vaihinger, *The Philosophy of "As If": A System of the Theoretical, Practical, and Religious Fictions of Mankind*, 2d ed., trans. C. K. Ogden (New York: Harcourt, Brace, 1935; reprint, Boston: Routledge & Kegan Paul, 1965), p. xli.

26. Ibid., 298-99.

27. Ibid., 308 (Vaihinger's emphasis).

28. See Ian G. Barbour, *Myths, Models, and Paradigms: A Comparative Study in Science and Religion* (New York: Harper & Row, 1974), chap. 3.

29. Ibid., 50-51, 57-58; Barbour gives references to Braithwaite's works.

30. See chap. 4, pp. 71-74.

31. Ludwig Wittgenstein, *Philosophical Investigations*, trans. G. E. M. Anscombe, 2d ed. (New York: Macmillan, 1958), pt. 2, p. 210.

32. I am indebted to a remark several years ago by Professor Michael Welker that first drew my attention to the frequency of "as" titles in modern works. Investigation of this hunch could be a fruitful research topic for a historian of modern culture; a model for such study is Wilfred Cantwell Smith's tracing of the term *religion* in the titles of modern books in *The Meaning and End of Religion* (New York: Harper & Row, 1978), 32-48, esp. 219-20, n. 63.

33. See chap. 7, n. 1.

34. Krister Stendahl, "The Bible as a Classic and the Bible as Holy Scripture," *Journal of Biblical Literature* 103 (1984): 3-10; Brevard S. Childs, *Introduction to the Old Testament as Scripture* (Philadelphia: Fortress Press, 1979); idem, *The New Testament as Canon: An Introduction* (Philadelphia: Fortress Press, 1984).

35. The term was coined by Kai Nielsen in his essay "Wittgensteinian Fideism," *Philosophy* 42 (1967): 191-209.

36. See Thomas S. Kuhn, *The Structure of Scientific Revolutions*, 2d ed. (Chicago: Univ. of Chicago Press, 1970), and my discussion of his ideas in chap. 3.

37. At least one nontheological scholar of religion agrees: "I have come to believe," writes Jonathan Z. Smith, "that a prime object of study for the historian of religion ought to be theological tradition." (*Imagining Religion: From Babylon to Jonestown* [Chicago: Univ. of Chicago Press, 1982], 43). This is as good an occasion as any to state for the record that, appearances notwithstanding, I did not crib the title of my book from Smith's. Slow writer that I am, I had already settled on my working title before I laid eyes on his. But it shouldn't really be a problem in view of the very different objects of *Imagining* in the two titles. Indeed, Professor Smith makes the point in his opening statement: "If we have understood the archeological and textual record correctly," he writes, "man has had his entire history in which to imagine deities and modes of interaction with them. But man, more precisely western man, has had only the last few centuries in which to imagine religion" (p. xi). My point in the present paragraph is that those engaged in the former activity (imagin-

ing God) cannot any longer avoid dealing with the latter (imagining religion) as well, but the two are nevertheless quite distinct.

38. Hans W. Frei, *The Identity of Jesus Christ: The Hermeneutical Bases of Dogmatic Theology* (Philadelphia: Fortress Press, 1975), 146.

39. Ibid.

40. Soskice, *Metaphor and Religious Language*, 131.

41. *The Works of George Santayana*, Triton ed. (New York: Charles Scribner's Sons, 1936), 3:8–9. It should be obvious that my borrowing of Santayana's image does not imply agreement with his ideas on religion or imagination. He does, however, make some intriguing remarks on both in "A Brief History of My Opinions" (ibid., pp. vii–xxvii). "I knew that my parents regarded all religion as a work of human imagination," he reports: "and I agreed, and still agree, with them there" (p. xi). Both he and his parents evidently meant that religion is imaginary, though he shows some awareness of what I have called the ambiguity of imagination. He asks rhetorically, "Does not modern philosophy teach that our idea of the so-called real world is also a work of imagination? A religion . . . simply offers a system of faith different from the vulgar one, or extending beyond it. The question is which imaginative system you will trust." But in the end Santayana remains skeptical of all imagination, even in science. "My matured conclusion has been that no system is to be trusted," except in a limited sense "as symbols." "Religions," he writes, "are the great fairy-tales of the conscience" (p. xii).

42. On the metaphor of religion as a "mapping" activity, see the title essay in Jonathan Z. Smith, *Map Is Not Territory: Studies in the History of Religions* (Leiden: E. J. Brill, 1978), 289–309.

43. Soskice, *Metaphor and Religious Language*, 97–98.

44. Frei, *Identity of Jesus Christ*, 144–45.

45. Karl Barth, *Evangelical Theology: An Introduction*, trans. Grover Foley (New York: Holt, Rinehart & Winston, 1963), 99.

46. The significance of this tension between the object of faith and the present experience of believers is overlooked by theologians who make "common human experience" one of the sources of theology. See, e.g., David Tracy, *Blessed Rage for Order: The New Pluralism in Theology* (New York: Seabury Press, 1975), 43–45.

47. See discussion in chap. 2, pp. 34–40.

48. *Søren Kierkegaards Papirer* (The papers of Søren Kierkegaard), ed. P. A. Heiberg, V. Kuhr, and E. Torsting, 2d augmented ed., ed. N. Thulstrup (Copenhagen: Gyldendal, 1968–1978), VII 1 A 181; unpublished trans. by Bruce Kirmmse. Cf. *Søren Kierkegaard's Journals and Papers*, vol. 2, F–K, ed. and trans. Howard V. Hong and Edna H. Hong (Bloomington, IN: Indiana Univ. Press, 1970), no. 1251 (pp. 62–63).

49. This profoundly biblical insight into the divine-human relationship raises serious questions about any anthropology that, like Schleiermacher's, identifies the creature's relation to God with its *dependence*.

50. Dietrich Bonhoeffer, *Letters and Papers from Prison*, enlarged ed., ed. Eberhard Bethge (New York: Macmillan, 1971), 360.

51. Ibid., 361. The stress on God's power comes through more clearly in the original German, since *Raum gewinnen* is a military metaphor, meaning "to gain ground or territory." Bonhoeffer is saying that God, precisely by means of his worldly weakness, conquers territory in the world. This passage from the letter of 16 July 1944, I believe, contains the key to Bonhoeffer's intriguing but puzzling proposal for a "nonreligious" or "worldly" interpretation of the gospel. He is reworking Luther's contrast between "theology of glory" and "theology of the cross" by identifying *religion* with the former.

52. Ibid., 360.

53. Martin Luther, Heidelberg Disputation 21, in *Luther: Early Theological Works*. ed. and trans. James Atkinson (Philadelphia: Westminster Press, 1962), 291.

54. This is a point clearly seen by Barth but little understood by his critics and successors. It comes vividly to the fore in his late essay "The Spirit," with which he concluded his first and only lecture tour of the United States. See *Evangelical Theology*, 48–59.

55. See my article *"Loci Theologici,"* in *The Westminster Dictionary of Christian Theology*, ed. Alan Richardson and John Bowden (Philadelphia: Westminster Press, 1983), 337–38.

56. I take this analogy to be the point of Wittgenstein's intriguing but unelaborated remark, "Grammar tells what kind of object anything is. (Theology as grammar.)" *Philosophical Investigations*, §373. See also §371: "*Essence* is expressed by grammar."
57. E. g., Matt. 11:15. Cf. Matt. 13:9, 43; Mark 4:9, 23; Luke 8:8; 14:35; Rev. 2:7; 13:9.
58. The seemingly trivial fact that television is one of the chief competitors of the church might in this way be given a persuasive theological grounding.
59. Mary Warnock, *Imagination* (Berkeley and Los Angeles: Univ. of California Press, 1976), 50. See chap. 6, p. 115.

Index of Names and Subjects

Index of Scripture References